they make themselves

they make themselves

WORK AND PLAY AMONG THE BAINING OF PAPUA NEW GUINEA

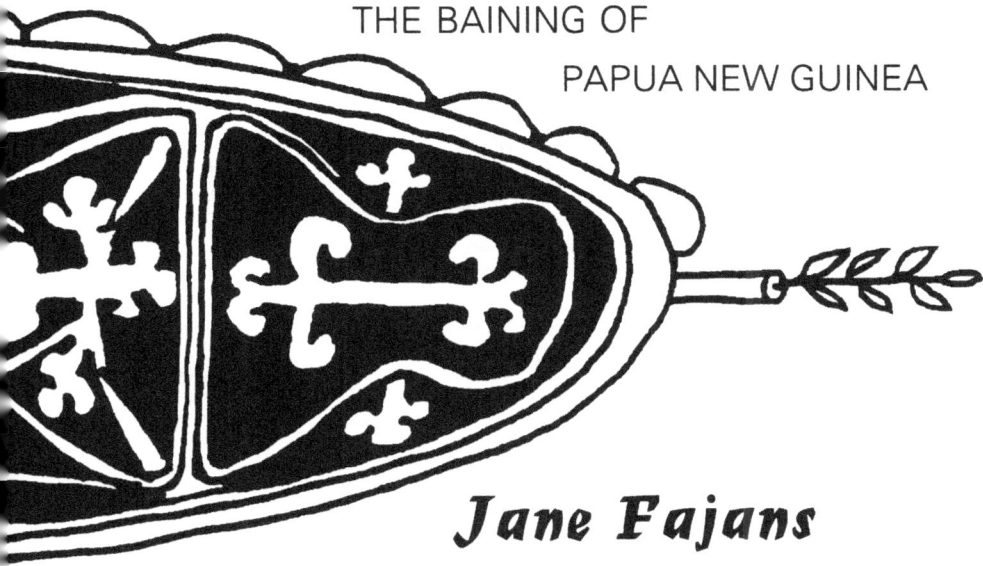

Jane Fajans

The University of Chicago Press ✳ Chicago and London

Jane Fajans is associate professor of anthropology at Cornell University.

The University of Chicago Press, Chicago 60637
The University of Chicago Press, Ltd., London
© 1997 by The University of Chicago
All rights reserved. Published 1997
Printed in the United States of America
06 05 04 03 02 01 00 99 98 97   5 4 3 2 1

ISBN (cloth): 0-226-23443-6
ISBN (paper): 0-226-23444-4

The publication of *They Make Themselves* was aided by
the Hull Memorial Publication Fund of Cornell
University.

Portions of chapter 6 were originally published in Geoffrey White, J. Kirkpatrick, *Person, Self, and Experience: Exploring Pacific Ethnopsychologies*, copyright © 1985 The Regents of the University of California, and are reprinted by permission of the University of California Press; portions appeared under the title "Shame, Social Action, and the Person among the Baining," in *Ethos* 11, no. 3 (1983), and are reprinted by permission of the Society for Psychological Anthropology.

Library of Congress Cataloging-in-Publication Data

Fajans, Jane.
    They make themselves : work and play among the Baining of Papua
New Guinea / Jane Fajans.
        p.   cm.
    Revision of the author's thesis (Ph. D.)—Stanford University,
1985.
    Includes bibliographical references and index.
    ISBN 0-226-23443-6. — ISBN 0-226-23444-4 (pbk.)
    1. Baining (Papua New Guinea people)—Rites and ceremonies.   2. Baining (Papua New Guinea people—Social life and customs.   3. Baining (Papua New Guinea people—Socialization.   4. Social structure—Papua New Guinea—Gazelle Peninsula.   5. Socialization—Papua New Guinea—Gazelle Peninsula.   6. Gazelle Peninsula (Papua New Guinea)—Social life and customs.   I. Title.
DU740.42.F35   1997
306'.089'9912—dc21
                                                                        96-37641
                                                                        CIP

To my Mother

Contents

Part Two: Play

x   Contents

Illustrations

Acknowledgments

As is the case with the completion of any work that has taken many years to complete, I am indebted to several people for their help and encouragement. I would first like to thank Jane Goodale for making me aware of the existence of the Baining, which knowledge lent them an air of familiarity when they were suggested as a potential field site by Ann Chowning and Andrew Strathern at the University of Papua New Guinea. My initial trip to the Baining was greatly facilitated by Rabbie Namaliu, then District Commissioner of East New Britain. Rabbie offered me continuous hospitality during my stay in Papua New Guinea, both in Rabaul and later in Port Moresby when he transferred there. I would also like to thank Chris and Tony Coase, the Reverend and Mrs. Willard Burce, Marta Rohatynskyj, and Tom Barker for their warm hospitality during my field breaks and travels around Papua New Guinea. I offer special thanks to Amy Burce for her friendship and collegial solidarity during our field initiation.

In the Baining area, my fieldwork was aided by the officers of the Lassul Bay Patrol Post, who received my mail and occasionally arranged transport. I also wish to thank the personnel of the Mission of the Sacred Heart, and especially Bishop Karl Hesse, who not only delivered my mail to me, but frequently stopped to chat about the anthropology of the Baining; and Mr. and Mrs. Jim Parker of the Summer Institute of Linguistics for sharing some of the work with me.

In the United States I wish to thank George Corbin, Jeremy Pool, and Gregory Bateson for sharing with me their wealth of material on the Baining.

My fieldwork was financed by grants from the National Institute of Mental Health, Fellowship Number 5 F31 MH 5750-02, the Center for International Research at Stanford University, and the Spencer Foundation. I thank them for their support. I have also been fortunate to receive grants that have allowed me to finish this book, and I want to thank the Spencer Foundation and the Society for the Humanities at Cornell University for their support.

Many people have read this book in various stages of revision. I would like to thank Jane Atkinson, Debbora Battaglia, John Comaroff, Charles Frake, William Hanks, David Holmberg, Billie Jean Isbell, Fred Myers, Renato Rosaldo, Steve Sangren, and Roy Wagner for their careful readings. I have not been able to address all their comments and critiques but I have learned a lot by trying. Portions of chapter 6 have been published previously, and I thank the University of California Press and the American Anthropological Association for permission to republish them here.

I cannot express in words the debt of gratitude I owe to my husband Terry Turner. He has given unyielding support, intellectual and otherwise, during every step of this project. His insights are so intertwined with my own that I conceived of this as a joint project. To our other joint projects, Vanessa and Allison, who have never known me without this book on my desk or in my computer, I thank you for all your patience and understanding.

I also want to thank the Baining, who not only put up with me for over two years, but adopted me into their families and shared their lives with me. A special thank you goes to Peni and Langerkan, Taluvian and Rauniram, Tangbinan and Tambas, Dembi and Dangerkan in Lan; and to Tovi, Inangaiyi and Uras, Pinam, Nguinga, and Nguingi in Yalom. *Meka atlo.*

Part One

Work

1   The "Baining Problem"

In Zen they say: If something is boring after two minutes, try it
for four. If still boring, try if for eight, sixteen, thirty-two, and so
on. Eventually one discovers that it is not boring at all but very
interesting.

John Cage

For years the Baining of East New Britain, Papua New Guinea were
(in)famous among anthropologists because of Gregory Bateson's judg-
ment that they were "unstudiable." As Bateson himself exclaimed to
me, fifty years after his own encounter with them, "The Baining broke
my heart; have they broken yours?" Although my answer then (and
now) was "No," I empathize deeply with the predicament Bateson
faced and the reaction he had. When I asked Bateson what it was about
the Baining that broke his heart, he responded, "The lack of any formulable culture or social organization." At the time I had no cogent
rejoinder to his evaluation. This book, however, is my response. In it
I address the question that Bateson raised and answer it, not
just by describing a "formulable" Baining culture and social organization but by examining why Bateson and others were unable to perceive
it.

Bateson was not the only anthropologist to work among the Baining—and abandon the attempt—before I started my work in 1976.
Over forty years after Bateson's departure, Jeremy Pool and his wife
Gail arrived in 1969–70. The Baining were not, of course, bereft of observers during the intervening period. They were regularly visited by
government patrol officers, and there were long periods when missionaries were resident in one or another community. As we will see
shortly, the reports of these non-anthropological observers are congru-
ent both with Bateson's and Pool's experiences.

Pool went to the North Baining[1] in 1969. Despite a stay of over a
year, he considered the results of his fieldwork to be negative.

---

1. Pool stayed for fourteen months and worked in two villages, the "coastal" village
of Puktas and the mountain village of Wiliambempki. In dividing his time between these
two regions his field stay mirrored my own, which was also divided between a "coastal"
and an inland community.

In more than fourteen months, . . . I was unable to define and fruitfully explore, to my own satisfaction, any area of anthropological interest. This is not to say that I found nothing; I gathered data on a wide variety of topics. Nevertheless, . . . I was unable to explore, in a thorough manner, any one aspect of Baining society which could be considered of central anthropological importance. (Pool 1971: 1)

The problem both Bateson and Pool had with the Baining arose from the apparent formlessness and lack of explicit norms that characterize Baining social and cultural life. There are no recognized social groups beyond the elementary family, unless one includes hamlets composed of a few related families, associated on an ad hoc basis without any conventional rules of residence or biases concerning laterality or filiation or descent. Social networks are amorphous and fluctuate tremendously in size and composition; there is no explicit idea of what constitutes a social group. Baining social life (with a few notable exceptions) is mundane and repetitive in the extreme, and holds little to seize the interest or offer pertinent meaning to the outside observer. It is difficult to take an interest—even a theoretically motivated interest—in boredom as a cultural phenomenon. The intermittent activities that spark interest and excitement, such as the dances and seances, are without conscious exegesis or referent. They seem dissociated from the events of daily life. Like Bateson (1931–32) and Pool (1971, 1984) before me, I was unable to get Baining informants to come forth with exegesis or commentary of a non-trivial kind for these aspects of their lives. The difficulty is further enhanced by the Baining's own attitude towards the dances, the surreal flamboyance of which they bafflingly dismiss as just "play." Beneath the dauntingly tedious and amorphous surface of Baining everyday life, however, analysis reveals a structure of interconnected values and meanings immanent in the most apparently trivial and ordinary everyday activities.

Baining Monotony: Entropy or Structure?

Despite the lack of normative forms of social grouping above the level of the family, despite the absence of social sanctions, political hierarchy, or sacred authority, and with no interpretation or exegesis of the meaning of their own rituals, the Baining have managed to maintain a distinctive social and cultural identity for over a century in the face of varied and often violent pressure for assimilation and change. In this sociological and historical perspective, the "Baining problem" appears rather as a Baining paradox: the maintenance of a coherent cultural identity by an incoherent culture, and the continued stability, resilience, and successful self-reproduction of a structureless society. The Baining case thus poses, in an unusually direct and compelling form, fundamental anthropological questions of the sources of sociality, commitment to shared values, and adherence to common cultural patterns.

The cohesion and continuity of Baining life in the face of often violent and oppressive incursions by a series of colonial regimes and other indigenous peoples clearly have implications that extend beyond the Baining case to the more general issue of the nature of social and cultural structures. In the case of the Baining, as I will attempt to show in this book, the structures of social relations and cultural consciousness are largely implicit, rooted in small underlying consistencies of values and ideas manifested in unpretentious activities and mundane beliefs. Nor can the apparent absence of normative structure in Baining society be accounted for, as some observers have suggested, as a result of the destruction of their indigenous system. All the information we possess from the time of the earliest European contacts and from missionaries and colonial administrators indicates that in the most relevant respects the Baining were essentially the same then as now. Rather, as I shall argue, the stability of Baining society is the result of the commitment of Baining people, as actors, to powerful and resilient patterns of orientation, meaning, values, and social bonding.

The content of everyday Baining social intercourse appears to a Western observer as monotonous and restricted in its range of meaning and expression; in a word, boring. The Baining, while friendly, accepting, and gentle, are neither inquisitive nor garrulous. Conversation is obsessively mundane, concerned primarily with food-getting activities and food-processing techniques. Gossip is minimal. Very little information comes forth spontaneously. Even the few traditional narratives seem to elicit little interest. I never saw one spontaneously told, although I could elicit stories relatively easily. I found no tradition of esoteric knowledge. Questions are usually met with a mixture of incomprehension, shyness, and passive disinterest. In addition to this, people are loath to put themselves forward by answering questions. Shame in such contexts is an important inhibitor. The cumulative effect of these characteristics of Baining culture, society, and personality is to strain the common assumptions and practices of anthropologists as participant-observers to the breaking point. Both Pool and Bateson felt stymied in their attempts to penetrate beneath the surface of Baining life, or even to find much in the way of interesting surface to penetrate.

I encountered the same problems during my fieldwork, and I experienced moments of profound discouragement. I was fortified, perhaps perversely, by the knowledge that others had failed to overcome these problems. The knowledge that the problems were not mine, but were "out there," stimulated me to try to deal with the "Baining problem" as an aspect of the research itself. When I found that interviews and elicitation techniques were far from successful among the Baining, I adopted a different tactic. Instead of continuing to prepare and ask endless lists of questions, most of which were answered with the phrase "I don't know," or just plain "No," I decided to follow the Baining's example and concentrate on learning, and integrating myself into, the mundane routine of everyday life. I spent many months sitting in the hamlet observing and participating in Baining family life. I tried to record the patterns and activities of hamlet life and garden work, of child socialization and casual visiting. This concentration on the mundane and the minute bore fruit. In the activities and practices I observed and queried I discovered patterns and consistencies which pervaded Baining life. These tendencies were the expressions of important Baining values, ideas, and motivations. They were not explicit, but they infused everything that happened. Through understanding these patterns of behavior and values I found that I could generate a systematic description of Baining persons, behavior, culture, and society. The Baining do not seem to perceive the system in these terms, nor in any terms I could elicit, nor did they recognize it in the terms in which I describe it here; nevertheless, the description and analysis I present in this work systematically integrates Baining actions and relationships with their values and beliefs.

My own insight into the underlying order of meaning which informs Baining social relations came when I realized that the Baining themselves felt their social life to be constituted of very few types of repetitive activities. Far from being amorphous, deficient in meaning or lacking in form, social interaction to them appeared rather strictly ordered, its constituent activities charged with meaning and value. The constriction of the range and content of Baining interaction, I came to see, is itself a product of the embedding of these values in a few cultural types of activities. The steady repetition of these activities continually reproduces and reinforces the values to which they are oriented. The "problem" of Baining amorphousness, it followed, was a false issue, an artifact of the theoretical and cultural lenses through which anthropologists, administrative officers, and missionaries had viewed them. The realization that despite its restricted range, Baining social interaction is saturated with meaning for the Baining themselves was the turning point in my fieldwork and constitutes the point of departure for this book.

Work, Sociality, Nature, and Value

The central concern of Baining culture is the transformation of natural products (food, babies, etc.) into social products through *work*. It is the multiple and intertwined strands of this process that produce, and hold, social value for the Baining. At the same time the Baining are preoccupied with the threat that aspects of nature, disorder, and entropy pose to society and themselves as social beings. Work therefore becomes the paradigmatic model for all social action; and for the Baining, the prototype of work is the humdrum routine of swidden gardening and food preparation. In fact, the Baining identify the socialization of children and thus the creation both of social persons and basic kinship relations with the work of gardening and food preparation (as phases of the process of food provision), not only in a metaphorical sense but in direct, substantive, and mechanically effective terms. One's social identity is thus in the most concrete sense the embodiment of work (both one's own work and that of others). Work (gardening, cooking, and child rearing) and its products (food, persons), therefore become the primary basis of interaction with other social persons, and as such the primary topic of casual conversation (see chapter 5). As I will show in this book, the processes that produce the social person are fundamentally the same ones that produce and reproduce society. Suffice it to say here that the Baining economy of cultural elaboration places a heavy weight on the simple and unadorned forms of these processes. That these activities are also the material basis of daily life makes it easier to overlook their social and symbolic significance.

With social value identified with "work," play lies outside normal social activity. In keeping with this dichotomy, the Baining attempt to prevent children from playing, on the grounds that to play is to behave as an animal (i.e., in an asocial or "natural" way). "All work and no play makes Jack a dull boy," and a society that fixates on work and suppresses play can become (at least through our eyes) a dull society.

Although the Baining suppress play in ordinary day-to-day social life, they classify their ritual dances as "play." Play emerges as a very significant counterpoint to ordinary Baining life. The Baining suppress play, conceived in our terms as spontaneous energetic activity unconstrained by normal social form, within the context of ordinary social interaction. Play as the spectacular expression of beings and powers opposed to the mundane world of work, however, is highly developed in contexts designated as outside normal social time and space: that is, in "ritual" (Bateson 1972b). The Baining world of play will be discussed in part 2 of this book.

Work for the Baining is not just a valued activity; it is the defining criterion of their own humanity. The Baining say "We are humans/people [akakat] because we work." Nonhuman others, like animals and supernatural creatures, do not work. The implication of this identification of work as the basis of human sociality is that things produced by work have positive social value. This is implicit in all Baining attitudes towards such products, although the Baining, not surprisingly, do not formulate a concept of value in such general terms.

Work takes the concrete forms of social activities (e.g., gardening, adoption, and socialization). What these activities have in common is that each transforms elements that are initially classed as natural (e.g., virgin forest or an unsocialized child) into social products (e.g., food, fire, families, and socialized persons). Work is a process that alters the materials it touches: it transforms them into "social" products. "Nature" and "society," as I use them, are not semiotic categories defined in terms of synchronic binary oppositions, but the starting and end points of transformative processes. In the simplest terms, "society" does not exist apart from the production of social products. "Nature" is essentially the domain of the not-as-yet-transformed; it is the source of raw materials that provide the substance and energy for socializing (or, which comes to the same thing, productive) transformations, rather than being primarily defined in terms of semiotic or essential properties.[2]

Gardening, cooking, adoption, socializing children, and preparing dance regalia, for example, are all processes that utilize natural materials for the creation of social products. They are, at the same time, the activities that form the core of Baining life. The value of these practices for the Baining is so ingrained and habitual that it permeates all aspects of life without any explicit recognition or expression. At the same time, this value is what motivates people to replicate these activities frequently. Value and motivation are dialectically produced through the same activities.

Work transformations, however, are not unidirectional, but reversible. If the Baining were to stop doing transforming work, their cultural order would quickly dissolve. Work as a highly valued activity is what produces Baining society. Its absence allows "nature" to dominate. The value of work is symbolically expressed in the high evaluation of sweat, as well as in the ritual uses of fire, ginger, and lime as embodiments of "hot" transformative energy. The energy needed for work is

2. This term is my own, not a translation of any Baining concept. In chapter 7, however, I suggest that the Baining concept of aios is a residual category, which includes the products of these reverse transformations.

derived from nature, which is the repository of both the raw materials and the raw energy necessary to produce and sustain society. Without this constant input of energy the social order would fall apart. Even with continuous energy input, certain elements of society become unable to maintain the "positive" transformations through which they are produced and begin to drop out of the social sphere. Such losses are the reverse, in terms of the Baining system, of the socialization process: they represent, in short, processes of naturalization.

All such "reverse" or naturalizing transformations have negative value. Naturalization occurs at death, when gardens revert to bush, when food decays, and when people run amok in the bush. The products of naturalization and the residue remaining after social transformations (a discrete but analogous category of social waste) comprise a distinct domain of natural phenomena, which is not conceived by the Baining as either identical or continuous with nature in its aspect as the domain of raw materials and potential energy. I distinguish these two domains of nature as "entropic nature" and "raw nature" respectively. Entropic nature is disordered and chaotic. It is the residue of society.

Activity as Descriptive and Theoretical Unit

In the field, I found that Baining social consciousness is formulated at the level of discrete activities and their overt meanings (i.e., gardening produces food, feeding people makes them your children, etc.). The more powerful and abstract principles and categories that ground and connect these discrete actions as parts of a coherent system of meanings are never made explicit. There are no Baining exegetes able and willing to provide interpretations of symbols or analyses of social patterns for the benefit of inquisitive anthropologists. I therefore had no alternative than to begin with the observation of everyday activities and social interaction, focusing both on interpersonal patterns and the ways individual social actors presented themselves through them.

Ethnographic necessity became the mother of theoretical invention. My theoretical perspective took form pari passu with my descriptive ethnography of Baining social interactions and their cultural meanings. As I attempted to formulate the relations among Baining patterns of activity, such as play and work, in terms of the Baining categories implicit in them, such as, in this example, nature and society, respectively, I found that my analysis increasingly assumed forms familiar from the work of theorists who have emphasized action, developmental processes, and self-regulating systems (e.g., Bateson 1972a; Bourdieu 1977; Marx 1947; Piaget 1967, 1970; T. Turner 1977, 1979, 1984), while both converging with and diverging from certain concepts and themes of symbolic anthropology and Levi-Straussian structuralism.

Before going to the field I had not been much exposed to the work of praxis or activity-oriented thinkers like those of the former group. The models of theoretical analysis and field methods I brought with me to the field all took for granted that the concrete contexts of field experience (from daily activities and conversational interactions to ritual performances), however primary in terms of the consciousness and lived reality of both natives and ethnographer, constituted a relatively secondary and derivative order of phenomena, from which it was the job of the anthropological analyst to abstract the theoretically primary forms of culture and society: from parole to langue, from behavioral regularities to structural forms or social norms, from ritual to symbol, and from symbolic action to classification. The forms and units of the theoretical models derived from this process (e.g., classifications, symbols, descent groups, normative rules, mythological structures) usually bore little resemblance to the concrete activities and communicative interactions from which they were "abstracted."

As I became progressively involved in the laborious process of understanding and relating the meanings of everyday Baining interactions and aspects of personal identity, however, the feeling grew that, at least for the Baining, these concrete forms of activity and personhood were themselves the fundamental units and relational forms from which a theoretical interpretation of Baining social and cultural existence would have to be constructed. To the extent that the Baining could be said to possess a social organization, it appeared to consist directly of a finite repertoire of types of interpersonal activity. To the extent that the Baining could be said to share a common culture, it appeared to consist of the meanings of these forms of interaction and the implicit relations among them. To the extent that Baining men and women possessed socially recognized personal identities, they appeared to be constructed out of this same relatively limited set of interactive relations in which they participated as role-actors. From descriptive units useful for organizing my ethnographic notebooks and my daily existence among the Baining, "activities" and "interactions" thus increasingly assumed the character of theoretical concepts and analytical tools.

"Activities," as I came to use the concept in this theoretical sense, are social interactions in which people transform their world to satisfy their needs, and in so doing transform themselves. Activities combine material activity and culturally defined symbolic forms (Vygotsky 1962, 1978; Leont'ev 1978; Wertsch 1981, 1985a, 1985b). They are intentionally directed toward a socially valued end. The notion of activity combines phenomena of signification and intention, cultural qualities usually associated with interpretation of meaning, with a set of objective conditions (situational context, technical aspects, and types of actors) which defines its material social form. Activity is at once material and ideal, objective and subjective, pragmatic and symbolically mediated. Activities, in other words, are the material processes which produce both social forms and cultural meaning. Activity, taken in this way, is the primary unit both of social and cultural organization and is central in the construction of personal identity. This definition of "activity" is a theoretical one, not merely a descriptive or ethnographic point of departure. A theoretical approach based on this concept of activity assumes that cultural meanings and material social dynamics must be analyzed as integrally interdependent phenomena, rather than discrete orders of reality. Such an approach does not focus on abstract classifications or paradigmatic "structures" of binarily opposed features, then, but on the processes or activities of their production.

The point is not to deny that "classifications," "norms," and "structures" may constitute significant types of cultural products or constituents of social systems, but simply to state that where they do exist (as I argue in the following chapters they do among the Baining) it is as products of social action, which must be continually created or recreated through key activities. Not all activities are equally potent moments of production and generative capacity. Some play a more structurally and symbolically significant role than others. Yet, activities that look very different may share significant productive aspects. The form of an activity, or "schema" (Piaget 1967, 1970), may be differently manifested in different contexts, but the underlying pattern may be similar. Among the Baining, the activities of gardening, cooking, adoption, child rearing, and dance are externally very different, but the transformative schema, the transformation from natural to social form, underlies them all. This master schema constitutes the structural frame of Baining society. The intercoordination of these different activities becomes the basis of a sociocultural "system." Both "systematicity" and "structure" must be understood as contingent products or outcomes of concerted social activity, not as a priori conditions of the nature of societies or cultures as "totalities." Nor, of course, does "systematicity" or "structure," to the degree it may emerge in a particular society at a particular time in its history, preclude the fact or possibility of conflict, disruption, and change. The degree to which internal conflict and change may actually occur in a society, or to which external events may stimulate internal transformations, like the society's degree of internal structure or systematicity, is an empirical question.

In the field with the Baining I gradually progressed from an understanding of simple acts and gestures to a grasp of more complex social relations and interrelated patterns of cultural meaning. In this way I ultimately arrived at a conception of the fundamental structures and principles through which the various activities, aspects, and domains of Baining life are connected in an interdependent system. I have tried to follow the same pattern in writing this book, and in constructing the ethnographic chapters that follow. Each of these chapters starts with descriptions of concrete activities of a specific cultural type, and proceeds to construct the general social form of this activity (in the term I use, its cultural "schema") and the value or values that serve as its cultural motivation. The succession of these descriptive chapters constructs a progressively more inclusive and mutually embedding account of the system of Baining activity schemas and values. This in turn leads to the abstraction of the more general principles and structures that integrate the system as a whole. This system is laid out in summary form in the concluding chapter, which also attempts to suggest some of the more general implications of my analysis for "practice theory."

My book, in sum, is an attempt to construct an ethnographic account and theoretical analysis as what Bateson (1972c) called a "metalogue" of the processes it describes, and through which it was produced: Baining social life as a series of activities which through their interrelations constitute Baining society and culture as a whole, and my own ethnographic experience of coming to an understanding of the Baining system through participating in these activities.

Part 1 pursues this analysis through an ethnographic account of Baining history, subsistence production, and social practices. The next two chapters describe the present situation and recent history of the Baining. Chapter 4 focuses on adoption and the formation of the Baining household, the subject that provided me with my first insights into the Baining system. This is followed by chapter 5 on the life cycle, chapter 6 on sentiments and the concept of the person, and chapter 7 on death and mortuary ritual, all of which deal with different aspects of the transformative qualities of work, cooking, and food giving, and the problematic nature of play. The contrastive domains of nature and society, and the oppositions between work and play are examined in depth in part 2, which consists of three chapters on ritual. The concluding chapter returns to some of the general issues raised in this introduction in the light of the material considered in the intervening chapters, and attempts to situate the Baining in a broader Melanesian context.

2   The Ethnographic Setting

Despite Bateson's and Pool's difficulties in studying the Baining, both readily recognized that the Baining exhibited certain patterns of behavior and activities that could be described in conventional anthropological terms (Bateson 1927–28; Pool 1971, personal communication). This chapter sets forth these basic patterns and processes of Baining social and cultural life. The problem that both Bateson and Pool had in going beyond this empirical level of description arose because (1) they did not feel that this material was specific enough or rich enough to add up to a minimally adequate or sufficient notion of cultural or social structure; and (2) the generative and regulative principles and mechanisms through which this pattern is maintained and reproduced were not in evidence. It is this latter category, the generative principles of cultural structure, with which this book is chiefly concerned and which will be discussed in chapters 4–11.

The North Baining are a Melanesian people who live in the northeast corner of the Gazelle Peninsula in East New Britain Province, Papua New Guinea (see fig. 2.1). They call themselves *akakat* (transcribed as *chachat* by the Germans and *qaqet* by the S.I.L. Bible translators), which means "the people" in their language. The name "Baining" is of Tolai origin and means "inland people," with the pejorative connotations of "bush" person. Although the term may originally have been derogatory and is not their own name for themselves, the Baining currently use it in all intergroup contexts. Since this is the name that is used in all official (e.g., administrative and mission) contexts, it seems as well to retain it in this work.

The North Baining constitute one of three related tribes spread across the Gazelle. The others are the Central Baining, who now live in the region around Galim, and the East Baining who live around Wide Bay on the southern coast of the Gazelle Peninsula (Whitehouse 1995). These three tribes are all related, although the extent of the relationship is unclear. Sources such as Rascher (1909) and Parkinson (1907), and many patrol officers have assumed a fairly homogeneous culture and social organization segmented into three mutually unintelligible lan-

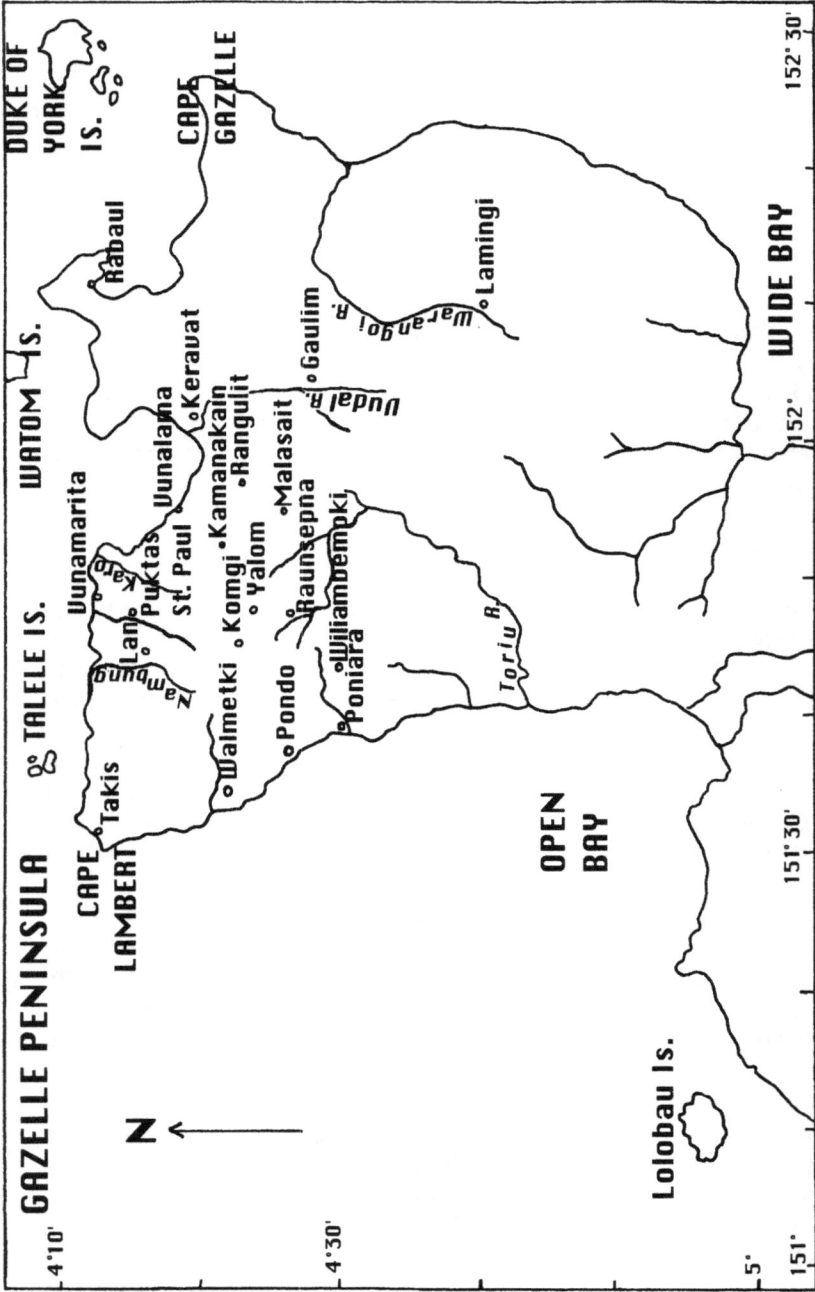

Figure 2.1 Map of the Gazelle

guage groups (and several dialects within each language). I am not convinced that these observers understood any one of these societies, let alone all of them, well enough to judge their similarity. This is a research project that is just beginning (see Whitehouse 1990, 1995, personal communication; Barton and Rohatynskyj, personal communication; Rohatynskyj 1992). All the Baining languages are non-Austronesian. It is evident from a cursory examination of Bateson's field notes (1927–28)[1] that there are outward similarities in the Central and the North Baining, and that the languages have a similar grammatical structure and many cognate words. Informants from each tribe contend that they cannot understand the language of the other although they grasp words or phrases; they prefer to speak pidgin with one another.

The North Baining, the subject of this work, speak a non-Austronesian language. Their region is divided into two dialect groups. These dialects are mutually understandable. The separation of dialects roughly conforms to that of the coastal and inland geographical areas, except that several groups of mountain dialect speakers have moved down to the coast within the last thirty years, stimulated by administrative and mission projects.

My description of the North Baining encompasses both dialect groups, since I lived and worked in one community in each area.[2] I lived first in Lan, a coastal community, from March 1976 until May 1977, and then in Yalom, an inland village, from August 1977 until May 1978. I returned to both groups for ten weeks in 1991. Although I speak both dialects, I became more competent at the inland dialect, where I could build on my previous language work with the coastal group. My description may be assumed to cover both groups, except where I explicitly refer to one or the other. Let me state at the outset that I did not obtain strictly equivalent data in both places, and in some cases failed to elicit types of data in one place that I had obtained in the other. Nevertheless, I am confident that where I extrapolate from data from one area, the description and analysis I construct are applicable to both parts. The difficulties I encountered in making sense of my Baining data arose not because the two regional sets of data are incomparable, but because of the scarcity of information and elaboration of all kinds from my Baining informants in both areas.

1. Bateson studied the Central Baining near Gaulim, a group seemingly closely related both culturally and linguistically to the North Baining. He stayed for over fourteen months. I have visited the Central Baining but have not lived among them.
2. Pool studied the same Baining group that I did and worked in both a coastal (Puktas) and mountain (Wiliambempki) community, as did I. I have visited both the communities Pool lived in and talked with them about Pool's stay.

Geography and Settlement Patterns

The Baining have traditionally lived in scattered hamlets across a large triangular geographic area bordered on one side by the Vudal and Toriu Rivers and the watershed divide between them, and on the other sides by the sea (see fig. 2.1). This area consists of very rugged mountains rising in parts to between 4,000 and 5,000 feet. The underlying rock is limestone and shows typical limestone formations such as sink holes, springs, and underground streams. Most of the area is covered with thick tropical rain forest. Rainfall is plentiful, averaging 120 inches a year, and falls throughout the year, although the season between December and May, which brings the northwest monsoon, is the period of heaviest rainfall and coldest temperatures. August is usually the driest month, and is the only time one can plan an event with a reasonable hope that it will not be rained out.

Within this environment the Baining recognize distinct districts, many of which cover very large areas. The residents of a particular district have rights to land, hunting, and mobility throughout their district. In the past (before the attempts of missionaries and administrators to concentrate them in larger settlements) they lived in dispersed hamlets throughout the area, each hamlet rarely containing more than one or two houses. For the most part hamlet residents lived independently of their neighbors (even those of the same district), although there were a few occasions for intercourse and collective action, such as marriage, raiding, collective work projects, dances, and death feasts. There was no recognition of kin or group ties between people on account of co-district residence. Intercourse between hamlets was more frequent within a district than across districts, but common district residence did not guarantee cordial relations. Raids and fights occurred both within districts and across district boundaries.

Individual hamlet groups practiced swidden horticulture, frequently moving their hamlets when they moved their gardens. They have sometimes, for this reason, been described in the literature as seminomadic or even nomadic (Rascher 1909; Parkinson 1907; Sangkol 1969), although this is a misinterpretation of the pattern. They did and do live in settled hamlets, but shift the location of these hamlets when they are no longer conveniently near their gardens. As a consequence of this residence pattern, the territory is dotted with abandoned hamlet sites, frequently overgrown, each of which is named. Since many of these sites also contain permanent fruit-bearing trees planted by their former inhabitants, they are natural loci for intermittent habitation or food gathering. The names and food resources of such spots in the bush are remembered long after the inhabitants are forgotten.

Plate 2.1   A Baining village

Since first contact there has been strong pressure both from the missions and the government for the Baining to settle in consolidated villages instead of dispersed homesteads. The populations that were collected in individual villages were gathered from the larger districts described above.[3] Consequently the villages are at quite a distance from one another, ranging from two to twelve hours' walk apart.

The history of Lan "village" might serve as an example of the forces and counterforces of consolidation. Originally, a number of small settlements was created by the missionaries. When these clusters were threatened with extinction through population decline, the response was progressive consolidation. Ultimately, what had been four settlements were concentrated into one at Lan (or "Luan" as it is spelled on administrative reports). During World War II the Japanese occupied the territory and moved everyone either to a work brigade in the mountains or to a camp near Guntershoehe Plantation. After the war the survivors began to migrate back into the mountains. Here they first lived in a consolidated settlement composed of the remnant populations from the four main areas. It was not long until the group divided into two subvillages located about a mile apart. The group at Raunit was composed of people originally from Ranga and Ruwa, while that at Kolkiaring came from Nacharunep and Lanivam. While everyone was still living in these communities, the government introduced cocoa as a cash crop. People began using the lands surrounding the villages for cocoa plantings. The government encouraged individual plantings of cocoa, and for the first time people claimed permanent ownership of the land they planted. At the same time, it was difficult for individuals to finance the construction of cocoa fermenteries and transportation to markets so they joined together for these projects. The Baining were, thus, moving in two directions at once. They were developing private plantations but were also engaged in cooperative processing ventures. By the time I arrived in Lan, the village had been abandoned. As people continued to plant and develop land for cocoa blocks, they tended to move outward from the village to live among their blocks. The settlement pattern was getting progressively more dispersed. Families tended to move back into districts where their families had lived before. At the same time they also considered themselves participants in collective projects (such as cocoa-processing fermenteries and small stores), which were located where the village used to be.[4]

3. The exception to this is the village of Raunsepna, which appears to be a conglomerate of several different districts whose people were brought together just before World War II.

4. In Yalom, the inland community, people have maintained a fairly consolidated village. It consists of five coterminous hamlets, and one hamlet about fifteen minutes' walk

The Baining have no indigenous corporate groups to organize activity in district or village life. There are no big men or chiefs, no men's houses or cult houses, no moieties, clans or lineages. The traditional pattern of social organization is based on the hamlet and household. Hamlets are now and previously were generally composed of extended families. These families might all live in one house or they might be divided into several houses. There was and is no particular rule of residence. At least some of the children were expected to stay on with their parents after marriage, but whether the son or daughter stayed, or whether a newly married couple lived with his or her parents was open to negotiation. Informants say these things are discussed in each individual case, and residence is determined by which parents need or want a child and his or her spouse to live with them. There is no concept of bride service involved. On the contrary, often the co-residential parents have to provide for the new couple until they have planted gardens that have begun to bear (see chapter 5).

Although the majority of Baining families are monogamous, polygamy was traditionally practiced throughout the area, and is still practiced to some extent in the mountains. Polygamy was originally prohibited by the Catholic missionaries but was tolerated in more recently missionized areas. One old man from Komgi, a leader in the Catholic Church, has six wives, which is generally assumed to be a record. A man with several wives may house them all in one household, but frequently they will live in separate houses. Commonly the logistics of polygamy are further eased by greater distance between the several wives. For instance, a man might house one wife in a house in the village, and another down on his cocoa block; alternatively one wife might live in a garden house, while the other is in the village, and

---

away. Hamlet size varies from one to more than a dozen houses, but the overall effect of concentration is greater because hamlets are within sight and hearing of other hamlets. Hamlet composition is less clearly defined in Yalom. Neighboring households may share kin ties or their placement may be based on friendship or convenience. Here, household configuration is more important, and it seems to be structurally equivalent to the extended family hamlet in Lan. It is common to find three or more generations in one household. There is great fluidity about these kin groups. They are neither matri- or patrilineal but are composed of both sons and daughters, their spouses (if married), and children. It is also acceptable for adult married children to have their own houses, and some single men live alone too, so although there are many extended family households, there are also nuclear family households and polygamous households. Residence within the format of village vs. hamlet is fairly flexible. In addition to the patterns enumerated above for each community, further fluidity is provided by the fact that each family builds houses at its gardens in which it might live for considerable periods of time. This too replicates the traditional residence pattern.

periodically they might switch. These strategies suggest that relations between co-wives are not always amicable. The general expectation, however, is that they do get along and cooperate.

Kinship and Adoption

I have been discussing Baining residence in relation to family and kinship relations, without describing the Baining kin system. The Baining have a cognatic system, recognizing relatives equally on both maternal and paternal sides. The kin terminology is a variant of the Hawaiian generational type, with separate terms for elder and younger siblings.

There is considerable difference between the mountain and coastal Baining in terms of the depth of genealogical reckoning. The coastal people can give terms upwards and downwards for four generations to great-great-grandparent / child (the terms are reciprocal). Since the system is classificatory there can be members of these categories who are not direct lineal descendants.

In Yalom, by contrast, there are fewer kin terms. The primary terms are mother and father, son and daughter, husband and wife, and brother and sister (the older / younger distinction holds here too). The term for grandparent is not widely known: one informant was unaware of the term so he ran next door to his grandmother's house to inquire. Kin relations tend to be collapsed in thought and language to those of the nuclear family; thus, people who are two or even three generations removed still tend to refer to one another as either parent or child. This is in some degree encouraged by the widespread practice of adoption, since it is very common for grandparents to adopt grandchildren. The collapsing of alternate into adjacent generations, however, is a more general phenomenon, as will be seen in detail in chapters 4 and 5.

There is no cohesive corporate unit like a clan or lineage. Since the reckoning of filiation is bilateral, the kindred is open-ended and overlapping. However, there is some sense, at least in Lan, that one's kindred constitutes a group. I was able to elicit a term for this group, *aninganingulta*, although I never heard it used spontaneously. I think this term can be translated as the "segments or pieces of one head" (*aningaka* [head]; *ingl* [parts of a whole]; *ta* [pl.] [humans]). In Lan, there are a few instances where this kin group can be seen to act as a body, but they are mostly occasions that are produced by acculturation and the interface with the outside world, such as the alienation or sale of land, collective activities relating to cash cropping, or planning for the purchase of a plantation. On these occasions, however, the actual term used to refer to the group acting collectively is the pidgin term "lain" (line) and not the vernacular term *aninganingulta*.[5] In Yalom there seem to be even fewer occasions for people to think or act in terms of the *aninganingulta* unit. There the term is interpreted as referring to a "group of brothers" acting collectively, but I found no spontaneous use of the word.

In traditional Baining society there seems to have been little need for definitions of ownership and cultural patterns of inheritance. There was little material property that survived death. As discussed in chapter 7, and for reasons which will be elucidated later on, the Baining feel it is fitting for the fruits of a person's labor to die with him or her; thus, gardens were destroyed, coconuts and areca palms chopped down, and pigs killed when their owner died.

The problem of inheritance emerged with the introduction of permanent planting for cash crops and store-bought goods. Lan and Yalom have responded to this stimulus in slightly different ways. Today at a death, gardens, betel nut, and pigs are still often destroyed or used for the death feast; clothing is frequently buried with the corpse; but larger investments such as cocoa blocks are not damaged. The accepted idea is that the deceased's goods are passed down to his or her children. In Lan inheritance is assumed to be bilateral, and goods should be divided equally between all children, male and female. In keeping with this idea of equality between the sexes, each individual in the society, male and female, plants and owns the produce from a cocoa block. In Yalom a different pattern has emerged. Only men "own" cocoa blocks. Women are said to derive the benefits of cash cropping through their husbands' blocks. Consequently, only men are heirs to cash and property. Thus far these variants have not made much difference in the life of the people, but there is the possibility they will in the future.[6]

The lack of an indigenous practice of inheritance has ramifications

---

5. On a few occasions, the members of a particular *aninganingulta* were seen to consult with the elder(s) of the unit about undertaking certain projects, for instance, opening a store, buying cocoa, buying a plantation, etc. They explicitly acknowledged turning to these elders for advice; but there was no sentiment that such elders had the power or authority to veto any proposal. Their contribution was to share their greater experience. Once again most, if not all, of these projects fit into the sphere of intercultural contact, and I am unable to offer examples from the traditional domain. Traditional occasions which would seem, in retrospect, to have offered opportunities for "group" activity and strong leadership, such as warfare and raiding or ritual dances, are not explicitly categorized as such by present-day informants. These informants state that warfare or raiding were often individual decisions made by impulsive youths, while dances could be initiated by whoever knew the magic spell. The latter were often but not exclusively older men.

6. The tendency towards patrilineal inheritance seems to be supported by the church in those areas in which it has arisen.

for adoption practices. In many societies, adoption is a means people use to provide themselves with heirs when natural ones are lacking. Despite the absence of this motivation, adoption is extremely common among the Baining. It is practiced by almost everyone, and is not restricted to orphaned children or childless families. As we will see in chapter 4, the Baining believe that adoption is *atlo* (good). They affirm that there is an extra strength in the affective tie that develops between parents and their adoptive children which is not present between parents and their natural children. These attitudes and practices have considerable importance for the Baining social and cultural system, and they have persisted despite the negative response they have aroused in both mission and administration.[7] Adoptions link families through the exchange of children. At the same time an adoption into a family transforms that family into a "social" unit. Through adoption the Baining create social relations and imbue them with cultural value (see chapter 4).

The adoptive link is created through the provision of food. Nurturance through food is more highly valued than that of mother's milk. Food that is the product of one's own labor is imbued with social value. All of the reports about the Baining's industry and interest in food are the result of the important role food plays in the creation and maintenance of social bonds. Food is the means by which one creates social relationships and is one of the most important media of exchange in the society. It is in this context that we turn to the horticultural system.

The Subsistence Economy

As mentioned above, the Baining are swidden cultivators. Their staple crop is taro (varieties of *Colocasia esculanta*), although since 1957, when taro blight invaded the region, the variant kong-kong taro (*Xanthosoma sagittifolium*) has become increasingly important and has virtually supplanted taro in some areas. At the time of the blight, the administration encouraged the development of sweet potatoes, tapioca, kong-kong taro, bananas, and beans, but they met with resistance from the Baining, who had never had any trouble with taro before and simply could not believe that their staple would no longer grow well (Haywood 1958: 3). As it was, this blight caused a major upheaval in Baining gardening and eating practices, since taro has never returned to the moun-

---

7. Nowadays some of the Baining leaders are also opposed to aspects of adoption. John Landi wants to restrict adoption to infants, so that children will not be adopted after they have learned to "know" their parents.

tains. On the coast taro still grows, but the plant is greatly reduced in size. To this day people reminisce sadly about how big and fine their taro used to be. Despite their reluctance to adopt new crops, they did adapt quite satisfactorily. In both regions a greater diversity of crops is known and used than before.

Taro and "singapu" (as the kong-kong taro is called in pidgin), are root tubers that can be grown the year around. The Baining cultivation cycle is, thus, for the most part not seasonally determined. Swidden farming requires the clearing of bush or forest. For the most part, this work is done by men, who chop the trees, pile the trunks and limbs into fences to keep the pigs out, and burn the dried debris. There is, however, no fixed division of labor, and women occasionally do these tasks as well. Both men and women participate in planting, using a digging stick as the main implement. Women are primarily responsible for weeding and harvesting, but there is no stigma associated with men doing these tasks. The Baining plant new gardens continuously, as old gardens are harvested and taro stalks become available. Sometimes the new plantings are just continuations of existing gardens, since the families keep clearing new bush areas adjacent to their old plots. This is particularly true of taro gardens. In such cases the plants in the garden range from newly planted stalks to mature taro plants. As family members harvest their taro, they immediately cut the stalk off the tuber and replant it in a new section. If their new garden is at some distance removed from the mature garden, they may carry both the tuber and the stalk back to their hamlet. If this is the case, they will let the stalks accumulate for up to a few weeks before carrying them all at once to a new garden. Stalks cannot be left unplanted for longer than a few weeks or they will die. Taro can be stored for several days or more, so people do not need to go to their gardens every day. However, raw taro tubers are quite heavy and bulky, and it is awkward to carry home more than a two- or three-day supply. In addition to this the Baining are very involved in their garden work, and they usually go back and replenish their supply before they run out. Having ample food supplies on hand is very important to them, and lack of food is a theme in autobiographies, stories, and songs despite the fact that since contact there has been only one period of scarcity (during and right after World War II). The vast majority of the time, the patrol officers described their gardens as plentiful.

Taro can be harvested five or six months after planting, but each plant produces just one tuber. Singapu takes up to eighteen months to mature. However, each plant produces a large number of tubers. Singapu gardens tend to be planted all at once, not continuously as are

Plate 2.2   Fence building

taro ones. As they are harvested, stalks are saved up and then planted somewhere new.[8] Families have a number of gardens in various phases of development at any one time, and these may be distributed over a wide geographic area. Since gardens are scattered, and are often at several hours' walk from village or hamlet, Baining gardens usually

8. Taro is a tuber that is not grown from seed, but regenerates when a small portion of the bulb (corm) is left attached to the stalk after harvest. If a certain proportion of the bulb is not left, the plant will not produce another tuber, and thus is effectively dead.

have a shelter in them. These structures vary from rough lean-tos, which provide shelter of sorts from the frequent rain, to regular houses. A Baining family, or part thereof, might spend anywhere from a night to over a month living in these gardens. Such extended garden visits often coincide with periods of intense garden work, planting or weeding, but this is not always the rationale for the stay. Moving off to gardens and staying there at will seems to be one way that the Baining maintain their precontact settlement pattern.

Certain old people, particularly old women, maintain a fairly permanent residence in such garden houses. Their excuse for this is that they have to live there to look after the family's pigs (since the administration prohibits pigs from wandering around the villages), but it also seems to be their own desire to do this. This residence pattern is in keeping with Baining concepts of space and time and will be discussed in chapter 5.

In addition to taro and singapu, the Baining also grow several types of green vegetables (the most important of which is called *aibika [Abelmoschus manihot]*), beans, sweet potatoes (varieties of *Ipomea*), sweet manioc (varieties of *Manihot*), bananas, pitpit *(Saccharum robustum)*, sugar cane, and papayas. Of these crops only pitpit is definitely seasonal. Pitpit ripens between late December and mid-April. This crop is the one that most clearly delineates the yearly cycle, and it is not surprising that the Baining word for year is the same as the word for pitpit. Pitpit is also very abundant when it is in season, and in Lan the pitpit season is one connected with certain types of exchanges and rituals. By coincidence the pitpit season spans the interval between Christmas and Easter so its association with ritual events has been carried over into Christianity.

Despite the plenitude of their harvests and their preoccupation with food (which is conceptually synonymous with taro), the Baining are rather indifferent gardeners. After clearing a garden, they are often thwarted in burning it by the frequent rains, and may omit this step. Even when burning is accomplished, they never spread the ashes across the fields. If they have seeds from introduced crops such as beans, cucumbers, squash, or cabbage, they may plant these in the ashy spots, but otherwise the fertilizing potential of the ash is unutilized. The field is cleared and weeded initially and then usually once more before harvest, but taro gardens are already becoming overgrown with secondary bush vegetation by the time they are six months old. This means that crops like bananas, pitpit, and singapu, which take considerably longer to mature, grow amidst the bush.

In Yalom, people are more lax about weeding (a fact which the coastal people observe and make derogatory remarks about). Once a garden is harvested it is not replanted; each swidden is only used for one cycle. Despite the perfunctoriness of gardening techniques and practices (the technology is also minimal, employing a digging stick, axe, and bush knife), the Baining food supply is plentiful. In fact, the few Baining who live close to the road to Rabaul are quite successful market gardeners, and others could become so if they had some means of transporting their produce to the markets. The coastal Baining also make some cash by selling produce to the plantations.

Garden produce makes up by far the largest proportion of the Baining diet. In addition to the garden food, they also raise pigs. Pigs are not accorded any special status in ritual or exchange functions as they are in other parts of Melanesia (cf. Feil 1984, A. Strathern 1971, Rappaport 1968, Rubel and Rosman 1978, and Goodale 1995). By contrast, on occasion they are even killed just for meat or cash, although they may also be saved for a wedding or death feast. The only other domesticated animals kept for consumption are chickens (dogs are kept for hunting but are not themselves eaten; cats were recently introduced and are used for catching mice), and they seem to get eaten by snakes, dogs, or thieves far more often than by those who look after them.

The Baining also obtain food from the forest, through both hunting and gathering. Wild pigs are the main game. They are hunted with a shotgun, cornered by dogs and speared with a heavy iron shaft, or caught in one of several kinds of trap. Cassowaries are also hunted in a similar manner. Possums and wallabies are the only other large prey. Flying foxes, marmots, bats, and various species of birds (hornbills, parrots, cockatoos, and doves) are also obtained. Certain other animals are gathered. These include caterpillars, grubs, freshwater shrimp, clams, and sea snails from the mangrove swamps.

Other foods are obtained from the bush or forest; these are mostly fruits and vegetables and are usually gathered seasonally. From forest trees come breadfruit *(Artocarpus altilis)*, galip nuts (Tahitian Chestnut, *Canarim indicum*), lapua fruit (species unknown), pau, laulau (Malay Apple, *Eugenia malaccensis*), and wild betel nut *(Areca)*. The Baining also plant and gather coconuts and domesticated areca nut *(Areca catechu)*, and they collect ferns, kalakal (a tree) leaves, wild yams (varieties of *Dioscorea*), and betel pepper (Piper betel) leaves.

As suggested above, gathering and food production are a major preoccupation among the Baining. Every family has numerous gardens in production at once, and people spend much of their time either going to their gardens or talking about them. Taro is a main topic of conversation. Food is plentiful although basically unvarying. The abundance of Baining gardens has been noted since contact. Only during and just

Plate 2.3   Carrying wood

following the Japanese occupation, when the Japanese confiscated the entire harvest and destroyed the means of reproduction, have the Baining been unable to feed themselves with the produce of their own gardens. Despite the abundance, the Baining seem obsessively worried about lack of food and starvation. Food is so greatly valued because it is an important social medium. The provision of food is what makes an adopted child one's own. Mortuary rituals and exchanges are based on the collection and distribution of food. Food must always be offered to guests to demonstrate one's good will towards them. However, people fear that a person traveling to another community will not be offered food and so will go hungry; this fear does a lot to constrain travel. The theme of a person arriving in another community and finding it empty and devoid of food is frequently portrayed in song (see chapter 6).

Intergroup Relations

As mentioned above, food is an important medium of social interaction. Food production may also, on occasion, be an arena for social intercourse. Most Baining gardens are prepared and worked by nuclear families. Sometimes, however, a family will offer friends or relatives plots of ground within a newly cleared garden, and will receive assistance in return. Occasionally an individual will ask help for one day and one task. For instance, a man will solicit help for constructing a fence around his garden. Other men will come and they will all build the fence, thus accomplishing in one day what would take one man several weeks. After this work party, the host will serve his helpers a meal in gratitude. The meal is not considered payment for their labor since the assumption is that the host will repay his friends by doing the same for them at a later date. A woman might organize a similar work party by asking other women to come and help her weed her garden. She too will serve them a meal. The same collective meal is served when people gather to help build a roof for a house.

These collective work parties are part of a small complex of interfamily/interhamlet activities. They are at the mundane end of a spectrum that includes more exotic activities such as raiding, large-scale food exchanges, and dances.

Raiding

In precontact times, the Baining used to undertake raids against other Baining hamlets. Raids no longer occur, and present-day Baining suffer a form of cultural amnesia, which wipes out most memory of this activity. What they do remember, however, are a few funny stories about raiding strategy and a great many moralistic lectures against warfare, which must have been received time and again both from missionaries and administrators. While the Baining will acknowledge that raids were performed and victims often eaten, they do so with great distaste, and rush onwards to affirm that they no longer do such barbaric things. Their attitude has much in common with that of religious converts who say "before we were sinners, but now we are saved (or at least do not sin so badly)."

The Baining had no recognized fighting leaders, although occasionally an individual got a reputation as a warrior. The elders tended to leave the action to younger men who were the ones to initiate and carry out a raid. Anyone could be the victim of a raid, so every individual had to be alert and on the defensive. Raids were often launched against people alone in their gardens, old people alone at home, or against a sleeping hamlet at dawn. The Baining used to raid and feud among themselves, but they were also special prey to the Tolai who inhabited the coast. Tolai occasionally hiked up and raided the Baining in their hamlets, but more frequently they waited until the Baining ventured to the coast to obtain saltwater (which they used as a condiment since they had no other source of salt), coral (cooked to make the lime used in chewing betel), and shellfish from the mangroves. Then the Tolai would attack and capture or kill them.

Food Exchanges and Feasts

A second type of intergroup/interhamlet organization involved food exchanges. These food exchanges are no longer performed, but I was told of two main types: *atit* and *akarrutki*. These exchanges were undertaken at the initiative of one hamlet or family group. Informants suggested that this was done to honor people that they respected and liked, or to whom they felt grateful, for instance allies from a raid, helpful neighbors, or the parents of an adopted child. The initiating group would solicit help from relatives and neighbors and amass a large quantity of food. In the case of *atit* the food would include pigs and taro; for *akarrutki* there would be no meat but huge quantities of pitpit. When all the food was gathered and properly displayed in the hamlet of the sponsor, he or she would send a messenger to the potential recipient. The messenger would carry a branch of areca nuts, which he would give to the recipient. Giving areca in a ritualized way is the Baining method of exchanging greetings. The intended recipient would gather his extended family and at the appointed time they would arrive as a group at the giver's hamlet. A small token of cooked food might be offered the guests at this time, but the bulk of the food was uncooked and was carried back to the recipient's hamlet, where it would be distributed and cooked. The recipient would be expected to return this food presentation at some point in the future. In the case of *akarrutki* this might occur some weeks hence, but for *atit* the sponsor would have to wait until he or she had pigs of the right size. No special gardens were prepared for this event, but since the pitpit season is one of relative abundance, many such feasts were held at this time, when they occasioned no particular strain. Extended family members who received food during the distribution would be expected to help contribute to the return gift when the time came. In this sense, the act of exchange generated a cooperative group, often an extended family group, but this group only persisted within the specific context so generated.

Food displays and presentations were traditionally used as a means of resolving disputes between groups. Occasionally one group would insult or shame another. The shamed group would attempt to reassert its pride through a prestation of food greater than the rival group could consume. The recipients of such a feast would be unable to leave until all the food was consumed.[9]

9. I have not seen such a presentation, nor to my knowledge has it been done in the last half-century, but older informants in Lan described it to me in 1976. In 1977 they threatened to perform such a food prestation on the occasion of a shaming incident involving food. I left the field before it came off. When I inquired twelve years later about whether this had been done, I found nothing had come of it. On this same return trip, however, I learned that the mountain Baining had had the same custom, and had recently

The Baining also amass great quantities of food for a large mortuary feast on the occasion of a death. This is another occasion when cooperation is solicited. For a death feast the host group is primarily composed of the close consanguineal and affinal relatives of the deceased. In addition to the sponsors, however, such a feast is attended by others more distantly connected to the deceased. These others do not act as a distinct group, since there is no need to reciprocate this kind of feast unless there is another death. Mortuary feasts are traditionally occasions that bring people together. Although there is a good deal more social intercourse at present than there was in the past, occasions for cooperative action are still not plentiful, and these feasts are among the few activities which require concerted efforts on the part of many people. Death and mortuary rituals will be described more fully in chapter 7.

Dances

Death feasts are matched only by dances as occasions for collective activity. The Baining are best known throughout Papua New Guinea for their dances. Coastal and mountain dances vary considerably. Coastal dances are almost never performed, having been banned over eighty years ago by the missionaries. There is still a collective memory of certain dances, however, and on my instigation the people of Lan performed the dances *Amambua* and *Asingal.* The other dances are now unknown in the coastal regions, although mention of them is found in the earliest accounts (Rascher 1909). Variants of these dances are still performed in the mountains. An interesting feature of the dances is how they have diffused from region to region. The coastal people used to perform dances called *Aharaigi, Amambua,* and *Akip* (see Rascher 1909; Corbin 1976). The mountain people claimed to have had a dance called *Asingal.* Nowadays the coastal people perform *Amambua* and *Asingal* and have forgotten *Akip* and *Aharaigi.* The inland people perform a variant of *Aharaigi* combined with *Akip,* a dance called *Akurikuruk*[10] adopted from the Central Baining tribe, and a dance called *Atut,* also originally a Central Baining dance. They have lost *Asingal.*

---

threatened to perform such an event on the occasion of an intervillage dispute. The people who described this dispute and its proposed sanction had never heard of this type of food presentation before it was resurrected on this occasion. Once again the actual presentation was not performed.

10. This dance first appeared in the North Baining in the late 1940s and diffused through the area over the next two decades. It was performed in every inland village when I did my original research in 1976–78. When I returned in 1991, however, I learned that it had not been performed in Raunsepna for at least a decade and was now considered to have died out.

In most cases these dances are done for fun, as the Baining say for "play," and not for any stated or recognized social, cultural, natural, or supernatural reason. There is no apparent association with social themes, calendrical events, or beliefs. In this chapter, I will describe the dances only in respect to their intra- and intercommunity aspects, since analysis and interpretation of the form and content of the various dances make up chapters 9 and 10. One important function of such special events is that they bring people together both during the preparations and for the performances. Baining dances are performed by a locality. People cooperate on this project, not because they are relatives or friends (although this might be the case) but because they are neighbors. The people of one locality (village or region) put on a dance and invite those from the surrounding districts. A community or region is always invited as a group. The invitation is reciprocated when the visitors turn hosts.

As we will see, these dances take a lot of work to prepare. They are occasions where large groups of men gather daily and work together, which is in contrast to the relatively isolated normal daily routine. The atmosphere in the bush camps where the preparations take place is the antithesis of normal social life; it is energetic, bustling, and colorful. People talk and joke with zest and move freely from one task to another. While not every man comes every day, and some men never come at all, it nevertheless takes a strong collective effort to put on one of these dances. A similar atmosphere of solidarity prevails in the song rehearsals held by women in the village. The Baining themselves recognize this invigorating and joyous aspect of their preparations and dances.

The dances themselves are occasions for large numbers of people to come together for the day to watch and socialize. This type of event is perhaps the one which brings together the largest group of Baining at one place and time.

Mission Influences

It is clear that the missions have played the most important role in the postcontact life of the Baining. Their role is not just religious but economic and social. The church has provided a new level of social interaction. Church services are a weekly occasion at which virtually all members of the community gather.[11] In a society where large gatherings of

11. This is less true in Yalom. Although services were held more regularly there in 1991 than in the past, not everyone in the community participated, and there was no tradition of weekly meetings following services.

any kind were extremely rare, as infrequent as once a year, this has greatly increased the frequency of social interaction. The Baining have taken the opportunity presented by the church gatherings to congregate for other reasons as well. After the service, everybody gathers outside to visit and socialize. There is a constant circulation of people among the seated groups, exchanging betel nut and talk. Eventually the scattered groups coalesce and a village meeting is held. Here are brought the disputes of the preceding week and the requests for the following week. People haggle over the garden damage done by a pig or the rowdiness of a group of men drinking. They discuss forthcoming events such as a church fund-raiser, a work party on the road, or a proposed dance. People wanting assistance building a house or garden fence make their requests in this forum.

The missions instituted communal work projects even prior to the administration's demands for labor. For many years the Catholics demanded one day of labor a week. This labor pool enabled the construction of churches, schools, aid posts, roads, hydroelectric schemes, and provided labor for mission gardens. It also gave people the incentive to cooperate on such projects. The Catholic mission in particular was constantly initiating new ventures to raise money for both the church and the community. They planted blocks of coffee, coconuts, and cocoa. They educated and trained people in carpentry, nursing, and teaching. Even when they did not have the money to employ these persons, they gave them skills that could be utilized by other agencies. In many Melanesian societies, this practice of education and training has worked to create a skilled labor pool. Among the Baining, however, most of the students have returned to their villages and taken up a traditional lifestyle. Only a few have continued to use their training either within the community or outside it. In the following chapters, I will be looking at what lies behind the Baining reluctance either to leave their communities or to distinguish themselves within these communities.

3   History

The Baining are assumed to be the original inhabitants of the Gazelle Peninsula. Their coastal neighbors, the Tolai, are Austronesian speakers who are believed to have migrated into the region from New Ireland around the end of the eighteenth century.[1] The Tolai settled most heavily along the Blanche Bay and Kokopo stretches of the Gazelle coast, but several groups moved north into the fringe of the Baining area. For the most part, these Tolai lived on offshore islands, where their mastery of canoe building and fishing could most benefit them.

From the time of the Tolai's arrival, but probably pre-dating that event, the Baining lived not on the coast, but in the mountains. Even the so-called "coastal Baining" actually inhabited the hills facing the sea. While it was undoubtedly healthier to live in the mountains because the altitude reduced the risk of malaria, it is also certain that here they were also less vulnerable to the raids of their Tolai neighbors.

Early historical accounts and the Baining's own reports of events suggest that relations between the Tolai and the Baining were mostly antagonistic and aggressive. Both the Tolai and the Baining were cannibals and devoured any enemies slain in battle, but it seems that the Tolai made concerted efforts to lure the Baining into ambush in order to obtain corpses or to enslave some Baining as workers. Although they lived in the mountains, the Baining needed to make periodic trips to the coast to replenish their supply of seawater and to gather various sorts of shellfish from the mangrove swamps. It was on these excursions that they were most vulnerable to Tolai attack. Mission accounts (Rascher 1909) suggest that these raids were not infrequent, and while it was mostly the local Tolai tribes who made the raids, they traded their slaves along the coast to other Tolai districts. According to observ-

---

1. The Tolai migration to New Britain is assumed to have occurred after a large volcanic eruption, which created both the volcano and island of Matupit. The Tolai are assumed to have arrived after this eruption because they have an origin myth that describes them coming out of the volcano. The myth suggests that the volcano pre-dates the people. Why the origin myth is of such recent origin is a question not addressed in this calculation.

ers such as Rascher (1909) and Parkinson (1907), the Tolai desire for slaves arose from the fact that they themselves hated to do any sort of manual labor, including gardening or building mission stations. Conversely, the Baining were praised as industrious workers. This trait, which as we will see later in this book is a central value in Baining society, was also one of the first characteristics to be noted by outsiders, and in fact was a key symbol of the Baining perception of themselves in relation to those around them. All these factors played a role in the ensuing colonial process.

The Gazelle Peninsula and all of the Bismarck Archipelago became part of the German sphere of influence in the late nineteenth century, first as part of the territory administered by the German New Guinea Company, and then after 1899 as part of the German colony Kaiser Wilhemsland. The Baining contact with the Germans was basically of two kinds: religious and economic. In the 1890s, the Catholic mission (Mission of the Sacred Heart) was vying with the Wesleyans (now the United Church) for religious domination. The Gazelle was divided so that each mission was granted absolute dominion in part of the territory (Rascher 1909: 55). The Coastal Baining area fell into the Catholic domain.[2] The German Catholic clergy, intrigued and attracted by the idea of missionizing these savage heathens, began exploring the area in 1894.

The Mission

In the early to mid-1890s there were only a few lone European traders in the hinterlands. One of these, an Irishman, was settled along the Baining coast at Massawa Bay. This spot became a stepping stone for expeditions into the area. The first mission station in the area, Vunamarita, was opened by Father Rascher in 1896, next door to Massawa.

The church was greatly advanced in its mission by an opportune series of events. Some time in 1896 there was a large Tolai slave raid on the Baining. It was reported that the Tolai had lured the Baining from around Gavit down to the coast whereupon they set on them and killed, ate, or enslaved about fifty people. Several of those enslaved were traded along the coast towards Blanche Bay where they came to the attention of the German administration. The administration, especially Dr. Hahl (then the chief justice, but later the governor) in conjunction with the Catholic Church (led by Bishop Coupe) decided to make

2. The same competition occurred when the inland area was opened, and that region was parceled out into several Methodist villages and several Catholic ones. Which village became which is traceable to precontact patterns of raiding and alliance.

an example of this case. They decided to return the slaves, seven Baining youths between the ages of sixteen and twenty, to their villages.
In doing this, they simultaneously served notice to the Tolai that raiding and enslavement were not permitted by the government, while
they demonstrated to the Baining that the government (and by association, the church) could be an ally in their long-standing struggle with
the Tolai. The expedition made by Dr. Hahl to return the freed slaves
to Gavit also brought Father Rascher, Bishop Coupe, and his associates
to Vunamarita to begin building their mission (Rascher 1909: 135–58).
The Catholic mission was thus clearly identified as a mediating agency
between the two tribes. Perhaps for these reasons, the Baining were
immediately more receptive and the Tolai were at first more wary of
the church than their traditional habits would have led one to predict.
Rascher sought to concentrate on converting the Baining.

In 1898 Rascher began building a new mission on a block of land
near the Baining village of Puktas, which was less than two hours' walk
from Vunamarita. This new mission was planned as a major mission
station, and prefabricated buildings were prepared for it by the church
carpenters at the Vunapope headquarters. In preparation for the movement of the big loads inland, Father Rascher began the construction of
a major road between Vunamarita on the coast and St. Paul's, the new
station. This road was the first of what was to become a fairly extensive
network of German roads in the coastal Baining region. Rascher's reports from this period describe the Baining as very industrious workers
who would work all day for a piece of tobacco, in explicit contrast to
the Tolai who demanded constant rests and were always begging for
things like tobacco (Rascher 1909: 155).

Despite this praise of the Baining's industry, neither Rascher nor
other observers had a very positive impression of their culture and
mental capabilities. Rascher writes that although the Baining are full
of good will, they are way below the other natives as far as mental
faculties are concerned (1909: 255ff.); Parkinson notes that they are
completely primitive and simple in all respects (1907: 155). They are
described as big, fearful, and untalented, although it is noted that these
characteristics are emphasized in the light of the unceasing hostility of
their neighbors. In implied contrast to the Tolai, they are described as
mere cultivators, engaging in no seafaring or exchange activities.
Rascher speculates that to their enemies they appeared as mere animals, creatures without a soul (1909: 265). By implication, the European
opinion was not much different.[3]

3. Compare this to Errington and Gewertz (1994), and Epstein (1968) on the various
ways that the Tolai and Duke of York Islanders were essentially pre-adapted to colonial
culture, values, money, exchange, etc.

Although Rascher never significantly altered his opinion of the Baining, he became more jocular in his characterization of them as dirty, fearful, and stupid savages as he became more fond of them. The Baining's perceived savagery only seemed to act as a stimulus to Rascher to work harder to raise them from this primitive level both spiritually and culturally. As a result, the St. Paul's mission station became a paragon of accomplishment for a few short years. What started out as a fifty-hectare plantation was doubled in size when the governor gave the mission another fifty hectares as a measure of his approval of its efforts. It later received another two hundred hectares when Dr. Hahl became governor and he too expressed his appreciation of the church's work.[4] On this ever-expanding plantation Rascher experimented with coffee, coconuts, and cocoa. Everything thrived. Because of its altitude, the missionaries were also able to produce such European delicacies as cabbage, potatoes, and beets, and for a while it became the market garden for all the German missionaries in New Britain. Such success led to expansion, and by 1902 the station was home to three ecclesiastical sisters and a brother in addition to Father Rascher. A second priest, Father Rutten, also lived at St. Paul's for two years, before moving on and setting up a second Baining mission at Nucharunep, two to three hours away.

One of the schemes this expanding group initiated was a Christian Village for many of the orphans raised by the mission. Since a large percentage of these orphans were Baining ex-slaves who had been freed by the church and then taken in and educated at Vunapope (the main Catholic station), Rascher was able to convince the church hierarchy that the Baining area was an appropriate place to found such a village (Rascher 1909: 358). He saw this village not only as a home for displaced persons, but as a model for the rest of the Baining. Consequently, great care was given to the construction of the houses and the planting of the gardens. It was not long before residents of this village began marrying local Baining. Whether it was the example of these new residents or the completion of a sawmill by the river, the natives of Puktas soon began to build better houses. This improvement, in conjunction with the donning of loin cloths, convinced Rascher that they were almost ready for baptism.

Despite the signs of success in all Rascher's undertakings, resentment, discontent, and misunderstanding were brewing. Rascher complained more and more about the cold-heartedness of the Baining, despite all he had done for them (1909: 419). These undercurrents became

---

4. Only recently (1991 is when I heard about this) have the people of Puktas and Lan begun to express dissatisfaction over this uncompensated expropriation of land.

stronger and soon coalesced in a plot against the missionaries. The leader of the plot, a Baining named Tomaria, was one of the inhabitants of the Christian Village. A former slave, he had been raised and educated by the Catholic mission from the age of fourteen. He had also worked on plantations on the mainland of New Guinea and was thus a good deal more worldly than his neighbors. Tomaria's immediate dispute with the mission involved marriage difficulties. Unhappy in his church-sanctioned marriage, he ran away with the wife of another Baining. When she was persuaded to return to her former husband, Tomaria began proselytizing against the life of "morals" and reminisced about the former "free" life and polygamous customs of the Baining. He incited discontent among the other natives by demanding pigs, taro, coconuts, etc., ostensibly as contributions to the mission but without mission authorization. When the mission failed to remunerate them, Tomaria used their anger to draw them into his conspiracy. On August 13, 1904, Tomaria led a bloody massacre at St. Paul's and Nucharunep, which killed a total of ten missionaries—two priests (Fathers Rascher and Rutten), three brothers, and five sisters.

The colonial administration took decisive retaliatory action. A reward was posted for each murderer killed or taken. The police made several punitive forays into the Baining mountains and eventually all the perpetrators of the deed were believed to be imprisoned or dead. The administration saw this uprising as a clear blow against all white colonials and insisted on making it an example for all native peoples by imposing heavy punitive action.

The church immediately proclaimed the dead to be martyrs, having died in the cause of the church. In the ensuing years, the victims have been presented to the Vatican as martyrs and are presently moving up the canonical hierarchy towards sainthood. The bishop prophesied, "[now that some] blood has flowed, the mission will flourish" (Rascher 1909: 453), and in this he was correct. To the Baining, this incident signifies the turning point in their relations with both church and state, and they became the good Christians that they remain today. To this day, they refer to the murdered white Germans as "our martyrs" and celebrate the anniversary of the massacre as an important church holiday.

Colonization in Earnest

In the first decade of the twentieth century, the German administration began expropriating land in earnest. Most of the Baining coastline was alienated as huge tracts of land were given or sold for commercial development. These lands were mostly turned into coconut plantations, and by 1908 there were eleven plantations listed in the Baining region (German New Guinea Annual Report 1907–8: 24). These grandiose land development schemes required a vast labor pool. The Baining were persuaded to provide a portion of this labor, but their small population could not provide the number of workers required. Consequently, many contract laborers were imported from other parts of the territory. The Baining were thus subjected not only to the European presence in their territory, but to that of many other New Guinean tribes as well.[5] Whole Baining villages were conscripted to work on the plantations, and particularly to construct miles of serviceable roads. Each plantation needed a network of roads for maintenance and harvesting, but there was also a grand scheme to link the roads through adjoining plantations and thus eventually to have a road link from the south side of the Weberhaven (now Ataliklikun Bay) all the way to Cape Lambert. This was a massive effort, which was very nearly accomplished before the outbreak of World War I. Many of these roads are still in service, and others are overgrown but discernable. It is an eerie sensation to be walking through deep tropical forest and realize that one has been walking for a long time on a completely straight and level path now completely overgrown with trees and brush and to be told that this was an old German road.

At the outset of World War I, in September 1914, the Australians invaded and occupied German New Guinea. The German forces surrendered almost immediately. German laws, nevertheless, remained in effect for the duration of the war (Jinks, Biskup, and Nelson 1973: 202). During the war, many of the Germans remained on their plantations. After the war, the German territories were taken over by the League of Nations, which gave the mandate for the administration of the New Guinea Territories to Australia. Civilian rule was not restored until May 1921 (Jinks, Biskup, and Nelson 1973: 230). For quite a few years after the war there was no effective colonial administration among the Baining.[6]

5. In the early twentieth century the government made a concerted effort to contact and pacify all the native tribes, that is to bring "the races into the union" (German New Guinea Annual Report 1904–5: 69). They sought to do this by contacting isolated tribes and drawing them into the labor force. As many observers of colonialism have noted elsewhere, the institution of a head tax was a device, not so much for raising revenue as for necessitating native participation in the cash economy. It was used to effect the same process in New Britain. The coastal plantations acted as a magnet for communities living up in the adjacent mountains (the villages further inland were still uncontacted) and whole villages moved to the coast to share in the cash and material items available there.

6. We know that in the 1920s and 1930s the life of the coastal Baining remained intertwined with the institutions of the mission, government, and plantation. The institutional

As mentioned above, for some time the trend had been for the Baining to abandon their mountain villages and move to the coast. This move was initially encouraged since it tied them more firmly into the colonial economy, but the government soon became alarmed at their apathy, ill health, and steady population decline. Different government officers had different ideas about both the causes and the cures for the Baining's ills. The interventions are cumulatively a comedy of errors. Several officials were disgusted by the Baining's scattered and semi-nomadic life and tried to get them to settle down in larger groups, preferably nearer "civilization." All too often these new settlements were at lower altitudes, which increased the prevalence of malaria. They were also in close proximity to the plantations, and there were problems with laborers from other parts of New Guinea Territory. Other administrators thought it was the Baining house style which was at fault, and ordered them to build "better" houses on piles off the ground. Unfortunately, these better houses were unsuited to the Baining climate, which could be cold and drafty. The Baining did not know how to build hearths inside raised houses, which meant that there was no warming fire at night. One patrol officer thought that the high infant mortality was due to an insufficient diet, and he introduced goats into the region with the expectation that the Baining would milk them and give the milk to their children. Unfortunately the Baining were disgusted by the idea of drinking animal milk and instead they killed the goats for meat.

In 1927 Gregory Bateson, then a graduate student at Cambridge University, arrived in New Guinea to begin anthropological fieldwork. Although his original desire was to work in the Sepik, he was persuaded by E. W. P. Chinnery to try a tribe closer to civilization on the assumption that it would be easier. He chose the Central Baining and went to live with the people of Latramat village. Although he pursued this research for over fourteen months, took pains to learn the language, and filled many notebooks with data, Bateson considered this project a failure. He was frustrated because he was unable to elicit even such basic information as genealogies or taboos. All information had to be "dragged out of them one sentence at a time" (quoted in Lipset 1980: 129) and even then did not provide enough information on which to

---

records (patrol reports and mission documents) from this period were all destroyed during World War II, however. The Baining situation between the wars would be completely unknown, except for an occasional mention in the Australian government reports to the League of Nations, if it were not for P. Pentony's thesis on Baining demographics (1940). As preparation for his report, Pentony read and digested all the patrol reports for these years. He summarizes them in his work, thus preserving a record of the Baining plight during this period.

base an analysis. He wrote, "I understand now what Malinowski meant when he said ethnologists must be able to withstand boredom" (quoted in Lipset 1980: 128). The Baining were undoubtedly boring, leading a "drab and colorless existence" except when they performed their dances (Bateson 1931–32). Since these dances were totally lacking in native exegesis, he was unable to use them as a focus from which to explore the culture. He abandoned his study of the Baining in 1928 and published only one article on them (Bateson 1932).

> The Baining increasingly came to have a reputation as a "timid and lackadaisical people" and, although they are well built and muscular and look strong and healthy enough, they appear to be lacking in stamina. They are somewhat filthy in their habits and appear to lack the will to fight any illness and their general attitude appears to be, "Oh, well, I am sick. If I die, I die. I am going to remain in my house and I cannot be bothered about anything." It would seem that this is the attitude to life generally. (Report to the League of Nations on the Administration of the Trust Territory of New Guinea 1938–39: 26)

To some other observers this perceived apathy was a result of "extreme stupidity"; they saw the Baining as a race suited only for simple laborious work. Others denied that they were stupid, and suggested that they appeared as such because they were extremely "introverted." As introverts they were reserved in the presence of strangers and lacked self-confidence. They therefore did not function well in acculturated settings such as in law courts or plantations (Pentony 1940: 22–23). They were extremely submissive to both Europeans and laborers from other parts of New Guinea, which was perhaps a carry-over from their aboriginal and persisting attitude towards the Tolai.

World War II

In 1942 the Japanese occupied the Gazelle Peninsula. Although their headquarters were in Rabaul and around the Blanche Bay, they also had important installations in Open Bay. The route between Rabaul and Open Bay lay across the Baining territory. The Japanese had a lot of cargo that urgently needed to be transported across these mountains, so they rounded up all the inland Baining (hitherto virtually uncontacted) and put them to work. The Japanese had several camps in the mountains, including a big wireless station on the mountain between Yalom and Raunsepna. There were other camps along the coast among the plantations. To support these installations, the Japanese demanded food and labor from every Baining person—men and women, the very old and the very young.

According to informants, the Japanese were exceedingly brutal to all the natives, killing and torturing anyone they suspected of disobedience. My informants told many stories of workers being forced to dig their own graves and then stand in front of them to be shot or have their throats slit as their relatives were forced to look on. Others described how a Baining woman was killed by having water poured down her throat until she drowned. Whipping and overworking were common. The Baining were forced to carry cargo for up to fifteen hours a day and were denied any food rations. In fact, many of them told stories of how hungry Japanese would rip food out of their hands. All their pigs and poultry were killed to feed the Japanese. Although the Baining were put to work growing gardens for the Japanese, there was not enough food, and hunger was rampant. Towards the end of the occupation, Baining gardens were stripped bare and nothing was replanted. In fact numerous individuals told me of an incident that must have been the supreme psychological torture to the Baining. The Baining were ordered to bring all their food to the Japanese. When they were confronted with these vast displays of taro, the soldiers deliberately cut the stalks off each tuber above the point necessary to regenerate, thus effectively, with one stroke, preventing any future harvest. The Baining described this as "cutting the necks of the taro." To them, this was murder, and the community mourned the dead foodstuffs, which as we will see literally and symbolically meant the ability to reproduce their lives. To this day, the hatred of the Japanese is venomous as the misery and racism is recalled.

The Japanese were not the Baining's only enemy, however. A number of plantation laborers from the New Guinea mainland were stranded in the area after the retreat of the Australians. Many of these Melanesians suffered the same fate as the Baining, but a number of them (mainly Aitape and Sepik natives) joined forces with the Japanese and assisted them as members of the Kempi (the Japanese native police). These collaborators took further advantage of the Baining by raping, stealing, and plundering things that even the Japanese did not want.

> The simple Baining native was looked down on by the foreign, and throughout the Japanese occupation, the Baining virtually lived a life of slavery, having to fulfill the slightest little want of the foreign natives who were living amongst them. (Parrish 1946: 14)

Following the devastation that the Japanese occupation wrought, and despite the Baining's relief at the Japanese departure, life did not get easier for the Baining for a long time. The most serious difficulty was the lack of food. Gardens had not been planted for months, there was virtually no seed available, and people were weak, ill, and depressed. There were virtually no children in the coastal communities since there had been no births during the war.

Postwar Experiences

The mountain Baining seemed to make a faster recovery than coastal Baining after the war. Patrol reports describe the inland villages as healthier and containing large numbers of young children.[7] From their short prewar contact with missionaries these inland communities had come to resent the need to support the mission personnel. Some of this resentment may have stemmed from the Methodists' practice of sending in Tolai missionaries, thus reviving old enmities. After the war these villages expressed a reluctance to become missionized, feeling that the missions had undermined the Baining way of life. Parrish quotes a native from Raunsepna as saying,

> Look at the mission villages with very few old people living to a ripe old age, women bearing very few children, all their tribal rites and celebrations have been forgotten whereas we still have these and they give an added zest to life. The mission natives do not enjoy life because they are afraid that they might do something wrong and their God will punish them. If we have the mission with us we will just become the same as the other mission natives and die out and we don't want this to happen. (1946: 10)

Although they were informed that they need not accept missionaries into their midst, in a short while all the communities were missionized, with Raunsepna itself becoming a big Catholic mission station in the mid 1950s. These mountain villages did, however, maintain their traditional dances alongside Christian practices.

The patrol officers during the postwar decade continued to describe the Baining as "docile, hardworking and obedient" and quoted the

7. Although the Territory was again mandated to Australia, this time by the United Nations, it was not until 1946 that administrative patrols again entered the Bainings. The Catholic mission preceded the administration into the area with the reopening of the mission at Vunamarita. Several plantation managers also returned to the area immediately after the war.

missionaries as saying that they had a "slave complex" inherited from the days of subjugation by the Tolai (Orken 1954: 7). Officers such as Orken suggest

> they are a people who will respond to firm control, but that control must be continuous, and it is not sufficient to send a patrol into the area once in every twelve months, and hope that the native situation will continue to be maintained or improved. (1954: 7)

After the war the Baining were visited by a succession of patrol officers. Rarely did the same patrol officer return a second time (the exception to this was Parrish, who patrolled in both 1946 and 1947). This lack of continuity prevented the officers from accumulating any knowledge and experience that would benefit the Baining. It does, however, give us a picture of the postwar Baining through many eyes. Each patrol officer to traverse the area felt compelled to record how the Baining seem to have been neglected by the prewar administration, the postwar patrols, and all medical practitioners (Parrish 1947a, 1947b; D'Arcey 1948; Williams 1949).

The patrol officers constantly harp on the themes of consolidating the villages, building better houses, digging latrines, and encouraging bathing, as the cure-alls for ill health, declining population, and apathy. Despite the government's desire to settle the Baining in real, centralized villages, their traditional tendency to fragment into dispersed hamlets persisted. Although the Baining continued to construct houses within the villages, they tended to live in smaller houses amidst their gardens. This meant that they were frequently absent from the villages when patrols visited. In 1954, Orken attributed the Baining's tendency to disperse to their habit of farming out newly born children to foster parents in distant hamlets.

> The feeling of cohesion which should inherently exist in a family, is thus not present right from the beginning, moreover, marriage appears to be an extremely simple procedure in which a man expresses a desire for a mate, and she goes to him without any ritual of "bride price" or feasting. (1954: 5)

Both practices were taken to be evidence of the lack of normal social values and economic drives among the Baining.

The Baining practice of adoption continued to frustrate and annoy patrol officers, who found it confusing when doing censuses and thought that it undermined the concept of the family. In 1957 Haywood writes,

> I had the opportunity to prove the old Baining custom of
> changing babies, at Yalom, during this patrol. The parents
> were rather embarrassed at the disclosure and I have hopes
> that this rather useless and undesirable custom will cease.
> (1957a: 10)

No one took the time to inquire into Baining beliefs about adoption to
try to discover why this practice was so prevalent. Orken was right to
attribute importance to it, but did not make the effort to ascertain its
significance. He and the others saw it simply as a problem to eliminate,
not realizing that its very endurance was an indication of its importance (see chapter 4).

The different patrol officers all comment on the Baining's avid interest in horticulture, their abundant and prosperous gardens, and their
keenness to obtain and try new crops and varieties (Parrish 1946;
D'Arcey 1948; Williams 1949). Work and gardening are important activities and values for the Baining, as this book will show, and ones
that could have been better used to stimulate the Baining to new activity. One patrol officer actually did conceive of helping the Baining in
this way. Williams was inspired to combine the Baining enthusiasm
for gardening with the skills that many of them had acquired as casual
labor on a number of the coastal plantations and suggested that the
Baining be given coffee seed to plant as a cash crop (Williams 1949:
4). Here, one runs into the problem of the lack of any administrative
continuity from one year to the next, as such schemes were not followed up and so they often failed, not so much from disinterest as
from ignorance and lack of administrative persistence. For example,
the idea of introducing a coffee growing scheme in the Komgi-Yalom
area is repeated in Orken's 1954 patrol report (7), so obviously nothing
had been done in the interim.

Despite the lack of government persistence in such economic
schemes, some Baining actually took matters into their own hands and
began to plant cocoa. Unfortunately their ignorance meant that they
planted it badly (without shade trees) and it did poorly. Nevertheless,
this initiative did in fact get them the attention they deserved, and in
1955 an agricultural officer came in to advise them (Martyn 1956: 2).
In addition to training several Baining in cocoa production, the government also encouraged the planting of coconuts (in areas below 2,000
feet) and coffee. The administration was very anxious to encourage
cash cropping among the Baining and thus to tie them into the larger
cash economy.

In 1954 it was reported that the population decline had been reversed. For the first time in probably two decades, births outnumbered
deaths (Orken 1954: 10). This trend was still very tenuous, and through-

out the 1950s the population increased only slightly. By the mid-1960s, however, the population definitely seemed to be on the rebound. In 1964 there was a population increase of 4 percent in the mountain areas (Hart 1964: 5). In 1976, my informants told me that the women were now starting to "fill up the place again" by having large families. The Baining area continued to show enormous increases in population, including a virtual doubling of population between 1980 and 1990, but these increases include not only in-migration into the area, but significant improvement in census techniques which give a more accurate count.[8]

From 1953 to 1957 there were several incidents of cargo cultism in the mountains.[9] In general, it was believed that the Baining were particularly susceptible to cult beliefs because of their basically primitive culture and mentality (Martin 1955: 4; Martyn 1955: 3). This primitivism was "enhanced by neglect by both the Administration and Mission bodies" (Martyn 1955: 1). The patrol officer in charge believed that the Baining "suffer from an inferiority complex" (Martyn 1955: 1). He further stated that although they are "apathetic and lethargic, . . . they are extremely good workers at gardening" (1955: 1).

In 1956 a patrol post was opened at Raunsepna as a result of this series of cargo cult incidents. It was felt that an administrative presence was needed to keep control in the area. Martyn believed that this post initially fulfilled its promise. He stated that

> the Bainings are well-known for their apathetic behavior. There has been a lessening of that apathy. A little more interest is being shown by the natives, reticence lessened and shyness decreasing. (1956: 1)

He believed that these changes directly reflected their confidence in the administration.

The location of the patrol and aid posts at Raunsepna established it as a regional center. Consequently the Catholic mission chose this site for a mission station and school for the inland Baining. This school was a boarding school, which attracted students from all over the region. The only other school in the area offering full instruction, including

8. The total population for the Lassul-Baining district was 8,804 for 1980 and 14,731 for 1990. This includes the population of the plantations in the area, as well as Tolai and others who have moved into the region. The birth rate was estimated at 4 percent with an overall growth rate of about 3.3 percent (East New Britain Statistics Office 1991). The population of East New Britain as a whole in 1990 was larger than projected a decade earlier for the year 2000.

9. Cargo activity in the North Baining area has been relatively scarce and short-lived in comparison with that in other parts of the Gazelle (cf. Whitehouse 1995).

English, was run by the Catholics at Vunamarita. It was not until the mid-1960s that the first government school was opened in the area, at Malasait, and only in 1988 did the last two villages, Yalom and Komgi, get funding for a school.

At the same time that the inland Baining area was beginning to get attention in the form of posts, schools, and missions, the desire to plant cash crops such as coffee, cocoa, and coconuts began to draw people down to the coast where these crops prosper. Most of the mountain villages had claim to vast areas of coastal or subcoastal land (which were aboriginally exploited for saltwater, seafood, and tree bark for bark cloth), and it was on these lands that they planted blocks of cash crops. The inland people insisted that this investment did not mean that they were abandoning their mountain terrain, but merely that they would migrate periodically down to the coast to care for their blocks. In actuality, however, since these blocks were at some distance from the mountain villages, people often spent long periods of time in residence in these secondary coastal hamlets. Over time, these residences often became permanent. Soon the once large mountain villages were reduced to clusters of several far-flung hamlets. For over a decade this de facto fission went unrecognized, and those living in the coastal hamlets were still officially registered in the census books for Komgi, Yalom, Raunsepna, and Wiliambempki. In the 1970s, however, the coastal communities were finally recognized as separate villages, and issued their own census books. Ironically, this recognition occurred just as a reverse migration was in progress. In the early 1980s cardamom was introduced as a new cash crop that could be grown at higher altitudes. Since it was an initially profitable crop, it drew people back into the mountains. However, since it needed to be sold to dealers, people attempted to plant blocks of cardamom within a mile or so of the few roads in the region. This meant that new settlements grew up on the margins of the territory by the roads. During this phase, some Baining had three residences: one in the old village, a coastal block for cocoa, and a third block for cardamom. A drastic fall in cardamom prices in 1988–89 meant a drastic fall in incomes. Many Baining abandoned these new blocks and returned to their traditional villages.

As the Baining began to engage seriously in cash-cropping activities they became increasingly aware that the continuous string of plantations along the coast deprived them of valuable economic land and even of a reasonable anchorage for their own use. For the first time they began to understand the value of land. This growing awareness of economics had other ramifications. This was the first time that individual Baining had ever needed or wanted permanently to alienate land. Since land was plentiful, this did not immediately cause problems. People claimed the land that they cleared and planted.

Although land consciousness increased greatly in the late 1950s, the Baining had been discovering the problems of ownership for some time before this. Right after World War II, the Baining in the vicinity of Vunapalading (Rangulit village) became involved in a land dispute with the Tolai from Kabaira who were moving into the area. These Tolai had planted some temporary gardens in the area after the volcanic eruption of Matupit in 1937, when their lands were covered with volcanic ash and dust. They left during the war, but after the war they returned and on the basis of their prewar usage claimed permanent ownership of the land. They did not just claim the land from the Baining but also extorted large quantities of food and firewood from them, as if they were slaves.

> The Baining having been subjected to this treatment for many years are reconciled to it; however, now they are coming into their own and realize that there is a law which protects their rights as well as the Tolais, the Baining resent the indignities that they have suffered so long at the hands of their neighbors. (Parrish 1947b: 9)

Whenever it came to directly confronting the Tolai or bringing a court case, however, the Baining tended to submit to Tolai domination.

> The Baining laid strong complaints to me but in the presence of the Tolai, backed down and eventually quietly withdrew their complaint saying that they had resolved their differences themselves. I cannot find the reason for this apparent intimidation. (Brereton 1965: 6)

Within the next few years, however, the Baining began showing stronger antipathy to Tolai encroachments in the area. The Baining realized that letting a few Tolai in would be like a hole in a dike. Soon all the land-hungry Tolai would be flooding the area. In 1967 the patrol officer foresaw that this grace period of plenty would not last forever. He recommended that a demarcation committee be established in order to fix boundaries between individual blocks so as to prevent future disputes (Chamberlain 1967: 5). In 1969 a Land Demarcation Committee was formed with representatives from several villages (Sangkol 1969: 2).

In the early 1960s the earliest blocks of cocoa finally began to bear, and the Baining began reaping some reward for their efforts. With the increase of income, several coastal Baining began investing in fermenteries to process the cocoa beans themselves rather than selling the wet beans to the coastal plantations. This potentially allowed them to reap much greater profits. In Lan the construction of a fermentery was developed as a collective project.

In 1975 Papua New Guinea became independent. A great effort was made nationwide to educate the population about this development. The political and economic changes were rapid and interesting but often incomprehensible to the Baining, who could not distinguish between local and national levels of government or between civil, land, or criminal courts. The Baining were at first opposed to the Local Government Council, since many Baining confused the national elections with the inception of local government councils. The Baining were afraid that the creation of a Council would mean abandonment by the administration and felt unready to be left on their own to rule themselves. The Council initiated a number of small community projects such as galvanized water tanks, extending and repairing several coastal roads, and buying hand-operated pulpers for coffee growers in the mountains. Unfortunately, until the 1980s most of the Council projects were located on the coast, which did not improve the inland communities' enthusiasm for the organization.

For years the administrative reports are filled with suggestions for improving access to the mountain villages and providing transport for any cash crops that the Baining grow. The patrol officers drew strong correlations between the difficulties in getting the Baining involved in any sort of cash economy and the difficulties involved in getting any Baining product to market.

Although on one level the potential of a road excited great hope and interest among the Baining, on another level they feared it. Many Baining expressed the conviction that once a road entered the Baining area an invasion of Tolai squatters would follow (Chamberlain 1966: 3). They believed that the only thing that had kept the Tolai out of their area for so long was its almost complete inaccessibility except by foot. Although Chamberlain allayed the Baining's fears during his patrol, the fears were far from unreasonable, as the following quote demonstrates.

> In a period where the District is suffering from land shortage for the expanding Tolai population, it is essential that a fuller knowledge of the lightly populated, but extensive, Bainings area, be held. . . . It is not the intention to develop the area for the Bainings people alone, as is sometimes implied. (Norton 1966: 2)

The administration made several attempts to buy land in the inland area, promising the likelihood of a road in exchange, but the Baining refused to sell for fear of Tolai incursion. Despite all the talk about the need for an inland road, it is obvious that the perceived need was stronger in the minds of the administration and missionaries than it was in that of the Baining. Although they acknowledged the desirability of a road, it is evident that they did not value its functionality over the threat of losing their land to their traditional enemy. Although preliminary survey work for this project began as early as 1956, it was only in 1966 that any actual construction was begun. Although the road reached to Malasait on my arrival in the Bainings in 1976, it was only at the end of my stay in 1978 that construction was once again under way and the road could be seen approaching Raunsepna.

Change and Continuity

There is a constancy in the Baining's orientation towards their lives and their land, which remains unshaken. This consistency reemerged when Jeremy Pool undertook fieldwork with the Baining in 1969. His experience echoed that of Bateson both in particulars and general mood, despite the intervening forty years. Pool and his wife lived and worked in two North Baining communities, Puktas and Wiliam-bempki. He learned the language and developed a good rapport with the people. Many of his informants told me stories of the Pools' activities during their stay. These focused on how the Pools lived as Baining—how they gardened, cooked, and ate Baining food. In short, the Baining remember the Pools through the activities they engaged in and their success in having assimilated to Baining life. Having read his field notes I also know that Jeremy Pool did careful and thorough ethnography. Despite this, he felt frustrated and stymied by his inability to penetrate deeply into any aspect of Baining culture or social organization. He could not recognize any pattern in the apparent diffuseness of Baining culture and society, or conceive of an analysis that would explain the lack of structure in their society.

There has been a consistency in outsiders' perceptions of the Baining throughout the group's ninety-year contact with European civilization. There has also been a consistency in the activities and occupations engaged in by the Baining. As the preceding historical summary indicates, the Baining have interacted with and reacted to European and Japanese societies (e.g., by engaging in wage labor and cargo cultism). They have adopted a number of customs and activities from sources outside their society (e.g., cash cropping, religion, and education).

Nonetheless, these intercultural exchanges have been tempered by a characteristically Baining approach to the new stimuli and opportunities.

The consistency of Baining interaction with the outside is most plausibly explained as the result of the influence of persisting indigenous sociocultural structures. This consistency is also manifest in the ways that the coastal and inland Baining groups, who have been separated since precontact times, speak distinct dialects of the language, and differ in numerous particulars of social and ritual practice, still share the same structure of cultural categories: nature, society, work, play, sentiments, affect. This consistency is itself strong evidence of the existence and persistence of such underlying cultural structures. As will become apparent in the account of these structures presented in the following chapters, they are both (1) highly general (taking the form of abstract categories such as nature, society, work, and play; and orientations including sentiments and affects, which are manifested throughout the main areas of Baining life); and (2) substantively concerned with aspects of behavior and relationships that have not been directly affected or contradicted by the forms of Western contact to which the Baining have been exposed. These two characteristic aspects of Baining cultural structures help to account for why they have remained relatively unchanged over the decades of interaction with the outside world.

I am not claiming that Baining culture is unchanged, but that despite Bateson's and Pool's failure to define a "formulable" culture for the Baining such a culture not only exists but persists. Above all, however, it is the commitment of Baining people to the values of their culture, their persistence in reproducing those values through their daily activities, and their determined resistance to the imposition of alien patterns of work, values, or politics inconsistent with their own egalitarian system, that accounts for the continuity. This is not to claim that Baining culture or society, as a reified collective essence or entity, has reproduced itself through the medium of the practices or "habitus" of individual Baining, but on the contrary that Baining culture and society must be seen as the products of the activities of Baining persons as historical subjects, in response to specific historical conditions.

It is certainly not the case that the Baining have not changed, or that Baining culture has resisted all the alien influences to which it has been exposed. The point is rather to account for why the Baining have accepted some influences and changes and not others. As I have reported, the Baining have more or less willingly adopted, or accommodated themselves to, a number of cultural, social, and economic patterns from the colonial and independent Papua New Guinean state administrations to which they have been exposed, for example, the Catholic religion, the schooling of children, community councils with elected leaders, and limited cash crop production. They have become bilingual in neo-Melanesian, although they continue to speak their own language to one another within their own communities. These are significant cultural and social changes by any standard; none of them, however, has been adopted or allowed to develop in ways that would conflict with the core egalitarian values central to Baining communal life and the forms of work and "play" through which these values are produced.

Many contemporary anthropologists have been concerned to emphasize the importance of the impact of Western colonialism and transnational capitalism on non-Western peoples of the periphery, and to avoid overemphasizing the coherence, self-sufficiency and change-lessness of non-Western cultures. It is possible, however, to carry such attempts too far. By representing non-Western societies and their cultures as mere products of Western imperialism, their members unable to maintain any authentic identity as historical agents in their own right, they may ironically reproduce the ethnocentrism and cultural arrogance of Western imperialism that they seek to expose. Anthropologists can make an important contribution to correcting this sort of oversimplified reaction by emphasizing that peripheral peoples and cultural minorities like the Baining, despite their often brutal and oppressive historical experiences of imperialism, remain historical actors in their own right. The value of the Baining case and others like it is to demonstrate that non-Western cultures, even very simple ones like the Baining, may be far more resilient and capable of maintaining themselves and their values, even while changing in response to coexistence with the Western-dominated world system, than most Westerners assume.

4   Kinship, Adoption, and the Production of Society

> Whoever wants to have children should, in my opinion, choose
> them from the family of one of his friends. He will thus obtain a
> child such as he wishes, for he can select the kind he wants. And
> the one that seems fittest will be most likely to follow on his natural
> endowment. The difference is that in the latter way one can take
> one child out of many who is according to one's liking; but if one
> begets a child of one's own, the risks are many, for one is bound
> to accept him as he is.
>
> Democretos

> For human beings it is one of the necessities of life to have children,
> arising from nature and primeval law. It is obvious in the other
> animals too: they all have offspring by nature and not for the sake
> of profit. And when they are born, the parents work and rear each
> as best they can and are anxious for them while they are small,
> and if anything happens to them the parents are grieved. But for
> man it has now become an established belief that there should be
> also some advantage from the offspring.
>
> Democretos

The negotiation of kinship is at the heart of Baining social production.
The Baining comprehend kinship on two levels: it is first a set of biological relations, and second a set of culturally created and defined categories and relations. It is through the constant juxtaposition of these two
levels of kinship that the key structural elements of Baining society
emerge. While the Baining recognize both aspects of kinship, they do
not value them equally. For the Baining, culturally constituted, socially
created relationships take priority over biological ones. The value of
the social and cultural kinship relations, however, is only defined by
contrast with natural kin ties. The crux of this distinction is in whether
the ties are socially or naturally produced. Kinship based on biology
is naturally produced; that based on adoption is socially produced. The
contrast between natural ties and culturally constituted ones is not
static. Relations are not permanently classified as one type or the other,

but must constantly be produced and reproduced and in this process their nature may be transformed. People's everyday actions and activities produce these transformations and thereby generate structure and values of Baining society.

Parallel processes of transformation occur within three integrated domains. First, individuals are transformed from natural into social beings. Second, the basic kin unit, the nuclear family, is transformed from a natural set of biological relations into the social unit, which I call the household. Third, the prototypical domain of nature, the forest, is transformed into gardens and thence into social produce. The same key activities produce all these transformations; the intersection of these three cycles in turn constitutes the reproduction of Baining society. It is not the social order alone that is created through this integration, but the social actor, and the cultural structure of values and symbols on which that social order is based.

The Nuclear Family: A Locus of Shame

While the nuclear family appears to be the principal unit of Baining society, it is imbued with certain characteristics and tensions that subvert this appearance. The nuclear family (the unit composed of a husband, wife, and their natural offspring) is for the Baining a repository of complex emotions and attitudes revolving around tension and shame. While these tensions are sometimes overt, more often they are evidenced by avoidances of behaviors and relations that are felt to be shameful. Nuclear family members, for instance, do not use kinship terms towards one another either in address or in reference. They refer to one another by name. Young children just learning to speak may address their parents as *nana* (mommy, mama, from the Baining *gunan* [my mother]), or *mama* (daddy or papa from the Baining *gumam* [my father], although the familiar term for father is less frequently used these days than the pidgin term "papa," since *mama* has the ambiguous connotations of father in Baining and mother in pidgin), but children give up these kin terms between the ages of three and four in favor of their parents' given names. Baining say that it would be bad or shameful for the children to continue using these familial forms. Husbands and wives and siblings also avoid using kin terms. A man who referred to his wife as *guanirki* (my wife), was described to me as a man who did not "have shame."

Nuclear family members are also frequently quite critical of one another and explicitly ashamed of the others' actions. In particular, parents are quite critical of their children's behavior. This is as true when the child is grown up and married as when he or she is still young.

Parents are often critical of their children's abilities and motivations to work. They frequently scold their children for laziness, even after the children have worked hard all day. Parents often reproach their married children for "forgetting" about their parents, that is, for failing to perform proper filial obligations to parents such as assisting in building a house, helping in the gardens, or giving their parents food, tobacco, or betel nut. Langerkan, an older woman with three married children and three unmarried children, complained several times to me that none of her and her husband's children had helped them to build their home. In my conversations with her children, all of them claimed to have given at least some help in the construction process.

Grandparents frequently criticize their own children in regard to how they care for their grandchildren. Langerkan was a frequent critic of how her daughter Taluvian, who lived next door, treated the grandchildren. Taluvian, although a very indulgent mother, would occasionally get exasperated and slap one of the children—so as to "teach" him or her. Whenever this occurred, Langerkan would accuse Taluvian of being a bad mother and thus fostering a bad child. Taluvian would counter with the defense that some discipline was necessary to prevent outrageous behavior. This kind of conflict was endemic between the generations. Langerkan's criticisms of Taluvian were reflected in and parallel to Taluvian's criticisms of her own children.

Parents also claim to be ashamed of their children's public behavior. Parents often said that they would not defend their biological children against criticism from others in the community, even if the children were innocent of any wrong-doing. They would allow the children to be chastised by others, or even join in the chastisement themselves, because to come to the defense of their natural children would be shameful.

In spite of the problematic nature of the family unit, the nuclear family as the basic unit of the household functions as the primary subsistence and social unit among the Baining. This social unit can be glossed in Baining by adding the suffix *-kana* to the name of the male head of a household, or the suffix *-kina* to that of the female (*-kana* and *-kina* mean "with" or "and" in reference to humans, so the literal designation is "so and so and . . ."). The husband-wife dyad is necessary and sufficient for almost all gardening and subsistence activities. Husbands and wives do, in fact, work closely together, and in so doing they provide for their household's needs and wants. As we will see, this is critical for our discussion of production and reproduction. Children gradually share in the work of their parents.

The majority of social interaction also takes place within the household. Although visiting occurs with varying regularity, there are no special institutions or arenas for social interaction in traditional Baining society. Except for the years between puberty and marriage, when single-sex interaction predominates, most visiting and social behavior is not constrained by sex; men and women visit casually, and often as a couple, in one another's homes, in their gardens, or on the paths between these places. Only large gatherings such as those outside the church tend to be sexually segregated. There are no collective centers such as men's houses, menstrual huts, etc. In most social encounters, people meet as complementary nuclear households, or as people whose primary identities are as family members. There is no association on the basis of sex, age, or knowledge, per se.

Beyond the Nuclear Family: The Kinship System

Relations within the nuclear family household thus have a functionally primary position, despite the tension and shame attendant on them. This is in part because they provide the point of articulation for the set of wider relations, and in part because they integrate natural and cultural kinship. Relations beyond the nuclear family are free of these aspects of shame, embarrassment, and denial. These more distant relations, while not on a level with those classed in some societies as joking or licentious, are more relaxed and culturally acknowledged.

Baining kinship is of the Hawaiian or generational type, and is bilaterally acknowledged. In Lan, where genealogical knowledge is greater than in Yalom, kinship categories are correspondingly more complex, extending to five generations in either direction. There are terms for child, grandchild, great-grandchild, and great-great-grandchild, and their reciprocals. There is also a term for the subsequent generation, *anirka*, which informants said was the word for children of *awusinga*, or great-great-grandchildren. However, in practice, this term is rarely used in a lineal context, that is to refer to descendants of that generation; rather, it is used laterally. Fourth cousins or beyond call one another *anirka* (masc.) or *anirki* (fem.). The term *anirka* is also the most common term in Lan for spouse, and the Baining say that it means that the relationship between two individuals is distant enough that they can marry. There is no sense, however, that one must or ought to marry within this *anirka* category.

Among kin outside the nuclear family unit, kin terms are more frequently used. While people can and often do use kin terms with their grandchildren, they ought to use kin terms exclusively with their great-grandchildren. This is said to be so that the great-grandchildren learn the path between them. The same would be true with any descendants below great-grandchild, should a person live long enough to see them.

In Yalom, kin terminology is much more constricted. Many people do not even know the kin term for grandparent. This reduction in kin terminology goes along with a corresponding constriction in genealogical knowledge. Many people do not know the names of their grandparents. Where grandparents and grandchildren, or even great-grandparents and great-grandchildren exist or are known, they are usually referred to as parents or children, thus collapsing the generations between them.

Although the Lan Baining recognize and can name kin of these different degrees, most people's own genealogical knowledge does not extend beyond their grandparents. They are better able to use these extended kin terms in a classificatory sense than in a direct genealogical one. People might call one another by kin terms such as *ahakugi* (grandmother), *aiga* (great-grandfather), or *ambarki* (elder sister), although they are unable to trace the precise connection. They do this because they have grown up using these terms.

These extended paths are ones people can use and cultivate. These are the relatives one can ask for food, betel nut, or even money. They are an individual's support network and exchange group. Their relationship and support are recognized as stemming from kinship, even if it is not traceable, and are seen as transferable to one's children. These are the people who will be responsible for one's death feast. In contrast with the ease and unselfconscious behavior that is the norm with such kin, people tend to be shy, restrained, and "ashamed" in the company of those considered unrelated, such as the spouses of one's extended family, and nonrelatives. One is also restrained in asking for food and other things from one's children. Parents say that their children should think of them and bring them food, but they as parents cannot solicit these gifts. In fact, parents do often ask for and obtain food, tobacco, and betel nut from their children, but the ideal rule remains.

Formation of the Nuclear Family

The contrast in social behavior and attitudes within and beyond the nuclear family underlies the structure of Baining society. In a more general sense, Baining society emerges out of the opposition between given and produced, or natural and socially transformed. These principles are embedded in the formation, creation, and continuity of the family unit. The family has two aspects: on the one hand, it is the point of reproduction of biological persons and units; on the other, it is the primary social unit of the society. The latter attributes emerge through social transformations, of which the most important is adoption.

The nuclear family consists of a relation between two partners or spouses of the same generation, and relations between parents and children of successive generations. Both relations are grounded in biology: the first is a sexual relation, socially sanctioned through marriage, and the second is derived from reproduction and birth. For the Baining, both of these relations are problematic.

Marriage: The First Transformation

Marriage for the Baining is culturally de-emphasized. There are no prescribed categories of marriage partners. There are no exchanges, payments, feasts, or services as part of the marriage contract. That the Baining do not emphasize marriage, especially the act of marriage, as a *rite de passage*, is in itself an important datum. The fact that the Baining do little to call attention to the act or the implications of marriage contrasts with the fact that the married couple is a strong, self-sufficient and complementary unit in the society. Elaboration of the marriage ceremony would seem to be inconsistent with the contradiction that marriage represents for Baining values and their cultural order of experience. The key to the contrast lies in the difference between what the newly imposed relationship of marriage grants to the newlyweds, and what they then go on to make of their lives together.

Pre-Marital Sex

Marriage for the Baining is a social and cultural sanction for the act of sexual intercourse. Among the Baining there is very little pre-marital intercourse. When a case is discovered, it arouses emotions of disgust and anger. Until recently a couple who were discovered to have committed an act of intercourse were then considered de facto married. Nowadays, in both Lan and Yalom, a fine is imposed on the offending party or parties in the event of a refusal to go along with the marriage, but in the past there was no choice. If either participant is caught more than once, however, he or she is likely to be publicly denounced as an animal (usually a pig). The reference to animals in the case of sexual offenders is strong evidence for an association between sexuality and nature. So also is the fact that young couples who do have intercourse usually go into the bush at night to do it. Sometimes a couple wanting to get married will take the decision out of their parents' hands by having intercourse and then telling their parents about it, thus forcing their parents to designate them as a married/engaged couple. In fact, a couple need not have gone so far as to have had intercourse for these sanctions to take effect. Merely being found together at night, or reporting back that they had held one another ("scratching one another's skin," as the Baining say), is thought to constitute sufficient intimacy to warrant a marriage.

Marriage

Traditionally, marriage was arranged by the parents of the couple. In Lan this practice has been dying out recently, and parents now tend to consult their children before making any such arrangements. They may ask whether or not their child wants to marry a particular person, or solicit outright suggestions from the child involved. Nowadays, the parents tend to mark a couple as engaged, but then they wait until the priest arrives before performing the ceremony that marries them. In Lan the institution of marriage has been taken over almost entirely by the church, which makes a good deal more of the *rite* than was traditionally the case. During this period of engagement, each one of the prospective partners is full of shame towards the other, and they do not interact if possible. This often contrasts with their behavior before becoming engaged. This shame is an expression of the underlying tensions that marriage involves. They are marked as prospective spouses (i.e., prospective sexual partners), but they do not yet have any social, productive relations. The aspects of shame override the socially valued relations, so the preponderant relation between them is shame.

In Yalom traditional arranged marriage is still the rule, but the single men in the village all expressed desires to change the pattern. They hoped their parents would take their likes and dislikes into consideration. A young man had recently run away from his new wife and stayed away until the parents agreed to void the marriage, and people took this as a sign of the times.

Before arranging a marriage, the parents of a son or daughter would look around for an industrious spouse. When a good mate was agreed upon, the father would broach the subject with the prospective spouse's family. If they were amenable to the marriage, it was set. Both sets of parents would ask their child if he or she wanted to marry the prospective spouse. If both children said yes, they were brought together, usually immediately, and given taro, which they shared between them. They were then married. According to informants, a child who did not agree was eventually coerced into saying yes. While the question was purely rhetorical, the parents persisted until they got at least verbal agreement. Once the agreement was reached, the couple ritually shared taro and they were considered married.

During the first week of marriage the couple might sleep sandwiched between the girl's mother and the boy's father, an arrangement that informants said was supposed to keep the newlyweds from being too afraid of their changed situation. This suggests that they spent at least a week sleeping side by side before initiating intercourse. If the couple had already engaged in intercourse, however, this phase might be shortened or eliminated.

Work: The Transformation of the Natural into the Social

Marriage, as I have described it, is quick and perfunctory. It is virtually free of symbolic content, with the exception of the shared taro, and is motivated by one of two things: either the couple's having engaged in intercourse, or the parents' desire to set their child up in an arrangement that quickly leads to self-sufficiency and stability. These two themes—intercourse and the self-sufficiency and stability of the marriage bond—are the key features for an understanding of Baining marriage. In a sense they are opposed. Intercourse is an activity about which the Baining feel comfortable only within the confines of the marriage bond, and not all that comfortable even then. Work need not take place only in marriage, but given the sexual division of labor, marriage is perhaps the most efficient way of organizing subsistence activities. These latter are activities that the Baining value as social, *atlo*, and in which they take pride, whereas sex is shameful, natural, and isolating.

My information on attitudes towards sex come partly from a few informants' comments and partly from observations of interactions where there were references to sexual relations or exploits. For the most part, my informants were loathe to discuss the subject, and my queries were met by extremely long periods of silence, which were usually closed with the response, "I don't know." Acknowledgment of sex is extremely shameful. Since sex is only permitted within marriage, marriage is considerably tainted by this association. The considerable cultural emphasis on the other activities (gardening, cooking, etc.) serves to balance or override the natural, shameful aspects of marriage. The qualities that people attribute to married couples (their industriousness and compatibility) are thus highly valued not merely in themselves but in contrast to this implicit, unspoken other side.

Life histories illustrate the ambivalence that many individuals had towards their own marriage (see chapter 5). Many informants confessed to having run away from their spouses shortly after marriage. The overriding reason given was that they were unready—too young, too lazy—to undertake the hardworking responsibilities of marriage. This is true of women as well as men, despite the fact that the transition required by marriage is greater for a young man than a young woman. Unmarried men typically do garden work only occasionally and then usually in the company of other men; they spend the rest of their time roaming: hunting and foraging with other youths. Unmarried women, however, customarily carry out all the daily tasks of a married woman. The fact that both sexes view marriage as hard work is an indication and expression of the collective values of the society. Although initiation into sex may have affected these early attitudes towards marriage, informants made no reference to it and projected their unease with the situation into the social responsibilities thrust on them by the new roles.

Married status, among the Baining, cannot easily be shed once it has been assumed. Even the informants who described running from their marriage partners conceded that they had eventually settled down with those same spouses. People gave no indication that their dissatisfaction with marriage had to do with the particular partner chosen, but rather with the new tasks and responsibilities thrust upon them. In similar fashion, once a marriage has solidified among the Baining, there is very little divorce. To some extent this pattern is ascribable to church and mission rules and beliefs, especially in Lan, which is a Catholic community, but there is evidence that the church practices merely reinforced underlying cultural patterns. There are cases where marriages break up—the most frequent scenario is when one partner runs off with another man or woman—but cases of divorce where the two partners simply take up separate and independent lives are much more rare.

The reason that marriage is essentially indissoluble, I would argue, is that it is perceived as a natural relationship and not a social one. The partners in a marriage bond engage in sexual intercourse, which, I suggest, is regarded as a natural act. The nature of this act is a mingling of the blood and fluids of the two partners. Having once shared this experience, the Baining see themselves as naturally connected in a way that is beyond the power of social action to separate. This is as true of their attitudes towards those who engage in pre-marital intercourse (they are de facto married after that act) as it is of their view of a married couple. Once the act has been committed the couple is connected whether living together or not. When they are not living together (e.g., divorced), however, it is only the natural bond that connects them; whereas when they are living together, they engage in numerous social and cultural activities and values that impart increased social value to their status.[1] The Baining transform the essentials of the

1. When the breakup of a marriage does occur, it is usually the result of at least one partner becoming immersed in a new sexual and marital relationship, which replaces, if not dissolves, the natural ties that connected him or her to the previous spouse. The shame that the Baining feel in reference to natural relationships serves as a constraint upon the relationship itself.

relationship by emphasizing the aspects of social complementarity to the point of rendering the natural aspects socially invisible.

Through the process of subverting the natural relationship between marriage partners, the social factors in the relationship are given greater value. The Baining stress the complementarity of spouses working together and value the industriousness of a person as the most important quality in the selection of a spouse. This set of values also accounts for the absence of any way of talking about physical attractiveness in Baining, and the shame that they feel in reference to terms such as "my spouse." The use of such terms focuses attention on the type of sexual relationship the spouses share.

Residence

Despite the fact that the parents of the couple are the instrumental actors in the marriage, marriage does not initiate ongoing relations between the two families. There is no payment or exchange at marriage. The married couple usually maintains ties with both spouses' parents, although these may be relatively stronger or more attenuated in individual instances. There is no prescribed residence rule, though the newlyweds usually live with one set of parents or the other at the beginning of their married life. The choice of which parents they live with is a decision to be made by the parents in each individual case and seems to reflect a number of factors. Informants are not agreed about which factors are more important. Some say it depends on which parents have the resources (essentially gardens and food) to look after the couple until their first conjugal garden begins to bear (this takes six to nine months in Lan but closer to one to two years in Yalom), although such living arrangements usually outlive these economic necessities. Others say that the in-laws decide among themselves which family has a greater need for the labor and support of the young couple, who, although a slight burden at the beginning, soon begin to contribute and may eventually support and look after the old people in the household. Other reasons tendered include the ability of the in-laws to help in the care of grandchildren—maternal in-laws seem to be slightly favored in this respect; or the location of various parents' residences—the Lan Baining feel a sense of superiority over the inland peoples, and if their children marry mountain Baining, they usually insist on their residence on the coast.

The Birth of Children: The Transmission of Natural Bonds

The second ramification of the underlying tension between the natural and social aspects of marriage comes in relation to the birth of children.

Children are much loved and valued in Baining society; nevertheless, relations within the nuclear family are filled with shame, tension, and denial. I interpret this ambivalence as arising from the origin of biological children in the "natural" act of sexual intercourse. As such, by their very presence, they call attention to the type of relationship that their parents share and thus the "natural" relations on which the nuclear family is constituted.

Just as married partners seek to subordinate sexual relations with one another to their "social" relations as a productive subsistence team, so the Baining seek to create social rather than natural/biological relations with their children.

The members of the nuclear family are prototypically thought to be people who share blood and substance with one another. The connection between parents and children is that of flesh and blood. The Baining acknowledge that children are the result of sexual intercourse; they are thought to grow out of the mingling of their parents' blood *(ambias)* and substance *(aminok)*. The child grows in the mother's womb *(angilki ara vutki* [the child's house]). It is thought that the child gradually coagulates and grows by absorbing the liquids in the womb—the products of the parents' intercourse. However, the fetus does not need to be constantly replenished during gestation. The growth of a fetus is compared with the development of a chicken inside an egg, or the meat and sprout of a coconut inside the coconut husk—both are solids emerging from a liquid base.[2] Parents are actually thought to give up some of their own flesh and blood to the child during pregnancy. The child grows from the mother's and the father's flesh and blood, not from the food that the mother ingests. Women are thought to lose increments of their flesh and blood to each successive child they bear. By the time a woman has finished child bearing, she should be somewhat wasted and "bloodless" (lack of blood is seen as an ailment of old age). Men also experience this gradual debilitation.

The Baining consider it shameful to speak of a woman's pregnancy, and husbands and others learn a woman is pregnant only when it begins to show. I tried to ask Taluvian when her baby was due (she looked about eight months pregnant), but she responded, "What baby?" When pressed to answer, she was very uncomfortable with the subject, but finally, after a long silence, said four or five months. She gave birth two weeks later to a baby who appeared to be full term. I believe this shame is felt because pregnancy is classed as a natural process, one not socially controlled or transformed.

Breast-feeding is also conceived as a direct physical transfer of sub-

2. I am indebted to J. Pool (1969–70) for this description.

stance to the child. The milk is thought to be present in the mother's skin and the child sucks it out. A lactating woman ought to eat lots of good food to keep up her strength during the term of breast-feeding. Breast milk is considered important for a child's survival, but it is not valued as much as garden food.

Adoption: Producing the Social Family

In contrast to the reproduction of the family through the natural processes of intercourse, conception, pregnancy, birth, and nursing, the social family is created through the process of adoption, which is the cultural transformation of the natural parent-child relationship. The Baining engage quite frequently in adoption.[3] In my genealogies, the rate of adoption was 36 percent. It may vary in different Baining villages, however. It is not, in any case, the incidence of adoption that makes it important but rather the role that it plays in the cultural logic of the system. Adoption affects and transforms the social order and is not confined to acts between individuals. Although not every child in the society is adopted, adoption touches virtually every nuclear family. Most families, that is, have either given a child away to another family, or adopted one. The term for adopted child is *atmiraka* (masc.) or *atmiraigi* (fem.), which literally means "the taken one."

The act of adoption is itself a social act. An adopted child is said to be one's "true" child. Parents call their adopted children by kin terms, *guaruimga* (my son) or *guaruimgi* (my daughter); they also refer to their children in conversations with others by these terms. Reciprocally, parents encourage their adopted children to call them *gunan* (my mother) or *gumam* (my father), and claim to feel pleased when they do so. Informants also say that adopted children should be favored with more or choicer food if such is available. They further remark that it is bad to hit such children: one should treat them well, and then they will grow up to be good productive members of society, and, not so incidentally, look after their adoptive parents well in old age. Parents are proud of their adopted children and will defend them from criticism or punishment from outside. The relations between parents and adopted children epitomize what is valued in Baining society.

These positive values are more clearly formulated and strongly emphasized as cultural ideals than they are actual patterns of behavior, and in reality parents' behavior towards adopted and natural children

3. Although this rate is high by Western standards, and affects almost every household, it falls far short of the rate of adoption in numerous Micronesian and Polynesian societies (see Caroll 1970; Levy 1973; Brady 1976) in which virtually every child is adopted.

is not that highly differentiated. This fact does not, however, detract from the cultural/symbolic importance that these adoptive relations and the ideals have. The Baining *say* it is impossible for a family to refuse a request from others to adopt their child. This is a cultural statement of a prescriptive nature, which they believe implicitly. It does not, of course, preclude ploys which some Baining use to avoid adoptions in select instances. The fact that this standard is not universally upheld does not diminish either the importance of adoption in the social system or the significance of the prescription that one must not hinder the adoption process. The Baining admonish younger adults to continue the custom of adoption, and not to "think too much of"—that is, value too highly—their natural children. The adoptive bond is stronger than the natural one in that once a child has been adopted, it is considered impossible for that child to be adopted away from its adoptive parents.

Adoptions

There are essentially three kinds of adoption in Baining society. The most common form occurs after a birth, when another Baining, male or female, single or married, sees the child and takes a fancy to him or her. The prospective adopter sees that the baby is *atlo* (in the sense of being pretty, healthy, does not cry a lot). If this is the case, the prospective adopter(s) may bring gifts of food, and nowadays baby items such as diapers and tee shirts, to the child's parents and give the parents the gifts while saying "this is my child." The parents are expected to agree and express no sadness or regret. Parents certainly never admitted to any sadness at this event, and one informant actually laughed at me for asking the question.

The child does not usually leave the natural parents at this time, but continues to live with his or her parents and nurse until he or she is approximately two years old. After weaning, the child will move to the adoptive parents' home. During the time when the child is nursing, however, the prospective parents will bring periodic gifts of food, and perhaps store-bought goods. These gifts are given to the child, even if they are later consumed by other members of the child's household. They are an expression of the nurturant role the adoptive parents feel that they have already undertaken. I remember being used as a carrier in one of these transactions before I understood the significance of the gift. I was puzzled at being ordered to take a gift of food to a three-month-old baby, and then being invited by the baby's parents to partake of the food. The experience, however, served me in good stead when the local school teacher's wife (a woman from New Ireland) told me that Awat, an older woman, had expressed an interest in adopting her infant. She thought she had refused the request and that the incident was over, except that Awat brought periodic gifts of food to the baby. The teacher and his wife were surprised and upset to learn that this meant that Awat still expected to adopt the child. I left before the child was weaned, but I expect that the teacher and his wife kept their child, if only because they developed a subterfuge by saying that the baby's grandparents expected to adopt the child.

A child much past the age of weaning is usually considered too old to be adopted, since the Baining say that he or she already knows his or her parents and would be unable to make a good adjustment. Although most adopted children seem to make a good adjustment, they also usually "know" their true parents, and on many occasions they run after them when they see them.[4] This does not seem so much a desire to return to their natural parents as a desire for acknowledgment. There is no secrecy in Baining adoptions. There is, therefore, no reason for parents not to acknowledge the children they have given away. In fact, people say it is good for a child to know both sets of parents so that he or she can know to help these people when they get old and infirm. Indeed this is critical for the later articulation of relations through food exchanges.

A second form of adoption occurs when the child is still an infant. If a woman is lactating (if, for instance, she was breast-feeding a child that died, or if her child was weaned before she stopped lactating), then she might adopt a child from another woman and proceed to nurse him or her. Children adopted in this way can be anywhere from one day to two years old. This form of adoption happens very swiftly in comparison with the first, since the woman must adopt the child within a few days after the preceding child has stopped nursing. While this sort of adoption appears more directly dependent on the desire and action of a woman than does the first, this aspect is diffused by certain cultural factors. The process creates a different sort of bond between the nursing child and the other members of the adopting family. Instead of calling the adopted child "sibling" as is normally done, the other children in

4. Adoptions are occasionally reversed, and the child is returned to his or her natural parents. There are several reasons given for this: if a child is constantly ill, he or she may be returned to the natural parents who are thought to be able to provide a cure; if the adoptive parents die (e.g., elderly grandparents who adopt their grandchildren), the children return to their biological parents; if the adoptive parents move to the coast, the child may be fostered by the natural parents in their absence.

When I returned to the Baining after thirteen years I noted that a number of children who I had originally recorded as adopted had "gone back" by the time I updated my genealogies. The percentage of cases is still small, but it confirms that this pattern exists.

the adopting family, as well as the parents, call the nursing child "my child" and say that they give him or her milk. It is not just the lactating woman who takes the initiative and responsibility for this child, but the family unit as a whole that adopts the child and commits itself, as this terminological usage suggests, to looking after him or her. In this way the Baining emphasize the social or collective aspects of adoption in contrast to the more private, individual relations of a biological mother/child nursing dyad.

If a woman does not have milk, but she or her family still desires to adopt a child in this way, there are two options open. The first and traditional solution is for the adopting parents to feed the child sugar cane. They squeeze the liquid from the sugar cane into the mouth of the infant. Informants say that this is an adequate substitute for milk. I never saw this done, but I saw people who had supposedly been adopted in this fashion. This was not very common, since growing great quantities of sugar cane was considered "hard work." The second solution has been provided by the availability of store-bought milk. Adopting parents occasionally adopt an infant and feed him or her with a solution of powdered milk. These two substitutes are considered identical to real mother's milk in terms of the relationships they create. The Baining see in these relations a structure that is substantively different from other relations; although interactive behaviors may appear normal, the conceptual bonds between family members are different in these cases. This difference has symbolic connotations, as in the example I give later in this chapter.

A third type of adoption occurs when two children are born simultaneously (within a day and a night of each other). In such cases, the parents frequently exchange children, each family breast-feeding the child of the other. These children are very closely aligned with their adoptive families, and occasionally do not know that they have been exchanged. Since the exchange is mutual and occurs very early in the child's life, the child's ties with the adoptive parents are almost complete. Nevertheless, there is no effort made to keep the adoption secret, and people's knowledge is usually revealed when they give genealogies.

Although only the latter type of adoption is considered an exchange of children, the idea of reciprocity lurks behind certain decisions so that a family that has given a child away to another family may return in a few years and adopt a child from either that family or a closely related one. There is no sense that adoptions have or ought to be balanced in this way, but in taking genealogies and life histories, I often found that one case of adoption or another would be "explained" as a reciprocation for a previous one. In these, as in all cases, the sex of the child has no bearing on the transaction.

Although most adoptions are motivated by choice and not necessity, there are also pragmatic adoptions. Children are, of course, adopted when they are orphaned or their parents are unable to take care of them. In the case of twins or children born close together, one child might be adopted to make life easier for the parents. If a woman's children consistently die in infancy, another couple might suggest adopting the next child to see if they can break the pattern of mortality. Langerkan explained to me that many of her babies had died (six out of eight at that point), so Uram and Garideran came and offered to adopt a child to try their luck at raising her. The child survived, and so did two of Langerkan's next three children. If a couple are unable to have children (which happened to be the case with Uram and Garideran) or if their children fail to survive, they may adopt a whole "family" of children. If a child doesn't get along with his or her parents, he or she might run away and ask to be adopted by another family.

While not a regular custom, it is fully possible for a single person to adopt a child. The most frequent reason given for such an adoption was that a child's parents had died and an older adolescent had taken charge of the child, continuing to look after him or her even after marriage. Another pattern occurs when a person looks after a child in his or her parents' absence (at school, etc.) and eventually the relationship becomes recognized.

An example of this occurred in my hamlet. Langerkan and Peni were looking after their grandchild Awat. Awat's brother Guadinam, who was about two years old and just weaned, also started spending more and more time around Peni and Langerkan's house. Dembi, the unmarried fourteen-year-old daughter of Peni and Langerkan, took on much of the responsibility for the care and provision of both Awat and Guadinam. People gradually started to refer to Guadinam as Dembi's child. Their relation fulfilled the Baining definition of adoption, since Dembi was already caring for Guadinam in the role of provider. She thus qualified as the child's de facto adoptive mother. I was told that while it was true that Guadinam was Dembi's child and would go with her when she married, in the meantime he remained in his parents' hamlet since they all lived in the same hamlet.[5]

Despite the fact that even adoption is constrained by the necessity for an infant to nurse, mother's milk is valued very lowly by the Bain-

---

5. Guadinam died before Dembi married, and I am not sure he ever lived exclusively with her.

ing. They say that mother's milk is "nothing," and that only "food," by which they particularly mean garden produce, is important for the growth and development of the child. As we have seen, this does not mean that the Baining eliminate nursing (except in the case of the sugar cane feeding); rather they go to great lengths to define and limit it in various ways. This social devaluation of mother's milk is consistent with the Baining devaluation of and shame about biological ties within the nuclear family. There is very little acknowledgment of the physical ties between parents and children; conception, pregnancy and birth are all minimally elaborated in both the belief system and social behavior and practice. Since the Baining see nursing as an extension of the physical (and thus "natural") connection between parents (particularly mothers) and children, a mother's tie to a nursing child is more likely to be shameful than highly valued. In short, while the Baining recognize the necessity for nursing a child (particularly with their protein-scarce diet), they do not perceive in it any positive attributes. The low value given to maternity per se, including pregnancy, birth, and nursing, is the inverse of the high value given to the social role held by parents of either sex.

Baining attitudes and values make it clear that the important status in relation to a child is that of provider. In stressing the role of provider, they are de-emphasizing the roles of both genitor and genitrix. For the Baining, being able to provide for a child is far more significant than being able to give birth to one. There is no stigma associated with sterility. If partners do not have children, they simply adopt them; and these children are more often referred to by their filial status, as "so and so's child," than by name as are other people in the society. Their adoptive parents are frequently said to "make good their children." Although the latter is the ambition of any adoptive parent in relation to his or her adopted child, the reference crops up most frequently in cases where the family has no natural children of its own. These households might be said to be "totally social."

Through the act of adoption and through their manipulations of the ways in which they can culturally and socially redefine the natural relations between mother and child, the Baining transform the natural and shameful aspects of the nuclear family into socially constituted and thus highly valued social relations. This transformation of natural relations into social ties applies primarily to dyadic relations within a nuclear family. However, through the transformation of the individual relations, the family unit as a whole is also transformed. The family, which is the principle unit of natural reproduction and primary socialization, is transformed into the *household*, a unit made up of socially related people.

Food: The Medium of Transformation

The household is the main unit of subsistence production and consumption. Just as married spouses subsume the "natural," shameful side of their sexual complementarity by stressing the industriousness of their complementary labor and subsistence activities, so too does the social family achieve its sociality through stressing constructed relations. The main types of Baining labor are analogous to the social production of the family. Swidden horticulturalists transform raw nature—the bush or forest—into a humanly designed and controlled environment. In their gardens the Baining cut down all the wild, natural vegetation of a plot, and plant domesticated crops in its stead. It is their labor that produces and cultivates these plants. This is particularly true since the majority of Baining crops are grown by vegetative propagation rather than from seed. These crops are grown by cloning. The plants are already sprouted or developed and are transplanted from one garden to another. They are analogous to adopted children who are transplanted from one household to another. Forest crops, which grow from seed, are more like biological children. Here again the Baining replace a substance that they see as natural with one they consider socially produced. The Baining say that they work in their gardens because they are *akakat* (humans), that is social beings. Work is what differentiates people from animals. Animals and nonhuman creatures *(aios)* do not prepare gardens, but frequently steal from them, and in this way they are opposed to workers. The amount of labor invested in these gardens is a sign not only of the work needed to cultivate a garden, but of the work needed to transform individuals into "human beings" and the physical relationship between husband and wife into a socially useful relationship.

The Baining establish gardens when they marry, and their gardens are destroyed at their death. Gardens are thus closely associated with an individual's mature, social persona. Socially valued work is also invested in the garden itself. As a result, the products of this labor, the foodstuffs harvested, are imbued with the essence of human values, work, complementarity, and production. These products are, therefore, apt media for the second transformative process that emerges out of the household.

Nature Transformed into Culture: The Process Generalized

The second transformation within the family is the transformation of the natural parent-child bond into a social one. While the natural tie between parents and children consists of shared bodily substance, flesh

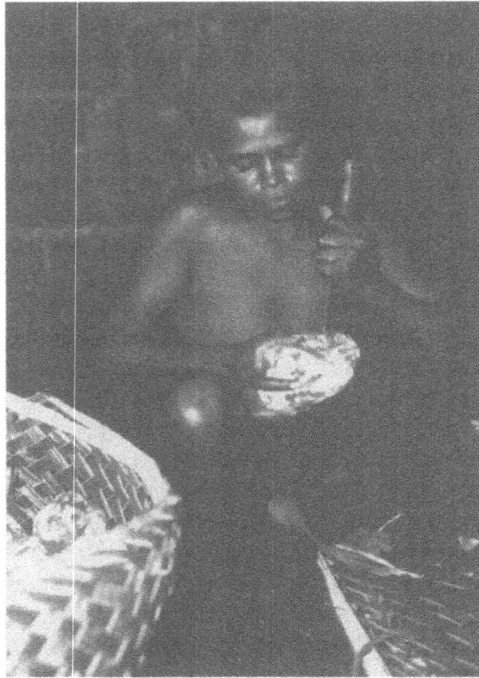

Plate 4.1   Serving taro

and blood, the social relationship is created through a socially designated medium, food. The Baining say that their adopted child becomes
their "true" child because they give him or her food. Nowadays,
money is added into the equation because money, which is produced
either from work or from the sale of food, is also an inherently social
medium. Feeding and providing for a child creates the bond. In this
process the natural nurturance of the parents in pregnancy and breast-
feeding is replaced by the socially valued (because produced by work)
nurturance of garden produce. Substituting natural substance with culturally and socially symbolic substance is analogous to the replacement
of the natural vegetation of the bush or forest with the domesticated
cultigens of the human garden. The fact that domesticated food is the
medium in both cases articulates these two processes.

When the Baining say that their adopted child is their "true" child
and their own child is "samting nating" (pidgin for a thing of little
worth), they are making a cultural juxtaposition between the two types
of bonds possible between parents and children. The same is true when

they say that mother's milk is nothing and food is the really important substance in the nurturance of a child. The contrast between natural and adopted children heightens the comparison between these two types of bonds and nurturance. With adopted children the parent-child bonds are entirely social. However, even with natural children, the Baining gradually transform the substance of the relationship. New-born children are mere projections of their parents' natural bodily substances, but over time they are fed and nurtured with increasing amounts of "social" food. While these children are never entirely transformed into social offspring—there is always a substratum of connectedness, and, thus, of shame between them and their parents—they increasingly add socially nurturant connections on top of the biological ones.

Adoption provides the model through which natural bonds are transformed into social bonds. The same processes involved in adoption, however, can be applied in other contexts. This is why the practice of adoption need not be universal among the Baining. Adoption epitomizes the process of transformation from natural into social relationships that makes it possible for all relationships in the society to become social. While nuclear family relations appear to have priority among the Baining, this analysis suggests that the primary social referents for these relations are the adoptive bonds and not the "natural" ones. Adoptive relations are imbued with the cultural values of sociality, industriousness, and reciprocity; it is these values that are connoted by the kin terms "parent," "child," and "sibling," when they are used as labels or metaphors for other types of social relations. By redefining the primary referents of kin terms within the nuclear family, the Baining complete the transformation of the nuclear family from a set of natural intrafamily relations into a socially produced unit, the household.

Coordination of Transformations

This transformation of the family into the household can be seen as the product of the two transformations already discussed: the transformation of the spousal bond from a natural relationship based on sexual intercourse into a social relationship based on the division of labor and productive subsistence activities; and the transformation of bonds between parent and children from natural substance into those mediated by the exchange of food. The household emerges as the organizing nexus of food production as well as the locus of food processing and consumption. It is the site of the key social activities of Baining life.

The processes that transform the nuclear family into the principal social unit of the society articulate with two further cyclical processes of transformation: the domestic cycle and the productive cycle. The coordination of these processes both produces and reproduces the Baining social system. While marriage initiates the process of natural reproduction—sexual intercourse, pregnancy, birth, marriage—it neither creates nor renews the social unit of society. The married couple is not yet a social unit; it has not yet produced a garden—a social creation based on the principles of social labor described above—nor has it reproduced itself socially. For this reason, young married couples generally remain associated with another family unit, a "social" household, usually that of one of the spouses' parents. While there is no fixed moment in the development of the family at which the new unit separates and creates its own household, this move generally occurs after several children have been born. It seems to occur about the time when the new family has begun to transform its own internal relations through the production of food and the transformation of natural parent-child bonds into social bonds, either through adoption or through the more attenuated form of substituting social food (itself a transformation of material nature into culture) for natural substance. This transformation is never explicitly marked by the Baining, but it is implicit in their sense of what an independent functioning family unit is. Married partners begin the process of social production through their creation of and work in their gardens; but it is only when the products of their labor are used to create social bonds within the family that the full effect of their labor is realized. Both processes are articulated by the use of food as the medium for transforming the nuclear family into the social unit of the society.

Reciprocity: The Process as a Cycle

The processes of transformation in the Baining system are not unidirectional. They can be reversed. Normally, adoption leads to nurturance through the assumption of parental bonds. The opposite is also true when an individual is already nurturing a child and therefore comes to be accorded the status of "mother" or "father." Although I have used the terms "parent" and "child," the significant roles for the Baining are those of food giver and food taker. The primary referent of a "food giver" is a nurturing adult while that of "food taker" is a child. It is not necessarily the elder who is the parent. In Baining society it is the relation between the two actors, and not their respective ages, that determines each one's status. For example, old people gradually give up gardening and participating in productive work, and consequently they become dependent on their children—both natural and adopted—for food. These people are thus food takers and not producers, and according to Baining criteria become childlike. The Baining frequently say that when they get old they become like children, and their own children become "parents" to them and give them food. Although the shift is frequently structured as a simile—old people become *like* children—the Baining take seriously the reversal of roles and responsibilities. We see that the terminology and the activity are inextricably entwined.

The interaction between people as food givers and food takers is a dynamic relationship that sets up a series of expectations and obligations; parents are expected to be food givers; thus, those who give food are parents. For the Baining, genealogical relationships are always subordinate to the social and creative relationships that people construct through their actions and behavior towards one another. This interaction also sets up a dynamic over time so that those who receive food are expected to reciprocate in kind later on, but in doing so, they acquire the status of parent, even in relation to their own genealogical or adoptive parents.

There is another element in the dynamic relations between food giver and food taker. We have seen that marriage and adoption bring out the Baining values of work, food giving, and social well-being, and to these we must add the value of reciprocity. The Baining say that they adopt children because when they get old their adopted children will look after them, in exchange for the care the adoptive parents gave them in their childhood. There are no sanctions to ensure that natural children will undertake this responsibility. Baining say that adopted children will continue to live with their adoptive parents even after marriage, and provide food for them, even though there is no residence rule specifying the pattern, nor is there any actual evidence that this is what happens. Natural children are more likely to move away; they might occasionally think of their parents and bring food, but they are not to be relied upon. These expectations do not correspond to the actual behavior of the people I knew; I saw both adopted and natural children caring for the aged. However, Pool (1969–70, 1971: 48–49) reports that when old people died in his village, their death was frequently attributed to suicide. People said that these old people committed suicide because of the sorrow they felt when their children did not look after them properly. Pool seemed puzzled by these explanations since there seemed to be no evidence of the neglect and rejection for which the children were blamed. Although I never heard a death attributed either to suicide or to the neglect of a person's children, the values I discuss here may underlie these explanations.[6]

The key to what one creates in the socially constructed and valued relationship with one's adopted children is the concept of reciprocity. Exchange in Baining society does not take very elaborated forms (Fajans 1993b). Most day-to-day exchange is almost immediately reciprocated. Whenever people meet in Lan, they greet each other by exchanging betel nut and pepper leaf. When several women in a household or in neighboring households are cooking, they will generally give a share of their cooked food to the other cooks and receive a share in return. Exchange of this sort is reciprocated immediately, and cultivates ongoing bonds between the participants. This pattern of interaction is in contrast to the patterns that are created by an individual over the life cycle.

The process of growing up in Baining and many other societies entails a status of dependency where one is constantly the recipient. In some societies, this "indebtedness" is never directly repaid to those who originally supported one; in such societies, like our own, the system is perpetuated through time as each generation repays its debt not directly to its parents, but to its own children. The Baining cycle is more complex; the move from child to adult is a move from food taker to food provider. In young adulthood, exchanges are with social equals—people who are also essentially self-sufficient and independent entities—and the exchanges are mutual and momentary, not reciprocated over time.

As a person's family grows and his or her parents age, other dynamics take precedence. The individual has obligations to support his or her parents, and become a food giver to these individuals. This is a form of delayed reciprocity for the indebtedness that was incurred in childhood. While feeding his or her parents, the individual is simultaneously acting as food giver to his or her natural and adopted children. This activity is the inverse of the former. The support and nurturance that the adults give to their children is the initiation of a debt that the children will have to reciprocate when they grow up.

This cyclical process of reciprocity is the key to understanding the order of Baining social structure. The Baining household is not a "corporate group." Rather, it consists of sets of domestic relations, which are not perpetuated through time but are maintained only so long as the activities that produce them are continued. When these activities change, so do the relationships between the participants. The patterns

---

6. I would hypothesize that the children referred to in Pool's data were natural children and not adopted ones.

of relations are structurally related and coordinated with each other; reciprocity is an important form of coordination. The household unit is produced through these exchanges. The household is conceptually closed by the death of the parents; a new unit is created with one's children. This closure is consistent with the lack of descent and lack of corporateness among the Baining.

Transformations across Generations

The segmentation of primary kinship and role relationships among the Baining into those of food giver and food taker has ramifications for all social relations. Since the transformation of biological relationships into social ones is produced by food, all relationships can become imbued with increased sociality through the giving of food. Food obtains its "socializing" value through the labor of the married couple in the horticultural cycle. Food producers are thus the principal agents of transformation (which includes socialization).

Relations between extended kin are more fluid and easy than those within the family. In fact, the absence of shame is compounded by a general expectation of support, nurturance, and recognition in accord with the social dimension of the relationship (for example, as mentioned previously, these kin are always permitted and frequently obliged to use kin terms with one another). Such acts of involvement and exchange become the basis for these relationships. Extended kin relations, insofar as they have importance, attain this importance by sharing in the idiom of all social relations in Baining society; they tend to develop out of food-giving / food-taking bonds.

The social potential of these kin ties is revealed by the fact that they are the most frequent adopters in Baining society. Adoption of grandchildren by grandparents is the most common type of adoption. The next most common adopters are other extended kin. Adoption of a grandchild by a grandparent collapses the two generations between them to only one. Similarly, adoption by lateral kin bridges a gap between families. The transformation of distant relationships through adoption into relations of parent and child is another instance of the primacy of the parent and child roles within Baining society. The act of adoption in these cases serves to consolidate more attenuated kin relationships, and to reconstitute these relationships as social bonds.

The incipient relationship of food giver / food taker inherent in extended kin bonds is made manifest in the construction of a full parent-child bond through food giving. This is another instance of the phenomenon mentioned above where implicit food giving and nurturance can be transformed into explicit adoption at any moment. In many instances the label "adoption" is merely used to help reinterpret the type of relation that already exists.

Adoptive ties create bonds, but these are superimposed on the underlying natural ties. This is evidenced over the generational cycle. When an adopted child grows up and has children of his or her own, the underlying natural ties reassert themselves. For example, if a grandparent adopted a grandchild, the child would call his or her grandparents "mother" and "father." However, in the next generation, this adopted child's own child would probably call his or her social "grandparents" great-grandparents. This reversion to the underlying biological relationship between the parties underscores the nature of the kin transformation for the Baining. Kinship is transformed only when the natural relationship is replaced by a social one—when flesh-and-blood ties are supplanted by nurturant and food-giving ones. Thus the grandparents in this instance had created a social tie with their grandchild, but the great-grandchild was not linked to them through this ongoing social process. New social relations can be created with these children; in particular, they can be adopted in turn by the great-grandparents. Should such an adoption occur, it would then serve to transform the kin ties between them into those of parent and child—the primary nurturant relationship. Grandparent-grandchild is not for the Baining a full social relationship, although it is for them one imbued with greater sociality than that of natural parent and child.

A woman, Tangbinan, was adopted as a child by a couple, Uram and Garideran, whom she called "mother" and "father." By classificatory genealogical terminology, the man Uram would have been a "brother" to her, and his wife would have been "grandmother." Her first child was just learning to speak while I was in the field, and he called Uram *gumam* (father), and Garideran *aigi* (great-grandmother) (the correct classificatory terms, not modified by the adoption of Tangbinan). This set of relations was on the verge of becoming more complex since Uram and Garideran had begun to care for the child Mengiam. This was seen as a prelude to adoption. I never heard Mengiam refer to Garideran as "mother" (although he was already classificatorily calling Uram "father"), but adults in the community referred to Garideran as Mengiam's mother and told me he would begin to call her that later (when I went back in 1991, both Uram and Garideran had died, and Mengiam had gone back to live with his biological parents).

When a couple adopts a child who is more closely related genealogically to one of them than to the other, the parents often take on different stances towards the adopted child. Tambas and his wife Tangbinan were going to adopt Isim, the child of Tangbinan's biological sister Taluvian, when he finished nursing. Informants told me that when this occurred, Tangbinan would scold and discipline Isim, but Tambas would not. Tambas was the true social parent; he was already being referred to as Isim's father, and he was the one who conscientiously brought gifts of food to him.

The underlying natural ties between kin are evident in the ties between natural parents and the children who have been adopted from them. From my observations, it seems that during the childhood and adolescence of an adopted child, he or she is wholly associated with his or her adoptive family. A considerable tension often results from any attempt by the natural family to "seduce" the child back, either for prolonged visits or for good. This refers to attempts by the natural parents to induce the child to renew social relations to them as parents, rather than merely temporary returns to the natural parents because of illness or for everyone's convenience during travel or work away from the community.

In contrast to such attenuated relations evident while the child is maturing, I have observed close relations between adult married men and women, and their biological parents. This increased closeness seems to accompany the birth of grandchildren. Peni and Langerkan said that their daughter Tangbinan did not come to visit them while she was growing up because her adoptive parents would not let her, but when she was big and married, she had her own thoughts on the matter and would come to see them and bring the grandchildren. The birth of grandchildren appears to be the link that reasserts the natural ties. The grandchildren are still one's grandchildren even if the intervening link (mother-daughter; father-son) was socially given away.[7]

The implications of these complex relations are important. What is clearly implicit in the relationships I have illustrated here is the constant interplay between biological and social relationships. Much of Baining activity and organization is directed towards the transformation of the natural into the social. This transformation, however, is a

7. In the particular case in question, Peni and Langerkan were planning to adopt Tangbinan's second child (her adoptive parents had adopted her eldest) as soon as he finished nursing. In keeping with this intention, they sent him occasional presents of food; however, the food they sent was less prestigious than the food sent by Tambas to Isim in the example mentioned above. Peni and Langerkan sent garden produce such as greens and corn instead of store-bought rice, tins of meat, or clothes. They themselves commented on the difference in the quality of the gifts, saying theirs were not as good; but I think that in a sense it was a truer expression of the tie they were fostering with the child. They were first reasserting a natural tie that had been undermined by the previous adoption, and then superimposing the social, adoptive tie on top of that. If there were a way to symbolize all this in the Baining system (and I am not sure there is), it would be to use garden produce with its underlying natural base, rather than store-bought goods, to show the underlying nature of the system.

process and not a single act. It takes continuous activity (work) to sustain and is never accomplished for once and for all. The natural and the social are in constant play with one another, and each derives its form and essence from its perpetual contrast and interaction with the other. The course of a particular process of transformation over time itself generates new relationships and dynamics, and these motivate the next stage of interaction and relations.

The Cycle Closes: Transformation of Social into Natural

As we will see in the next chapter, individuals become progressively more socialized as they mature. The height of sociality is achieved when one is socializing others as an adopter or a food giver. This preeminent social status, as we have seen, is not maintained forever; old people become increasingly more dependent, and in so doing lose their status as socializers. This will be more thoroughly discussed in the next chapter. The culmination of this process is the reversal of the nature-society transformation, that is, the reversion of an individual from a fully social being to one less social, or increasingly natural. For the Baining the final transformation occurs at death and is marked by the symbolic destruction of all sociality and social bonds. As seen in chapter 7, death is the one life passage that the Baining elaborate ritually and cosmologically.

After the death of an adult, his or her kin go to the gardens of the deceased and destroy some of the food in each garden. They will go and chop down bananas or pitpit, uproot and slash taro, and sever the stems of greens. Then they will gather quantities of food to take back and make into a "feast." On the way back to the hamlet, they mark various places along the road with slashed taro or some other food. They do this at any point where two paths converge or divide. It is interpreted as a message to all who pass that way that someone has died.

The destruction of an individual's garden is quite clearly the negation of much of that person's social persona, since gardens and work are what set men and women apart from animals and spirits. The destruction of a garden brings out the implicit association of *aios* as dead men with the creatures and spirits who steal and damage Baining gardens. At death the garden is damaged as if by *aios*. Just as the once social person is now part of nature, the social garden is now naturalized.

The produce that comes from a person's garden is the medium through which that person has in the past made and maintained social relationships. At death those relationships are severed, and so is the food. Cut food is displayed along all the paths and intersections in the community, overtly mapping on the ground the rupture of social bonds that has occurred. The matrix of paths through the hamlets and bush becomes a physical representation of the social relationships of the dead person and the way food mediated relations between individuals and households.

Back at the deceased's hamlet (or that of his or her kin), a small feast is made with food from the dead person's gardens. At this feast, individual members of the community make clear their intention to taboo certain foods during the mourning period out of sorrow for the death. However, not everybody can taboo food. There are certain categories of person for whom it would be shameful to taboo food. These people are the biological members of the deceased's nuclear family. The people for whom it is good, expected, and appropriate to taboo food are the grandparents, grandchildren, adoptive parents, adopted children, distantly related kin and in-laws. These are precisely the people with whom—during life—the dead person had created social relationships that used food as the medium of relationship formation. These were social relations maintained through food; at death the process of creating social bonds is inverted through the very refusal of food.

The idea that someone would taboo food for a close relative, a child, parent, or sibling, elicits the same sort of dissociation and discomfort (which the Baining gloss as shame) as would the use of kin terms, or the expression of nurturance or pride among those kin categories. Death reasserts the asocial characteristics of a person and his or her relations, and disrupts the valued processes of social transformation. Mortuary rituals are designed to provide a social closure to relations with the deceased and to reconstitute social relations among the living.

Adoption as a Mediator in Relations with Outsiders

The production of society through the transformation of natural ties into social ones is the process underlying most Baining activity and values. These transformations take a number of different forms, but they share a pattern or schema. This schema works on the symbolic as well as the material level. It is through symbolic generalizations of the principles described here that the Baining manage to incorporate outsiders into their social order. These processes are essentially the same as those used daily, but rely more heavily on a conscious manipulation of the symbolic transformations. This is seen most clearly in relations with plantation laborers.

Chapter 3 describes how Baining land was alienated during the early years of German colonization and was given over to extensive coconut plantations. Since then there has been a steady stream of labor from other parts of Papua New Guinea into the area. In recent years, influenced by such factors as self-government and independence, the introduction of cocoa as an additional cash crop much more profitable than coconuts, and the increasing land scarcity elsewhere in Papua New Guinea, many of these plantation laborers have decided not to return home at the end of their contracts. Some sign on for further contracts on the plantations. Many of these long-term laborers are on friendly terms with the Baining in the communities nearby, and a number of them have been adopted by particular Baining families. These adoptions are made manifest through visiting and food exchanges. In general, the Baining bring gifts of garden produce and betel nut to their "children" on the plantations, and the plantation laborers reciprocate with store-bought rice, tinned fish, tobacco, and sometimes liquor for their "parents." Visiting occurs back and forth, with the laborers occasionally spending weekends in the villages. Recently, some of these laborers have begun buying parcels of land from their Baining parents, which they plant with coconuts and cocoa and from which they will eventually earn a living.

On one occasion when we were with some laborers who were now landowners, my Baining adoptive father turned to me and, pointing to Yakan (a laborer) and the others, said that they were his children and that he had given them milk—had nursed them. I was by then familiar with the idea of adoption between Baining and such outsiders to the community as me, the school teachers, or these laborers from other parts of Papua New Guinea. I understood these adoptions to be analogous to those of a child taken after weaning who was socialized with food. The food exchanges between Peni and these laborers, or between Peni and me, were frequently mentioned in this vein, and we were frequently commended for being good children because we reciprocated concurrently with receiving, not waiting until our parents were old and infirm to help them out. I did not, however, understand the allusion to breast-feeding. On inquiry Peni said he had given them milk because he had given them land, and they had planted coconuts on it. If they had just used the land to plant gardens on it, that would not have constituted a nursing relationship among them. That was all the exegesis I could get from informants, but I gradually constructed the following explanation.

The Baining say that the earth (land, ground) is their mother, because it gives them food. This statement is on the order of a symbolic analogy for them. There is no further elaboration of the point. They also have a myth that describes the origin of the coconut (see appendix for the full text of the myth). In this myth, a man tells his two sons to watch over his grave after his death, and something will come up that will provide them with food (nowadays they say money too, since coconuts are a major cash crop). After the father's death, a coconut tree grows from his head (the nut of a coconut is perceived to look like the head of a man). Coconuts are thus symbolically analogous to fathers.

In the construction of the relationship between Peni and the plantation laborers, these various elements take on more concrete relationships. Peni is parent to these laborers because he has adopted them and given them food. He has also given them ground, which stands in the relationship as symbolic mother to both him and the laborers (Peni's relationship to the ground does not change, even after giving it away). The laborers then go ahead and plant coconuts on the land, supplying the element of father to the equation. The coconuts supply the laborers with food and money as specified in the myth. Since the medium of adoption is just these elements of food and money, the laborer is thus in an adopted-child relationship with the coconuts he planted on the maternal land. This leads to a double adoptive relationship. The laborer is the child both of the Baining Peni, and of the ground (mother) and coconuts (father). The Baining is also the child of these same symbolic parents, the earth and the coconuts, although we may assume he is the natural and not the adopted child since the connection cannot be cut. The situation that emerges is that the Baining and the laborers are both children of the same symbolic parents, but one is also the parent of the other. The only context in normal Baining society where such a set of relations can obtain is when a family adopts a child and the mother nurses it. In such instances the whole family becomes parents in relation to that nursing child. An analogous relationship had been built up between Peni and the laborers, but through a different path. Thus, what Peni had done in telling me that he had nursed these laborers was to construct the missing link which made the other relationships cohere (see fig. 4.1).

This whole example is an instance of a reverse transformation. In this case, a set of relations obtain, and because these relations are normatively the result of certain transformations, the relations can be conceptually reversed to posit the missing link. In the example given earlier in this chapter, an adoption was said to have occurred because the nurturance associated with it had been provided; here, the breastfeeding is posited because the social relations that exist are more easily understood if they are seen as stemming from that fact.

The Work of Kinship

In the beginning of this chapter, a distinction was made between the Baining concepts of natural and social kinship. The distinction between natural and social is itself a product of Baining cosmology. For the

A. "Milk" Adoption

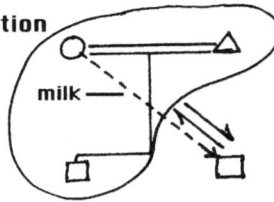

Reciprocal "parent-child" terms used between nuclear family of adopting mother as a whole and adopted child

B. "Adoption" of Adult Non-Baining Worker

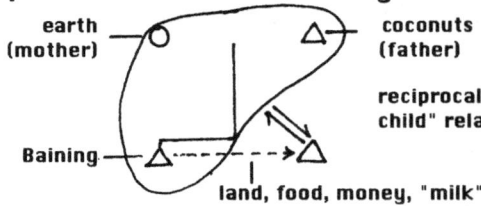

earth (mother)

coconuts (father)

reciprocal "parent-child" relationship

Baining

land, food, money, "milk"

Figure 4.1   Adoption

Baining the natural is not culturally mediated. The social is socially and culturally mediated through activities the Baining call work. These categories are not equally valued for the Baining. The Baining relegate biological relations of kinship, which radiate from the nuclear family with decreasing intensity, to the domain of nature. The culturally constituted system of social kin is analogous to the former, but it is valued very differently. This difference in value is due to the fact that work has been performed to construct the relations. These work activities have high value for the Baining.

Value stems from the work of transforming the natural into the social, and all the activities the Baining call work share this quality. This same underlying schema is repeated in the production of gardens, where nature is transformed into social products, and in socialization, where children are transformed from natural offspring into social children (as the next chapter describes). These activities all have social value for the Baining. They are all processes of social production and reproduction.

5   The Life Cycle and Socialization

Baining narratives about their lives are quite stereotypic, and reveal more about cultural values and expectations than they do about particular personal experiences. This stereotypic quality is important both for what it reveals about what people consider important to relate and what they do not. The following life history expresses the essence of a Baining autobiography.

> Before when I was small, my parents carried me; I was very small. Then I went around on my hands [crawled]. Then later, I stood up, and I was as big as Salangun [eighteen months]. I went around and I played, and I did this [splashed] outside in the mud. And I went. I ate only a little. I was still small. I did not know [understand] things. I went around, already I went around [to steal] for cucumbers from my "other" parents. My parents were angry at me because I should not go around to the others; that is bad. I went for cucumbers and I ate them, and my parents were angry at me. I should not steal from others, it is bad.
>
> My parents and I went to the gardens, and late in the afternoon we pulled up taro and picked greens and carried firewood and came back to the hamlet. Then my parents cooked; and I cried for food. They gave me food. Again I cried for food, and they gave me food. I ate and I grew and I grew. Later I worked in the garden. I planted taro stalks, I weeded, I mounded the taro, I harvested the food.
>
> Later, when I was big, the same as Wingi [about eighteen], already I went and I did all this [garden work]. And I carried cargo [for the Japanese]. I went and I thought of men. I wanted a husband. Later they arranged a marriage for me. I was big then, the same as Wingi [Wingi is still unmarried]. I was married, I stayed with him, on and on. Then later, a while ago, he died; and I lived and I am old.

I was afraid to marry. I wanted to stay [as I was]. I ran
away to the bush. I slept there. My husband did not come
after me, he stayed [at home]. Later I came to him. We two
lived [together], we did not live with others. We stayed and
later I gave birth. I gave birth to Pataip first, followed by
Tuknygit, but she died; the Japanese policemen killed her
when she was as old as Salangun. She was followed by
Nguarem, then by Uras, then by Langmutki, but she died.
Then later came Sumumga, followed by Kamisarum, followed by Ratkinaigi, then Lumbak, then Leram. That's all.
Uras's parents took her [she was adopted]. Her parents died
and then she stayed with me. When she was big, yesterday
[recently] she married. Ratkinaigi lived with me, but Lumbak's parents took her [she was adopted]. I stayed with Sumumga and Kamisarum. I was not angry when others
adopted them. They take their children and I went to take
mine, Dlaung, the only one. It is good. This is good, you
exchange with each other and it is good.

I live and I go and I work; we work for the singapu [Singa-
pore taro] and the taro. We work/clear the bush. I burn with
fire, and I plant singapu and taro and we work. I help my
children—I work their gardens while they stay on the coast.
And we do all this for ourselves. Then I cook some food and
I eat. I go and I work all this; I work for myself, and for
the aswain [vegetable], the greens and the bananas, and the
pitpit. I go and I work all this for myself. And already I am
old and I will stay here. I will stay here completely, and they
[the children], they go down to the coast, and I work all this
after they have left.

My husband died and I was sad. Before he died, he was
blind. When he died, I did not want to die too. I want to
stay as I am. I did not think that I too should die. I will stay
like this, and my children will look after me. I told them
that they will look after me. Already I am old, but I still
work in the garden, but I do not work for real. My children
look after me, and they work for me. Later, I want to stay
completely in the village, and they will look after me. But
not yet. I still want to go. I still want to go to the gardens.
(Pelas [elderly widow], life history)

The lack of personal detail in Pelas's account and the way she skims
over what, by our standards, are important, distinctively individual
experiences and events (such as her marriage, her husband's personality, the birth and rearing of her children, etc.) are evocative of the Baining ethos of de-emphasizing distinctive individuality in favor of conformity to a common ideal of sociality.

I originally found the Baining life histories disappointing because I was expecting a rich fabric of events and details. I wanted people to tell me how particular events in their own experience taught, influenced, and motivated them. Instead, I found people unable to personalize their narratives to any great degree. Most of the particulars in the biographies were the result of questions from me. Even with this instigation, the responses tended to be very detached; for example, when asked how they felt when a child was adopted or a spouse died, people responded "It was good," or "It was sad"; when I asked people to relate their experiences in having children and raising them, rarely did I get anything more detailed than a list of the children. Not a single informant spontaneously made any mention of the dances or bush preparations despite the fact that these occasions are obviously the most colorful and marked events in the Baining social world. Personal experience is not what these biographies illustrate, and I became less disappointed in the material when I realized that there is another level of information being offered here. In their totality these life histories are an important key to understanding Baining culture, values, and focal activities.

What emerges from the life histories is the Baining perception of the ideal social personality, and the progress that individuals make through their lives towards this social goal. As we have seen in previous chapters, the Baining conception of an individual is that he or she is "natural" at birth and is only gradually transformed into a social being, a "person," through processes and activities such as the ingestion of garden produce, adoption, and productive labor.

This chapter analyzes the Baining life cycle and the social processes that accompany it. The first section presents Baining concepts of the physical development of individuals throughout the life cycle. The second section is a description of the life cycle drawn from a corpus of over twenty-five life histories taken from people of different ages, sexes, and marital status. This same corpus is used to abstract attitudes, values, themes, and symbols underlying the production of the person in Baining terms. The third section weaves together the patterns illustrated in the first two and places them in a model of socialization, production, and reproduction.

Physical Developments during the Life Cycle

The life history given above is a cultural characterization of the life cycle. Very few physical changes creep into the life histories. The Baining are more concerned with socially produced changes than with those they consider natural. Nevertheless, the social changes are wrought on a physical body, and the ensuing body is a cultural product. I will begin my description of the life cycle by discussing how the Baining conceptualize physical aspects of age and bodiliness.

As we have seen in the previous chapter, the Baining attribute conception to sexual intercourse. The fetus is the product of the combined fluids of the parents: the semen (often called blood) of the father and the blood of the mother. The child gradually coagulates from the fluids of intercourse. During pregnancy the child absorbs the flesh and blood of the mother, thus growing at the expense of some of her substance. Birth is the physical rupture between mother and child, but the dependency, even parasitism, of the child continues. The nursing child still draws sustenance from the flesh of the mother. The Baining say that a mother's milk is contained in her skin and is drawn out through sucking. They recognize a connection between the food a mother eats and her production of milk, since there are certain food taboos applied to nursing women, but the general conception seems to be that food is converted to flesh and then sucked by the child, and not that food is directly converted to milk. The child is still an extension of his or her parents' skin.

Physically, a young child is characterized by having little or no hair, no teeth, little ability to see or focus and no strength. While these characteristics predominate, the baby is hardly human. The Baining say "its eye is not clear," meaning that the child does not know or understand yet, or is in darkness, meaning the same thing.[1] The first signs of a developing consciousness in the infant are correlated with seeing and recognizing people and objects, and with the beginnings of separation and independent activity. One informant said that a child becomes a person when he or she lifts up the mother's breast to suckle. I suggest that this one marker symbolizes the beginnings of physical and muscular coordination in the child, and a separation between child and mother in that the child recognizes the mother (the mother's breast) as an object to be manipulated, not just a physical extension of him- or herself. This transformation is paralleled by a new form of locomotion.

The Baining use mode of locomotion as a means of delineating physical age. A newborn baby is carried in an adult's arms or in a cloth tied across the chest. In answer to the question "How old is he [or she]?" a child of this age is described as *ta tal ka (ki)* (they carry him [her]). After the age of five or six months, parents begin to carry their children on their shoulders. This form of transportation requires that the child have some sense of balance and support, and take some part in maintaining his or her posture, usually by grasping his or her parent's hair (although parents frequently support the child with one hand if neces-

---

1. This is the same expression they use for their ancestors who were pagans.

sary). Children of this age are described as *ka (ki) kalak* (he [she] sits on the shoulders). An older child is identified by the phrase *ka (ki) tit* (he [she] goes). This term is ambiguous since it means progressively different things for individuals as they grow, and to derive the age of the child one has to remind informants to specify which criterion they are applying. The first sense of *ka (ki) tit* refers to crawling, and informants will usually specify *ka (ki) tit prama angurigit* (he [she] goes with his hands). A toddler goes on his legs. An older child who has become even more independent (e.g., boys and girls of the seven to nine range) is said to *ka (ki) tit mas* (he [she] goes fully), meaning that he or she goes for water, firewood, gathering, wandering in the bush, etc.

Beyond these, age distinctions are not specifically made among children. They are generally classed as *engilta* (small), as opposed to adolescents, who are vaguely categorized as *ambarta* (big). *Ambarta*, however, has multiple connotations, signifying anything from adolescent to elder, depending on the context and who is being described. No notice is given to puberty in a classificatory sense; no rites of passage surround it. People do, of course, notice the growth of breasts in a girl and the change in a boy's voice, but they do not spontaneously use these as markers. The onset of puberty does not initiate any new phase of the life cycle. Adolescents essentially continue the same lifestyle as before, with a gradual increase in both work and responsibility. The transition to adulthood, marriage, and parenting comes later for the Baining. If puberty is the onset of certain physical processes of maturation, the Baining are more concerned with the fulfillment of those processes. While they recognize that adolescent girls develop breasts and in general get plumper and heavier during adolescence, it is only when a girl's breasts begin to fall and she is definitively "big" that she is ready to marry. A boy is ready to marry when he is "big," shaves, and can do a man's work.

The idea that men and women are relatively heavy and hearty at marriage correlates with several Baining ideas. The first of these is that as a married couple begins a life together as a productive unit each partner must be physically capable of upholding his or her share of the work. There is a belief that work and sweat are both necessary ingredients for production. Sweat for the Baining is not just a by-product of work but a component in the work itself. Sweat emanates from the blood of the skin and is an indication of internal heat or transformative power. Labor that does not produce sweat is somehow believed to be less effective. The flesh of the young adult is believed to be replete with blood and sweat-producing capabilities.

The second reason why robustness is required is the belief that flesh and blood constitute the raw material from which come conception and nourishment of offspring. As mentioned previously, each child born is believed to reduce the parents' flesh and blood by an increment. As people age and have children, therefore, they are thought to diminish in size. Informants say that children "pull" flesh and blood from their parents. Old people are frequently referred to in the diminutive (e.g., *aurananini ma Pinam-ini* [our little mother, little Pinam]). The diminished quantity of blood in their skin renders them less capable of sweating and their work suffers on this account. Old people are less productive because they can no longer sweat so much. Their internal heat (their transformative energy) is diminished. The process of aging is, thus, a process of enfeeblement, which is ultimately connected to the cycles of production and reproduction.

Although the aging process is conceptually derived and explained through this physical process, the same debilitation and wasting away can be seen to happen to individuals who have either never married or have not borne children. This is not perceived as a paradox by the Baining, who attribute to these individuals the same effects of age as they do to others. Thus Pinam, who bore only one child in her life, still diminished as she aged, and she called attention to this fact about herself. The fact that old people lose weight, muscle, strength, and blood is seen by the Baining in a cyclical mode as a return to the frailty of childhood. Although she is now thin and tiny, Pinam herself explained that, "Before I was big [fat] and now I go back/return/reverse myself to being small [like a child]" (the word "small" is also the word for "child" in Baining). This concept of reversal is strengthened by several other characteristics attributed to old age, which are also shared with infants and young children, such as the loss of hair, teeth, eyesight, and hearing, the latter being associated with understanding (the verb to hear, *nari*, is the same as the verb to understand). The social dependency of the old on their adult children is thus accompanied by the symbolic physical transition from adult to childlike being.

Despite the fact that the Baining do not believe in spirit reincarnation (in which the next step after being a "child" again would be that of being a baby again), it does seem that death is for them the logical next step in the cycle. The relations between the social life cycle and the "unsocial" characteristics of *aios* as dead people, spirits, and bush creatures will be further examined in the next chapters.

The Life Cycle

Growing up is more than just a succession of physical stages; it is a series of social stages that are produced by various social processes.

At each stage the individual acquires new capacities and is accorded new expectations. Such new capacities, however, are learned in social contexts. The social person is constantly produced through interactions with others.

Infancy

The individual at birth is a natural being, untouched by social expectations. "Before when I was small, my mother always carried me, and I used to urinate on her and defecate on her. I was just a baby" (Masnari [young married woman and new mother], life history). A baby is a bundle of uncontrolled natural processes, constantly carried by the parents. An infant starts out as a "physical" extension of the mother and father. First he or she is carried in their arms, still close to their bodies. Later he or she is moved to the shoulders. When placed on the shoulders, and subsequently on the ground, the child begins to assume a bit of autonomy. He or she can be physically separated from his or her parents but is still a relatively natural being. The process of crawling on hands and knees is animal-like. The Baining do not encourage their children to crawl; in fact more often than not, even when a child is at the crawling stage, he or she spends most of the time on an adult's lap or being carried by a sibling. Should a child be set on the ground and start to crawl, it frequently happens that one or another of the adults present will reach out, almost unconsciously, and lift the child into his or her lap. Crawling and toddling are not periods of exploration and learning for a Baining child; they are periods of passivity.

In addition to physical immobility, a baby does not understand the spoken word that is used to restrain, educate, and socialize. "When I was small, they spoke to me, but I did not hear" (Winga [married man], life history). The Baining say that a child begins to become a person at around six months of age. At this point the infant acquires several attributes that they use as markers. One of these is the child's ability to lift up his or her mother's breast to suckle. Another is teething. Informants say that adults begin speaking to a child when he or she shows his or her first teeth. When all the teeth have come in, the infant starts talking back. At about this time, they say that a child's "eye becomes clear." This is a Baining expression for being oriented and able to understand. When addled or confused, the eye is not clear (being lost in the bush or running amok [akambain] are examples of activities described as unclear). Things that are clear are relatively social: "a clear place" is a term used for the village or hamlet; it is opposed to "unclear" places such as the bush or forest.

Childhood

Children are socialized in clear places, either the village or the garden, which is also a clear place. The child ventures out into these clear spaces as he or she grows, and increasingly learns spatial and mental orientations. Young children often remain in the hamlet with older siblings or grandparents during the day while their parents go out to the gardens. If they accompany their parents, they are carried through the bush, an unclear place, until they reach the gardens. When they do venture away from their parents, however, young children tend to do "natural" things. In the village, many children described their play as "splashing outside in the mud," an activity that parents did not encourage (as we will see in the next section) perhaps because it is reminiscent of pigs.[2] When they go with their parents to the gardens, the activity which they recount most frequently is that of going to other people's gardens to steal food, particularly cucumbers (which can be eaten raw).[3]

Stealing food (which is done in a hidden, "unclear," way) is antisocial behavior. Stealing is the antithesis of giving, the act of sociality par excellence. Stealing food is also analogous to what animals do when they break into people's gardens and eat the crops. Again the behavior of the child is most closely comparable to that of pigs, since pigs are the primary "natural" destroyers of gardens through their food-stealing activities. Although stealing from gardens is animalistic, what children (and pigs) are stealing is the very food that in other contexts is given to them to socialize them. The symbolic characteristics of food as socializer and mediator between nature and society make it an apt target for children in this quasi-social, quasi-natural state.

Whether or not a child accompanies his or her parents to the gardens, the routine on the return from the gardens is the same.

> My parents worked in the gardens, and I cried for food. Later we came home to our house, and my parents cooked. They cooked our food. My friends and I played in the village: we ran around, we splashed, we chased each other. When I was hungry, I came and I cried for food, and I ate. (Winga, life history)

2. Pigs are the principal domesticated animal, natural beings in a cultural setting. They are socialized by being fed by their owners, a process analogous to that of socializing the young child.

3. The Baining eat very few foods raw: primarily coconuts and cucumbers, and both of these are frequently eaten cooked as well. There is something asocial about raw food that makes it dangerous, especially to people in a vulnerable condition: the young, or the sick. Social food is always cooked.

Always I cried and cried for food, and my mother was angry
at me. There was no food yet, she was still cooking the food,
the taro and the greens. When it was cooked, I ate. Later I
would wander around (play), then I would come and again
I cried for food, and she got taro for me. Later when I was
big, and they arranged a marriage for me, and I gave birth
to all my children, they were the same, and they cried to
me for food, and I got food for them. (Kwatnan [married
woman], life history)

One's parents are the people who are socially recognized as one's food
givers. To steal food from others is to rob these people of their socializing power, and thus of their social status. The dictum "Do not steal
food from others" ("other parents" in the Baining kin terminology)
thus grows out of (1) the need to socialize children away from their
asocial tendencies; and (2) to internalize in children the proper attitude
towards the social relationships in their environment.

The process of feeding and caring for a child over time results in the
gradual growth of the child both as a physical being and a "socialized
self." As the child matures, he or she is more and more tied up in the
web of social relations that are produced through the giving of food.
Physical development is entwined with social embodiment. The emphasis is on feeding a child. Informants' memories of childhood re-
volve around how they took food illegitimately and how they cried
for food from their parents.

Why is there a dearth of other activities described? People mention
that they used to go outside and play with their friends: "I went and
I played outside. I saw my age group outside and I went to them and
we played. Afterwards our parents were angry at us" (Masnari, life
history); "I played, and when I came in they [her parents] were angry
at me. Don't play; you cannot play in the village. Then we were quiet"
(Kwatnan, life history).

My friends and I, we played; we went to the village and we
chased each other just like you see [the children nowadays].
We did all this too. Later my parents were angry at me. I
should not play. It is bad. We should not play because their
ears hurt [from the noise]. And later when we were big, we
did not play like this. We were big, so we did not play. (Suvanan [elderly woman], life history)

There is very little child culture among the Baining. There are only a
few games that seem indigenous to the area. In general children seem
merely to run and chase each other out of doors. This sort of general
exuberance is not appreciated by the adults in the society, as the quotes

above indicate. Informants over forty years old describe how they were punished as children for playing. Their parents would take a piece of bone or thorn and pierce either the septum of the nose, the sides of the nose, or the ear lobes. Children were then supposed to keep a long pointed object in these apertures so that when they engaged in some sort of active game or rambunctious activity, the bone, thorn or whatever was in the hole would interfere with the play, and perhaps hurt. This would serve as a constant reminder to them that they were not supposed to play. This practice is no longer carried out, and has not been for some time. Almost all the older people in the community, however, have holes in their nose or ears dating from childhood. One old woman still wears a long curved cassowary bone in her septum, as if it were a form of decoration; this example misled me for a number of months into thinking that all such scars were a form of decoration, and I was quite startled to learn that they were signs of punishment. Informants could not explain or speculate about why playing is so objectionable to the elders of the community. They could only say that their parents complain of the noise.

One explanation might be related to the fact that the games played by children are not very structured or organized. They do not involve social values like work or reciprocity. Most of the games are forms of running, chasing, splashing, and throwing things. Such activities are both noisy and disorderly. They seem more animalistic than human. I hypothesize that it is this aspect that parents object to. Their punishment is meant to discourage the "natural" activities of children. In contrast, the few games that are most elaborated and appreciated in Baining culture are those that are indoors and sedate, particularly the making of a wide array of string figures.

The Baining do not consider that children learn from play. Parents do not make toys for their children. They do not give them miniatures of adult objects such as spears, baskets, tools, etc. They rarely play with their children either in a verbal or active way (although they are generous, loving, and physically in touch with them frequently). Other children occasionally teach the younger ones in a playful way. Two children of age eight to nine were seen on several occasions playing with a 3½-year-old. Their "game" consisted of calling the names of things and people for the younger child to repeat.

Parents proceed from the principle that children learn from work. Consequently they teach children to work in the garden as soon as they show the interest and capability. These are the lessons people recount in their autobiographies.

When I was bigger, my father and I went to the gardens.
He taught me about gardens and we worked. We built a

fence and we worked the garden. Then he said this to me:
"You climb the tree and cut down the branches over the
taro sticks and the singapu." We went to the garden and he
taught me all this, and I did it all. He taught me to catch
crayfish, and he taught me to make traps in the bush, and
I made them, and I did all this. (Nguinga [unmarried man],
life history)

What did my parents teach me? To work. I went with them
to the garden and I saw them working. Later I worked just
like that with them. (Kwatnan, life history)

They and I went to the garden, and they said I should go
work in the garden, and I did not want to. Later I went there
by myself. I did not want to work. I was tired of working.
I wished we did not have to work. Later I saw my friends
and I went to them, and we played. (Masnari, life history)

People recount these experiences as educational ones. These are the
processes that transform a child into an adult; the biographies name
these processes quite explicitly.

Adolescence

As children grow and become better able to work, they develop into
a resource not only to their parents, but to the community as a whole.
Adolescents described by the Baining as "big," although already productive workers, are not yet responsible for their own family or household. They are called upon to contribute to collective work parties,
where a big job is done in one day. In exchange for their work, the
laborers are given a meal after their work.

When I was big, we went for food. We carried singapu and
firewood, and we filled the water [bamboos] for our parents
for them to eat and drink after the communal labor. The
next day our parents would cook for the men who built the
fence in the garden or who planted the taro sticks or who
cut the bush. Then perhaps one of our parents [relatives]
called us and we worked. We worked weeding. Or perhaps
another of our parents called and we weeded a garden in
preparation for burning it. Then another parent called on
us to cut pitpit for her roof. (Uras [married woman and
mother], life history)

Adolescents are full adults but are not yet married and self-sufficient.
During this phase, they are engaged principally in lateral relationships
with their peers and with others in the community, helping all who
ask. Their efforts are immediately reciprocated with food. This is in

contrast to the next phase—that of marriage and child rearing. Married people are entering the phase of linear reciprocity, repaying their parents for what they gave previously, and looking out for their children in anticipation of reciprocal payment later in their lives. During these adolescent years, a person's relationships are broader and more varied than at any other point in his or her life. Not only do people work more frequently in communal groups, but they work for a wide range of people.

This work pattern fits in with the social pattern mentioned earlier: this is the one time in the life cycle when people associate more with people of their own sex than in sexually complementary dyadic units. They both socialize and work in bigger units. In Yalom, the young men even live together in a men's house.[4] When they marry, they move out of the communal house, back into an extended family household (either their own parents' or their wife's parents' house) with their wife. While the women do not have their own communal house, they often gather in groups in the evening for a short social period, and they sometimes gather together at night for an informal sing. One house, that of a widow with three daughters, was often the locus of these events, and it was common to find several other girls and young women sleeping over at Sumitki's (the widow's) house.

At this period of their life, youths do not want to marry and assume the responsibilities of a spouse and parent.

> As for me, I say I don't want to marry. I want to roam. I want to work on a plantation. I want to stay like this [as I am now]. I will work on a plantation: I will work, I will find money and I will wander. I will work, then later I will marry. (Kwanukndum [adolescent male], life history)

> I do not want to get married. I am still small. Later! Our parents speak, but we do not want to. They talk in vain. I do not like men. I still do not want to. I still do not know about gardens. I do not know how to work yet. (Karamang [adolescent female], life history)

Although these are adolescents speaking, many older informants who reflect on their feelings before marriage share these emotions. They recall wanting to stay single and remain with their friends. They pre-

---

4. This house is a recent innovation borrowed from the idea of men's houses learned from plantation workers on the coast, and from the model of laborers' dormitories on these same plantations. These young men eat at their parents' houses, but they sleep and frequently socialize in their "haus boi" (pidgin for plantation laborers' house; there is no indigenous term).

ferred the sporadic communal work to the everyday routine of the married. They expressed a dislike of the opposite sex. An old woman tells,

> My parents spoke and I, I did not want to get married. I wanted to stay and have them cook for me, like before. Yes, I ran away, to my other parents [relatives]. Later they came for me. My husband did not run away, and later they and he came for me, and we lived with my parents. (Suvanan, life history)

> My husband did not want to get married, he was scared and he ran away. He ran to the Tolais [the neighboring tribe who live near the town]. I did not want to get married, but it was our parents who decided it. I did not run away, I lived with my parents. Women don't run away. Where could they go? The men go to the Tolais. They do not want to marry the women. He is scared, he wants to stay as he is, and they give him a wife, and he is scared and he runs away. If not for this, he would not go. He will not be able to work for his wife. All of us, we want to stay with our parents and have them cook for us. (Uras, life history)

People object to marriage because they do not want to have to work so hard. The men do not want to have to make gardens all the time, and the women do not want always to work in the gardens and to have to cook for their family all the time. They want to remain dependent. Their parents, however, see that they are already socialized and productive members of the society, and so they arrange the marriages. Despite the fears people have and their initial reaction of running away, virtually all the wayward spouses come back and settle down with their chosen mate.

Marriage

Marriage is a moment of transition between two positions in the household cycle. Those who are not yet married are still dependent on their natal household's production and labor cycles. These people state their commitment to that unit through such phrases as wishing to stay unmarried so their mothers will continue to cook for them. One informant said he had talked his adoptive father out of arranging a marriage for him by asking "What? Don't you want me to help you in your gardens anymore?" (Tovi [when he was still unmarried], life history). Despite their position and sometimes significant labor input in their natal families, adolescents are not involved in keeping that unit functioning. Marriage is the process of transition from a position of cog in the natal family household to that of initiator and responsible actor in a new family unit.

The transition from being a socialized person to that of an active socializer is not easy.

> After I got married, then I worked some gardens. But we were hungry. Before I was married I did not make gardens. I used to wander. Then later I planted gardens for us, but there was no singapu; it was not ready yet. There was no taro; it was not ready yet. I worked gardens but we were hungry. Then later they began to be ready. First the sweet potato was ready, and then the taro, and we went and got them and we ate; but the singapu was not ready yet. Then later it was ready and we ate. I tell all of this [that happened before]. Men who are just starting marriage, they are hungry because before they did not work. Young married people are hungry and they eat ferns. (Inangaiyi [married man], life history)

The state of self-sufficiency, which is attributed to a married couple, is an acquired state. It is attained, in the Baining view, through garden labor, and the fruits of that labor: the garden produce. Self-sufficiency is a social characteristic; it is opposed by hunger, which is not social (as I discuss in the next chapter). Hunger is associated with isolation and asociality.

The phase of marriage and child rearing does not bring forth much comment in the majority of the life histories. People just mention that they lived with their spouse and did not fight. This steady state is usually seen as continuing to the present, unless the spouse has died. When asked what they did with their spouses' informants responded,

> We did not get angry at each other and our children are the same. They do not get angry at one another. We talked about the food we would eat. We cooked and we talked about the food we would eat. And we would eat when the sun was going down. Also when the sun came up, we ate. We told our children this, and we and they ate. In the evenings we taught them. We did not tell stories. We were quiet and lived like this. (Suvanan, life history)

The relationship between husband and wife, except in the context of preparing gardens and feeding the children, does not receive much attention in the life histories; but the gardens and feeding are of paramount importance.

> We work for ourselves, each couple like this. We two go. My wife pulls out singapu and later she cooks for us. The

people work hard for food for themselves. Those who do nothing will die, because of themselves, because they did not do any work. We two go, my wife pulls up singapu and she carries vegetables. She cooks the singapu until it is done; she puts the greens in the bark steamer [aluska]. When she finishes that she goes to fill the water containers. This is women's work. She does all this for us; she works hard. If she did not work for us, we would die. I am a man. I do my work [in the gardens] and we come home and I am tired from my work and I rest. But my wife, she works in the garden, but later she cooks and gets water. If a friend or a child comes up, my friend and I, we sit and talk and she does all this work and then we eat. . . .

My children and I, we cry to our mother for food and she makes food for us. Always she is our mother, and she gets food for us. She is my mother because of this. (Inangaiyi, life history)

We work for ourselves, and soon our children will do the same. When they are big, they will follow after us, and they will do all this, and so on. Always we do these things, and we do not have one among us who does not. All of us, when we are big, we work the food for ourselves. And so we eat, and we finish all this, and it goes on and on. We work the gardens; we go every day. During the day, we work, on and on, and it is over. The same the next day, we do all this again. Later they do this for themselves. (Suvanan, life history)

Parents

The period between marriage and old age is the phase in which people individually and in couples are most important in socializing their children. They do this by feeding them as well as by teaching them. We have already seen how children cry to their parents for food. Parents spend their days at their gardens planting and harvesting, and then they come home in the late afternoon with garden produce. It is usually the women who cook and provide food for the children in this context (although it can be either), and who mention over and over that their children cry to them for food. Some men, however, see themselves as responding to an additional aspect of this relationship by hunting and providing meat occasionally.

My child cries for meat and I go and I hunt something. The child speaks and I go; I do not want to go, but the child cries and I cannot not go. All of this I do because of my child. It cries over and over for meat and I go; sometimes I bring back a little meat, sometimes I go in vain. (Inangaiyi, life history)

Both parents are thus constantly involved in and responsive to their children's needs and desires. Feeding, however, is not just a physical and mechanical process. The Baining see it as the model for creating and sustaining the social aspect of family relations: thus a mother is a mother because she gives food. She is not only a mother to the children, but also symbolically her husband's mother because she feeds him. The Baining are quite explicit about how this relationship works: "My wife/mother works and cooks all the food and gives it to us, and she is our mother because of this. She is my wife and mother" (Inangaiyi, life history).

Socialization of children is not accomplished merely through feeding and looking after them. Teaching often has to become a good deal more explicit. In so doing, Baining teach their children the things they learned while growing up: in particular how to work, and how they should eventually reciprocate the food they are presently receiving. The dominant parental role in these years is as socializer, which is more important than merely that of adult.

> I teach my child the good ways. I cannot teach him another way. I said to him that he can not steal things; that is not the way that my father taught me, so I teach my son the way my father taught me. I teach him to work. I look after my children. I look after my own child, and I look after my adopted child. I teach them both. I cannot show all this to my true child alone. I show it to my adopted child too, and later I will talk to him and he will hear me; and these you gave birth to, you will talk and they will not hear you. (Winga, life history)

> I teach my child[ren] to work the gardens. They plant the food in them, the greens, vegetables, cucumbers, and pitpit. I tell them they will look after me, and I teach them all this. (Suvanan, life history)

> Later when I am old, my children will look after me. I talk like this, and they will do well by me. (Naramitki [widow], life history)

Parents are primarily responsible for the success of their children in becoming full social beings. Therefore, parents who in other contexts will deny that they discipline their children, can be seen disciplining or punishing their children for laziness or irresponsibility. This contradiction is explained as being necessary for the education of the child, without which he or she will be looked down upon by the neighbors, or will not be chosen as a spouse for someone's child.

Langerkan was looking after a child who was staying with her family while in school, but who was not really an adopted child. Her daughters, aged eleven and fourteen, teased this child, Pelangut, by saying she did not know how to cook. They told her that she could not just stand around and watch lazily; she would have to learn to do it too. Langerkan said that Pelangut was afraid of the fire (i.e., that the heat of the cooking food would burn her). She said that previously her adopted daughter Danggekan had been afraid of fire, and that she Langerkan had scolded her and shoved her hand in the fire, and that "taught" her. She said that she would have to teach Pelangut too. She would have to learn and could not just remain without working. Langerkan said that formerly all mothers had done this with their children—shoved their hands in the fire. It was bad for them to be afraid of fire, because later they would not know how to cook. They would not be able to look after themselves.

While the Baining are raising and teaching their own children, many of them are also showing by example how the other side of this system works. Many of these adults are looking after their own aged parents.

They thought "our son, he will marry and look after us! He will look after us well, and we will live." Before they gave me food, and now we give it back and look out for them, as before they looked after us until we were big, until we got married like this. Now I look after my father and mother as before they looked after me. (Winga, life history)

In many of the life histories informants discussed how their parents had died before they had a chance to look after them. They did not have a chance to reciprocate in this direct way, or serve as an example to their own children. It is probable that in the past this was the normal case rather than the exception; people did not routinely outlive their usefulness and therefore did not often become dependent on their children for support. One old woman, a grandmother, mentioned to me that until recently most adults did not live long enough to know, look after, and adopt their grandchildren. She said that now people are living longer (increased longevity may be due to greater access to medical care). The fact that this pattern was not always fulfilled in practice does not detract from its importance as a cultural ideal for the Baining. It does, however, underline the importance of the fact that these reciprocal attitudes and orientations are taught as moral lessons, and not just through example.

Old Age

The attributes of old age are a decrease in mobility and a lack of self-sufficiency. These characteristics develop gradually, not all at once. Except in the case of illness or accident, people progressively lose their skills and self-sufficiency. As their children grow up, they gradually unburden themselves of the responsibilities of looking after a large family (although they may continue to care for an adopted child or grandchild), and can concentrate on maintaining themselves alone. In the opening life history, Pelas says she is already old; however, she goes on to tell us that she still works in the gardens. She is still self-sufficient; she works "for herself and the foodstuffs." The phrasing of her statement makes an implicit equation between herself and the products of her labor (an implicit equation between her life cycle and the productive cycle). She says that although she is old she still works, not only for herself, but also for her children. The children in this case have not yet become fully independent of their mother's labor (although they are married), let alone undertaken the responsibility of supporting her. While the tenor of Pelas's remark is that of being proud of her sustained capabilities, there is nonetheless an underlying critique of the children.

There is, perhaps, in this a tinge of the Baining pattern of being critical of their own children. Pelas maintains that when she becomes incapacitated her children will look after her, but on another level she tells us she is old and still helping them. Another woman in a similar position is Suvanan. She is also old but still active. She says, however, that her work is no longer real. It is becoming a lie, a pretense. She merely goes through the motions, and in actuality she is more and more dependent on her children. Pelas confesses that she goes only to the gardens that are close to the hamlet. When people go to those far away, she stays home with the young children.

Araninda

Attitudes towards old age are complex and ambivalent for the Baining. People see old-age dependency as in one way an ideal. It is the way your children repay you for your labor, etc., and therefore it is something to be anticipated with pleasure. It was given as a goal by most informants. However, at the same time, it is a recognition of degeneration and nearness to death, which provokes ambivalent if not totally negative responses from the Baining. All but two of the villagers in Yalom maintained at least a token participation in gardening and pro-

ductive work; the two who did not were both blind and very, very old.
These two were held up as the ideal by the others.

> Later when I am too old to work, I will stay home all day
> in the village, and my children will look after me for food
> and clothes and money. I will stay home as does our little
> mother Pinam [Pinam is one of the old women who does
> not do any productive labor]. (Suvanan, life history)

> Now I am losing my teeth and I am old. Already I am losing
> my teeth, and later they will all be gone. When I am old,
> my wife and I, we will stay completely here, in this place,
> close to the fire, and our children will go for singapu, and
> to fill the water containers, and they will cook for us. We
> will just stay sitting by the fire. This happens to all of us.
> There is not one of us who does not go to the place by the
> fire when we are old. It is the same as before when I was
> small. I am old and my child will go for food, and will cook
> for me, the same as before when I was small and my parents
> cooked for me. We will change places, and my children will
> be my parents and I will be their child. I will stay and they
> will make food for me, just like Pinam; she stays and her
> children look after her. (Inangaiyi, life history)

> Today I do not look out for myself [his children look after
> him]. I stay in the village, and it is good. Before we heard
> talk, and they told us that later you look after your father;
> and I looked after my father. They said to me, later you will
> have children, and you will look after them well, and they
> will be good to you later. (Kamisarum [elderly blind man],
> life history)

Old age is more than just a collection of physical characteristics (although these are also diagnostic). It is also a product of the lifetime
activities of the person. The processes of production and reproduction
take a physical toll on the person so they are no longer capable of full
participation in society. When this occurs the old person gradually ta-
pers off his or her gardening, hunting, house building, wood gathering,
and perhaps even cooking tasks. Instead of leaving the village or hamlet, he or she remains at home every day. Such people are called *araninda* (pl.) (*araninga* [masc.]; *araningi* [fem.]), which essentially means
"stay-at-home."[5] As an *araninga/araningi*, the old person is frequently
left at home with the young children, from toddlers to seven- and eight-

---

5. *Araningi* is the same term used for the constant drizzle that fills the gaps between
fierce monsoon storms in the months December to March, because this rain tends to
keep people at home. Another meaning of the term is as a reference to "our people,"
"the people from here."

year-olds, when their parents go to distant gardens. They are ostensibly left to look after these children, although frequently it is the children who get firewood, water, and even food during the day. In fact, the old and the young share many attributes. They are both dependent on adults for food and livelihood, neither having the strength or skills to participate in productive labor. Those who stay at home engage in taking care of each other in the adults' absence.

Death can come at any time in a society such as the Baining, and few people survive past the period of their own productiveness; thus the group of *araninda* is relatively small. As I mentioned, there were only two old women in Yalom and one old man in Lan who were true "stay-at-homes." There were several other men and women who participated in some but not all of the productive tasks. Several other old people took an alternative course and lived entirely alone in garden or "pig" houses.[6] Here they lived near a source of food, and they tended pigs, often not only their own but those of their children or siblings as well. Such people have to be reasonably self-sufficient to live alone, although many of their needs are filled by their children and grandchildren, who routinely bring them food, water, and other necessities. This is another instance where people are associated with pigs. This time a relatively socialized person is marginalized in an increasingly natural context. Here the association with pigs thus becomes a metaphor of desocialization.

Despite the fact that there are statistically few adults who survive long enough to become dependent on their children for food and livelihood, this stage of life is conceptually important in the Baining view of the life cycle. Virtually every informant responded to inquiries about maturity and old age with a discussion of how people "retire" to the hearth after their productive years. In these discussions, the *araninda* phase is overtly portrayed as something of a reward for labor time served. People ostensibly look forward to it. "I will sit by the hearth, by the fire, and my children will care for me" (Suvanan, life history). As in attitudes towards retirement in our own society, however, there is actually considerable ambivalence. Pelas and Suvanan, both old and relatively debilitated, thus maintain the fiction of working. They say

6. The Baining frequently try to keep their pigs out of the village, on order from government and medical authorities. To do this, they often build huts in the bush (anywhere from one-half to several miles from the village) where they train the pigs to come for food each morning. Occasionally the family owning the pigs will sleep in this hut and feed the pigs each morning; otherwise, one family member will carry food out to this house most mornings and feed the pigs. The pigs are fed only a portion of their diet by their owners—merely enough to keep them trained to return to their "home" daily. For the rest of their sustenance they forage in the bush.

their work is a pretense (*ngu kok di ngu matna* [literally, "I lie that I work"]). What they do not say is that they work to forestall complete dependency, which is so clearly a prelude to death. For Pinam, who stays home all day, the days are long and boring. Although she never complained, when I asked her directly what she did and how she felt, she confessed to tremendous boredom during the day. I observed that she either slept or sat catatonically with a glazed look in her eyes most of the time she was alone. The presence of an anthropologist who frequently spent the day in the village was clearly a delight to Pinam, whose face lit up whenever I entered her house. Although she never spontaneously talked about dying, she was clearly nearing death. Her time seemed to be divided between an almost living death during the day when she was alone and relatively catatonic, and the social mornings and evenings when she was in the bosom of her family and was their dependent. When asked how she felt about her impending death she said, "I don't want to die; I am afraid of dying. I want to live [stay] just as I am."

Death

Although the *araninda* phase is obviously a transition to death, death is for the Baining a relative unknown. Culturally, it is poorly elaborated except for what the missionaries tell them; they do not have, or do not remember any pre-mission beliefs. Death is a state to be feared and avoided and certainly to be ignored. Almost all my informants answered questions referring to their own death as did Pinam, admitting a real fear of dying (expressed often as a fear of the "hole," the grave) and a desire to "keep living as I am now." Although other accounts (Pool 1971; Klemensen 1965) state that husbands and wives used to want to die along with dead spouses, my informants reacted with revulsion and incredulity to the idea, reiterating in no uncertain terms that the thought of death or suicide had never occurred to them at such times.

> My wife died and I cried. I was very sad for her, but it was not possible for me to think of dying with her. It was not possible for the thought of dying to stay in my stomach. No! I am afraid. I don't want to die. Forget it! She alone, she dies and I stay. (Arigini [elderly widower], life history)

This fear of death and fondness for life is not so uniformly attributed to others by informants. For instance, they mentioned that Ilavut, a relatively young man who died a month or two before I arrived, had refused offers to carry him to the aid post, expressing his resignation to his death. Although I did not ever meet Ilavut and hear him say this for himself, I did hear Inangaiyi, during an illness, say he had dreamt that a ghost had revealed his impending death. Inangaiyi told me he thought he was going to die, and he expressed fear at the prospect. When I offered him medicine, he accepted the offer gladly, with no qualms at thus "defeating his fate." A few weeks later, he could barely recall the psychological certainty of death he had felt before. Informants also said they had had to watch Pinam after her husband's death to make sure she did not kill herself in sorrow. Pinam, however, responded to questions on this topic with categorical denials that the thought had ever occurred to her. The cultural model and expectation of the transition to death seems to predict a smoother and easier process than is often psychologically the case.

Cold and Heat

There is a dimension of well- or ill-being that is connected not only to one's physical state, but also to the context one finds oneself in. Space and time affect a person's physical and mental well-being and his or her relative sociality. These qualities are elaborated through metaphors of heat and cold. Hot and cold appear frequently as Baining descriptions of environmental states, but opposition of hot to cold goes beyond physical temperature. The word for cold, *awis* (pl.), can cover all of the categories of cold (except illness) in English. It is used for cold evenings, cold river water, cold food, etc. The concept hot is slightly more complex, since there are two kinds of heat. In Lan *angungi* means hot for all connotations, but in Yalom it merely means physical heat. A hot taro is *angungi*, as is a fire, but people are not *angun*; they are *awilas*. Sitting by a fire or sweating in the sun produce *awilas*. *Awilas* is also associated with a certain state of excitement and energy: a somewhat heightened state most frequently referred to during dances. *Awilas* might have connotations of sexual excitement. Circumstantial evidence suggests it does, but informants did not produce or acknowledge the association.

In addition to these physical qualities, hot and cold have other associations for the Baining. Nature and natural things are cold. The bush, the water, and wild animals (also domesticated animals) are essentially cold creatures and places. In a story I heard told in both villages, the villagers discovered a "bush woman" living in or by a water hole where she ate raw taro scraps soaked in cold water. When this woman was captured and brought to the village, the first task was to warm her up. She was fed warm spicy foods, and gradually she vomited all the cold elements out of her system. (The rest of the story detailed how she was socialized into women's productive roles and then married a Baining and bore children.) In contrast to the bush, the village is a basically hot place. This is attributed to the presence of fire in the village and to open space where the sun can shine.

In addition to these spatial domains, people are relatively hot and cold. Old people are believed to be relatively cold; therefore, they need to huddle by the hearth to keep warm (or bask in the sun). This was mentioned in the life histories as the fate of the old. I believe the idea is that old people have little or no internally generated heat (fire) and are therefore dependent on fire as an external source of heat. They are restricted in movement to the heat-giving radius of the village fires. If they venture beyond the boundaries of this space, the internal and external states of cold would merge. They would then be totally cold, natural creatures: a state resembling the Baining concept of death. The old are therefore kept in the village and sustained through external heat sources.

Young people and people in their prime have internal sources of heat, couched in the idiom of flesh and blood and manifested in their ability to sweat. These people carry their own heat with them into the bush and can, therefore, garden and hunt successfully. They can also transform parts of the bush into gardens both through fire and their own heat manifested as sweat. In this way, gardens are transformed spaces and loci of heat; consequently they are classed as social (village-like) places rather than as bush.

The village is more than just the locus of heat and fire. It is the place where certain natural and bush elements are transformed into sociocultural products. Raw materials such as food, water, and firewood are transformed in the village into products for human consumption. Many of the foods are called by different names after being so transformed (in the same way that English "pig" becomes "pork," and "cow" becomes "beef"). For instance, taro in the field is classed as *anat*, whereas a cooked taro is *andaka* or *andum* (a diminutive suggesting a portion of taro). Meat products in their wild, whole, and raw forms are called by the name of the animal from which they derive. When butchered and cooked, however, they are almost all classed under the rubric *asarik* (meat).[7] The village is the locus of this transformational process. That is why it is an apt place for people undergoing transformation.

Children and old people do not contain in themselves the means of their own transformation. They are the products of others' transforma-

7. The taxonomy of animal foodstuffs begins with a generic label, *asarririrung* (glossed as "meat-things"), under which all potential meat products are classified by animal name. When prepared for consumption, however, all of these become *asarik* (meat).

tive activities. They are made or kept social by those who garden, cook, and feed them. They are social products but not social agents. They are, therefore, safer in a context where sociality surrounds them. The village is, thus, both the fitting locus for socialization in the case of children and the necessary supplement and reinforcement for the sociality of the old. When young children are taken out of the village (the social setting), they are frequently carried through the bush and only set down when they reach the gardens (a social oasis). Although this behavior can be explained in terms of pragmatics (distances are long and children tire easily), I believe that it is also rooted in Baining conceptions of space and agency.

Another aspect of hot and cold beliefs has to do with their relation to water. The Baining are not particularly compulsive bathers. The environment tends to be dirty, muddy, ashy, and smokey, and water is frequently some distance away. Many people bathe only about once a week, on Sundays before church. Youths bathe most frequently, often when returning from collective labor outings or walks in the bush, or when filling water containers. Bathing, however, is not considered merely as a cleansing operation. If I complained of being cold in the evening, I was told it was because I had not washed that day. Although no informant could elaborate on this, I believe cold represents the impingement of nature on the skin, and washing restores the heat of the social person. An informant said that if a person does not wash, then he or she will not sweat because he or she is dirty. I interpret this to mean that dirt is seen as blocking the passage of sweat from the body; sweat is, perhaps, the excretion of cold from the body (water is basically considered cold), leaving only the internal heat behind. Perhaps relating to this, I observed that old Pinam, who stayed at home every day (and was consequently grey with ash), never washed. When I mentioned this, I was told it was because it was too cold for her to wash. My informant said that if they lived on the coast (where it is warmer) people would bring water for her and she would wash and dry in the heat of the day. My interpretation of this is that the internal and external coldness of Pinam were essentially one. Since she had no internal heat there was no generation of sweat, and therefore no need to wash to clear the skin. She would not regain heat by washing off the external cold of the bush (as represented by dirt) as would younger people. The dirt on her skin was, incidentally "social dirt" (ash and house dirt), although the Baining made nothing of this. I also observed that parents usually heated water before bathing babies. I believe this was done as a substitute for their body heat; perhaps it was an external transforming agent—the heat applied to the skin might be believed to pass inside and initiate the generation of heat.

Another distinction important in Baining spatial classification of bush and village, is that of clarity. The bush is a place of obscurity. Trees, branches, vines, stones, and other things obscure long-range vision and make locomotion difficult. These hazards, compounded by darkness, make night travel virtually impossible. By contrast, the village is classed as a "clear place" where one can see for distances, and travel at night is possible because there are few or no obstacles. These distinctions correlate with phases of the life cycle. Children and old people have less internal clarity and vision and thus need to be surrounded by the external clarity of the village. Mature adults with internal clarity can deal with the challenges of the bush.

In Lan there are two occasions when events in the life cycle may be marked spatially. This occurs at birth and death. Informants say that a child's placenta is frequently buried at the edge of a hamlet clearing. A betel nut (areca) or coconut palm is then planted to mark the place. As the child grows older, this tree is pointed out to the child as the place where his or her "rubbish" is buried. The tree is given to the child and he or she matures along with it.[8]

At death, a similar act occurs. The survivors of the dead person frequently plant a coconut or betel nut palm at the foot of the grave. This act is related to the same myth mentioned in chapter 4, where the coconut tree grew up from the head of a dead man (see appendix). In transposing the act to one of human intention and action, the coconut is transposed from the head to the foot of the grave. The tree is used to mark the grave. Since traditionally graves were dug adjacent to house sites, clumps of coconuts and betel nuts found scattered through the bush and forest are recognized as former house sites. Individuals, especially descendants, make claims to the fruits of these trees on the basis of kin ties with the former inhabitants.

Coconuts and betel nut palms share certain symbolic properties for the Baining. They are the vegetal counterparts to domestic pigs. Just as pigs express quasi-human, quasi-natural characteristics, so do these palms mediate between nature and culture. They are one of the very few plants that can be grown in or adjacent to the hamlets: that is, within the "clear" places. They can be eaten both raw and cooked; this is particularly true of coconuts, although betel nut when chewed without lime and pepper leaf is considered almost raw (*ngu sis* [I eat it alone; *sis* is also the verb used for eating raw food]). Both are clearly recognized as plants that reproduce "sexually" (that is, they go

8. This is true in Lan but not in Yalom. One reason for this is that coconuts and betel do not grow in Yalom—it is too high. There is, furthermore, no substitution of another plant in Yalom. The placenta might be buried, but its place is unmarked. Ornamental plants may be planted on the grave.

through a life cycle from nut to tree to reproducer of seeds [nuts] to old age).[9] They are strongly associated with human social space. Coconuts are almost never considered wild; they are always associated with human occupation. Some betel nut palms are recognized as "wild," but such trees are often assumed to belong to *aios*.

Betel nut is the principal item of social exchange among the Lan Baining. Betel and a pepper leaf or fruit are supposed to be exchanged at the beginning of every social encounter. My first lesson on arrival in the Baining area, on the hike up to Lan, was that when you encountered another person on the path, you stopped and exchanged betel. Each person digs into his or her coconut basket or string bag and removes one or two nuts and a pepper leaf. The giver must remove the stem of the nut(s) and lay it (them) stem side down on the broad or stem end of the leaf. He or she must then rip off the very tip of the leaf. Only when all these steps have been completed is the prepared bundle handed to the other person. If there is more than one person in the opposing party, a bundle is given to each individual adult in the other group. The prestation is immediately reciprocated. To forget or leave off any of the above steps in the exchange is an indication of anger or dispute with the other person. I never saw anger or a feud expressed in this way, and I came to assume that the various steps represent patterns of politeness, for which I found no Baining word other than the general words for "good," *amuris* or *atlo*. I assume that the use of the words *aheirein*, *aseirein*, glossed as "anger" and "dispute," when used in reference to betel nut exchange might suggest that these words have a secondary meaning of merely impolite behavior.

No Lan inhabitant likes to venture forth without a supply of betel nut, both to cope with the exigencies of social form and incidentally to slake his or her desire for betel during the day. The preparations for a social outing—to church or to a feast—almost always include sending a child up an areca palm for a branch of betel nut, which is then distributed among all the adult household members. The transition between child and adult in this case is gradual. When I first arrived in Lan, Dembi was just fourteen and had recently finished sixth grade, which was the apex of the local education. She was still considered a child, and only rarely chewed betel nut (at least around her parents) and still frequently got high when she did.[10] As my stay progressed, I

9. As mentioned earlier, most Baining cultigens are not grown from seeds, but from cuttings. This is true of taro, singapu, sweet potato, the principal greens, and pitpit.
10. Children do not regularly chew betel, but they are allowed to if they ask. Young children (three to six years old) frequently cry to be allowed to chew and often get both high and sick from it. I think this teaches them a lesson, which lasts until adolescence since children of seven to twelve seemed to chew only rarely. In Yalom one three-year-

noticed that she was increasingly included in the family distribution of betel and occasionally, but increasingly, recognized in public as an adult and thus worthy of betel exchange. This was especially true when she was away from her parents (e.g., when accompanying me on social forays). When I returned to Lan after my ten months in Yalom, there was no doubt about Dembi's adult status in the society, at least as marked by betel exchange, in which she participated fully.

Coconuts, although edible raw, are most frequently eaten cooked (as coconut milk). The most prestigious food, which is cooked for feasts, consists of a very rich cooked coconut cream. The Baining worry about the effects of eating raw coconuts and say that anyone who is sick (e.g., with a cold) should not eat them. The converse of this concern is that colds and other ailments are often attributed to the eating of a green coconut or plain grated coconut. Raw coconuts are taboo for lactating women. It seems that people who are vulnerable, through sickness or as a result of closeness to nature (nursing children), should not indulge in raw (natural) food. Sick people are often restricted in their use of betel nut too. Cooked coconuts, as used in feast food are the epitome of social food.

Betel and coconuts are, in sum, socially important plants in Lan. They are closely associated with the margins of the human life cycle, being planted at birth and death. The spatial position of coconuts and betel parallels their social position; they are planted on the margins of social space, as mediators between nature and society. They are fully utilized during the adult years as items for exchange or collective consumption. People working in gardens take frequent breaks to chew betel, because it is said to make one less tired, and thus to help one work. After chewing it, they are stronger and more awake, and more able to work productively. When betel nut is scarce, people complain about work and say that social talk becomes more difficult.

One of the impediments of old age is the difficultly in chewing betel when one has lost one's teeth. Old people cannot chew the hard nuts. They solve this problem in two ways. The first is to construct a mortar and pestle out of a bamboo tube and a stick, in which they pound their betel, lime, and pepper until it is soft and chewable. The second is to depend on others to chew for them and then give them the masticated pulp. The children of people without teeth are often recruited to do this; Dembi frequently chewed for her father. This act symbolizes several aspects of the parent-child relationship and old-age dependency.

---

old cried to her mother for betel, and her mother forced her to chew it "hot," with lots of lime and pepper. It was as if her mother wanted to "show her" that this was for adults only.

Children who chew for their parents are symbolically beginning the pattern of looking after their parents. The old who take this pulp are also symbolically returning to an infantile state. Parents frequently feed children aged six to eighteen months with food they have premasticated for them. The betel nut that is being masticated is itself a symbol of the margins of sociality. The role of betel nut and coconuts in Baining cosmology will be further elaborated in the discussion of mortuary rites in chapter 7.

Socialization and the Life Cycle

The most important product in a society such as the Baining is the social person. The production of the person is also the reproduction of the system since it is through persons that the system perpetuates itself. For this reason the process by which social actors are constructed— the socialization process—is of paramount importance in the system.

The Baining life cycle can be grossly divided into three phases on the basis of the relation of the developing person to productive activities: (1) the period of growth and development when the child is not a fully productive member of the society; (2) the period of full maturity when "blood and flesh" are at their prime and the individual is fully productive; and (3) the period of waning productivity, attributed to the physical decrease of blood and sweat.

These three phases, however, are only part of the picture. While the phases of production in the life cycle are important, they are supplemented and offset by the phases of social reproduction (that is, the process of socialization). For the Baining, the process of socialization does not terminate when an individual becomes a socially adapted member of society, but continues into adulthood and old age.

In this sense, the socialization cycle can be seen to have seven phases. Drawing on the life histories and discussion presented earlier in this chapter, we can delimit these phases. In the first period of life, infancy, the individual is perceived by the Baining as an asocial being. Untouched by social concerns, the infant is capable of only natural behaviors and urges. The second period, that of childhood, is when primary socialization occurs. One of the most important aspects of this process is feeding, through which the child ingests the social products (food) produced by his parents. The child also learns to work and gains increased understanding of social life. By phase three, the adolescent is essentially a fully socialized being. He or she has mastered the basic skills and attitudes necessary for life and survival in the social milieu. Although the adolescent has grasped these complex patterns, he or she has not yet internalized them well enough to replicate them in his or her own behavior or teach them to others. The pivoting that occurs between merely internalizing beliefs and values, skills and patterns, and the ability to replicate them by socializing others has not yet occurred. Adolescents are full members of the society, but they have not yet achieved the position of reproducers of the social order. Their abilities are concentrated in their own self-sufficiency.

It is only during the fourth phase, marriage and full maturity, that the individual is invested with the responsibility of transferring sociality, that is, of socializing others. The true adult in Baining society is not just the perfect social actor, but the socializing agent. These are the people who are able to reverse the roles learned in their own socialization and apply the experience to others.

As people get older, their energy and skills gradually diminish and they enter phase five. This phase usually coincides with the maturation of their own families of procreation. Their involvement in the active role of socializer fades proportionately. The activity of socializing, feeding, and schooling children and grandchildren never disappears, but the "grandparent" generation, like the adolescent generation, relinquishes primary responsibility to others. During these later adult years, there seems to be a gathering together of forces, a focus on subsistence and stability. Individuals in this phase are no longer replicating themselves but are merely sustaining themselves as socialized beings. As they get older and more enfeebled, they increasingly lose the attributes of the adult social being, becoming progressively "desocialized" as they lose the ability to feed, clothe, wash, and look after themselves. In phase six, they "return" to a status similar to childhood, not only in the social responsibilities between generations, but in terms of the physical qualities and abstract values associated with personhood. The old person, while not yet a natural being, is but one step removed from it in death. It is because of the concrete perception of this state that the elderly are reluctant to retire gracefully into old age. The ideal of retirement as the reciprocal reward for a lifetime of productive activity is marred by the negative implications of desocialization. Those who have not yet neared this phase tend to anticipate it as a social reward for productive work; those who are descending into it, however, realize its negative evaluation and thus face it with ambivalence.

The final phase of the cycle is the transformation of the socialized being into a natural one after death. We have seen above that if the full cycle has been traversed, this transformation is less radical than it seemed in chapter 4. As mentioned earlier, however, only a few members of the society actually survive into full old age, thus declining gradually into a natural state. The transformations associated with death are more complex and culturally more elaborated than those of any other phase in the Baining life cycle. For this reason, death and mortuary practices will be discussed in and of themselves in a later chapter.

It is through the elaboration of the life cycle that the Baining express and confront the social and cultural dimensions of their system. By using their own lives and bodies as markers, they negotiate the boundaries of their social world. This mediation is both an individual and a collective activity. It is expressed in temporal terms in the form of the individual life cycle, but it is also manifested in the ways that individuals and groups are located spatially. Nature and society, life and death, individual and group are not static and separated domains, but are transformed and mediated by the actions of individual Baining. In producing themselves, their households, and their environment they are reproducing the society in which they live.

6   Sentiments and Motivation in the Social Person

The Baining Concept of the Person

As the life histories show, the Baining are not prone to using personal experience or subjective states to describe themselves, nor do they reflect on such attributes in others.[1] Their descriptions are much more clearly tied to aspects of social roles, interpersonal interaction, and the general nature of social behavior and action. The relevant social entity among the Baining is the person. In this chapter, however, I will go beyond the Baining's own perspective and examine instances and accounts of more idiosyncratic, even deviant, personal experiences to analyze the categories of person, self, and individual in the Baining context.

The absence of expressions of emotion or subjectivity does not imply the absence of motivation or affectivity, but merely the absence of cultural emphasis on them. The Baining project and experience affective states through sentiments. Sentiments are culturally constructed patterns of feeling and motivation that define, extend, and contract the boundaries of the self, and can be socially interpreted by others.

The Baining see the development of the person during the life cycle as a progression defined by the gradual acquisition of important social characteristics and powers, and then by the erosion of these characteristics during aging and dying. Throughout the life cycle a Baining is constantly negotiating his or her status vis-à-vis the natural world. A human infant is not automatically considered a "person" (*akakaka* [masc.]; *akakaigi* [fem.]), but is accorded this status only when he or she attains certain social characteristics and behaviors. Gradually, through the labors of his or her parents, the child is socialized. From the age of about six months, a person gradually acquires more social attributes

---

1. The Baining do not express affect and motivation as part of their discourse. As I discuss in this chapter, they do not value individuality as a criterion for attaining prestige and / or power. Their concept of what a social person is contrasts with the descriptions of persons from a number of other Melanesian societies (Battaglia 1990; Goodale 1995; Maschio 1994).

and greater control over social action. Socialization is accomplished through the giving of food and the teaching of work.

The Baining person is characterized primarily by his or her engagement in social relationships predicated on productive labor, food giving, and food taking. As a child grows up he or she is continuously nurtured as a social being by being given food from the gardens, and by being taught to participate in daily tasks such as getting water or firewood, gathering food, and working in the gardens. Once a child attains adolescence, he or she is a full social being capable of performing virtually any garden work; he or she also attains growing independence in social relationships, culminating in the pivotal transition between the roles of food taker and food giver. This is the moment when people engage in community-wide relations of a reciprocal nature. As married people and subsequently as parents, they are more than fully social beings in themselves, since they have successfully reversed their childhood roles and dependencies, and have become the inverse—providers and food givers for others. Food giving is of tremendous significance in the status of the person. A food-giving person is again engaged in asymmetrical social relationships, but now he or she takes the dominant role. Such people are the true actors and agents in the society. The processes building up to this role of socializer are reversed during the process of aging, and individuals become progressively desocialized as they become older, more helpless, and increasingly dependent.

The whole life cycle is perceived in terms of the social and cultural values of food giving/food taking, production/reproduction, and reciprocity. These values form the criteria on which judgments about the status, effectiveness, and behavior of others are made. For example, the Baining say, "She is a good [atlo] prospective bride because she is industrious"; "He is my child because I give him food"; "He works hard, so he is ready for marriage"; "She is lazy so no one wants to marry her"; "I scold her so she will work hard and people will think well of her"; "I give them food, and later they will look after me." These are the sorts of personality descriptions and motivational statements the Baining spontaneously give. Occasionally one can elicit other descriptions or judgments by offering information as a provocative stimulus. For instance, if I reported "so-and-so told me this," an informant might respond, "Oh, he is a liar"; or if I announced "My rooster disappeared," someone might volunteer "Those boys were hanging around yesterday," or "X's wife was caught stealing a rooster last week." But without such contextual incentives most personal descriptions reflect judgments not on the "personality" of the subject, but on his or her social, relational, and productive characteristics.

As described above, the culturally patterned phases in the life cycle alternate between the natural and the social. In addition to these broad cycles, people move between nature and society at many points in their daily lives. These movements are related to and influenced by spatial, geographical, or social criteria. For the Baining, the village is the social space par excellence. It is clear, warm, and easy to move about in, and it is where visiting, food exchanges, and dances occur. The bush is the opposite: obstructed, visually unclear, cold, and filled with natural and supernatural beings. People are said to have to keep their wits about them in the bush or they become *akambain* (crazy; "longlong" in pidgin), and get lost or trapped by bush spirits. The bush is a place where you can only walk or roam during the day; at night it becomes impassable. It is the source of raw materials for bark containers, mats, cane belts and dyes, and dance masks. It is not a place for prolonged social intercourse. In fact, it is where people test their wits and strength against asocial, animal, and supernatural forces. The garden is an intermediate place. It is a clear space produced through human labor and sweat, which is surrounded by the forest with its antisocial agents and forces, which continually threaten to penetrate it (e.g., pigs breaking into gardens and stealing food). The garden produces the raw materials that people take to the village and transform into social food. The garden is transformed from forest to clear space through two agencies that the Baining consider socializing: fire and sweat.

The contexts of village, forest, and garden are seen as affecting the internal states of people located within them. Thus, hunters are thought to be vulnerable to the disorienting properties of the forest and may *kambain*, that is, become inwardly as disoriented as the world around them. There is some idea, although it is not explicitly expressed, that men are better able to survive and hunt in the bush than women, who, especially when burdened with children, are considered more vulnerable. Women are not barred from any forest domain (except ritual places, see chapters 9 and 10) but are less likely to frequent them alone. By contrast to the bush, inside the village people are surrounded by social products and the agencies of social transformation, such as food and fire. This environment protects them, to a degree, from their own internal "natural" properties. This is why the village is an apt place for children and old people to spend the day, while those who are more fully social can brave the natural elements. Adolescents and adults have enough social and transforming properties, such as "heat," to act as buffers against the forces of nature. Old and young lack this internal heat and thus have little resistance to forces from the outside.

The symbolic properties of old and young, natural and social, hot and cold, night and day, are important as defining characteristics of the Baining person. They are the properties that mediate the boundaries between internal and external, and thus help define the boundaries and

nature of the person. In different circumstances, they work to expand
or contract these boundaries. As mentioned earlier, sentiments are another class of phenomena, which also act on the boundaries of the person, helping to define, expand, mediate, and contract these boundaries.

The Role of Sentiments in Defining the Person

Sentiments are culturally constructed patterns of feeling and behavior,
which demarcate and mediate the boundaries of the person (Durkheim
1972: 219–20). They provide forms of affective interaction between a
person and his or her environment (which, of course, includes other
people). These standardized affective patterns include both reactive
and active forms of feeling: both responses to events and motivations
projected outward from the individual onto the social order. The interplay between reaction and projection formulates and demarcates the
affective boundaries of the person. The acquisition and expression of
sentiments during socialization is how an asocial (natural) individual
is transformed into an affectively controlled and disciplined culturally
motivated person.

Sentiments may be differentially weighted in importance and value.
Among the Baining, "shame" (*angirrup* or *akalup*) emerges as the most
important sentiment. Shame is particularly salient because it functions
to maintain the separation between the natural and the social. In this
analysis, the presence of shame indicates a disruption or failure of some
of the key processes of transformation and coordination.

Shame has been analyzed as a form of negative sanction and constraint (Piers and Singer 1953), but it may equally be viewed as a positive means of reasserting the normal order of relations. Such a positive
value is also visible in accounts of similar sentiments among other Pacific groups (White and Kirkpatrick 1985). Not all sentiments are
equally powerful in ordering and motivating the Baining actor, but
sentiments in general play the structural role of motivating and gener-
ating contextually acceptable behavior, or adjusting to loss or damage
to the relational boundaries of the person. The other sentiments discussed in this chapter, hunger and "lassitude," also extend and contract the boundaries of the self, but they do so within more restricted
contexts. While not as salient as shame, they combine with it to form
a set of sentiments that inhere in kin and food-giving relations.

Shame

I became aware of the importance of shame in Baining culture in the
context of adoption. Shame inheres in certain relations and actions,

many of which are situated in the nuclear family. Under ordinary circumstances, the members of a nuclear family work, eat, and sleep together in a relatively social milieu. Only when the relations within the family are contrasted with external relations, which are predicated entirely on social ties, does the naturalness of family ties become shameful. Shame crops up where the relation between two or more people relies more on natural bonds than on socially determined ones, so it reflects the different value given these ties. Ties that do not elicit shame are valued more highly than those that do.

The Baining say that their adopted children are their "true" *(araik)* children, and that they are "ashamed" of their natural children. Similarly, they say it is "good" *(amuris* or *atlo)* to use kinship terms reciprocally with their adopted children, but they are "ashamed" to use kin terms with their natural children. They are prepared to support and come to the defense of adopted children in public arenas, but say they would not defend a natural child because they are "ashamed" of what their natural children do. While friends and some relatives of a deceased person may undertake food taboos to express their sorrow (see chapter 7), members of the nuclear family would be ashamed to do this. For adopted children and more distant relatives, however, such expressions are appropriate.

Such examples of shame between family members led me to investigate this sentiment, but I quickly learned it is not restricted to family contexts. Other occasions that produce shame are as follows: coming upon a person of the opposite sex bathing; being discovered in the act of sexual intercourse; a man discovering that a woman is menstruating. Shame also inhibits behavior; it is shameful to enter someone's house without being invited (visitors often lurk, out of sight, near a house they want to visit until they are glimpsed or some slight noise is overheard and they are invited in). Informants say they would be ashamed to request food or gifts from people not related in any way. Because of this, people are reluctant to travel to places where they have no kin or close friends. Key aspects of the sentiment are constant throughout this range of examples. Briefly, shame inheres in contexts where natural and social relationships, and the boundaries between them, are constructed and contrasted, and where private and public spheres are delimited.

Shame is evoked principally in contexts where the untransformed, natural connections are juxtaposed with relations that are socially and culturally defined. Thus, speaking up for a close kinsperson in public produces shame by intruding the private into the public. In much the same way, shame is felt by people who want to visit someone, a social act, but are stopped from entering the other's house without invitation because of the shame of invading the other's private sphere. People arriving at another community are ashamed because they see before them a social nexus with which they have neither natural nor social ties, and, therefore, no means of entrée. After a death when a person's social network is disrupted, people following food taboos are ashamed to speak of them because they are a private matter, not to be discussed in public.

The dichotomy between natural and social in the Baining family parallels similar distinctions between private and public spheres. Nuclear family relations (except for adoptive relations) are natural; they are also private and ideally not made explicit. Direct reference to the nature of the relationships, as for example, through kin terms, is avoided. Within the private domain people are connected, but such connections are not socially formed or transformed. It is here that shame inheres, but it is only implicit until it is contrasted with other relations. Shame is expressed when aspects of the private sphere are extruded into the public domain or, conversely, when those of the public domain are intruded into the private sphere. Shame is a reaction to a disorder of the boundaries or margins, whether potential or actual. Andrew Strathern (1975) has reported that shame is said to be "on the skin" in another New Guinean society. While the Baining are not so explicit about the bodily locus of the sentiment, it is clear that the cultural locus is also the boundary of a social entity, the "person," the household or the community. Shame is, however, more than just a reaction to a transgression of boundaries between equal domains. The domains here are not structurally equal. Individual and private domains are less social and thus less highly valued than the more public and collective arenas.

Shame results when a set of relations normally opposed or separated is contrasted with relations or actions that deny that separation or collapse the opposition. Relations that have been created through social action (adoption, exchange, etc.) are more valued and more complex than those that are natural or private. Shame occurs when more complex relations are juxtaposed with simpler ones. The complex, social arena defines the context and the private level becomes the intrusive element, which is accordingly the focus of the shame. In this view, shame is not merely a negative sanction and constraint on behavior, but a positive force, which restores the boundaries of these separate domains. As a result, shame is the principal sentiment in the Baining repertoire. That is why it can be opposed to *atlo* in the examples cited above. Other Baining sentiments also negotiate boundary and category oppositions, and I class them with shame as part of a set of sentiments that locate people in natural and social space.

Hunger

One particularly important sentiment in Baining attitudes and orientations is that of *anaingi* or *airiski*. This is literally translated as "hunger."
It might seem that hunger should be classed as a physical state and
not as an emotion or sentiment, but I would argue that for the Baining
it is both. The experience of isolation and hunger is the subject of a
number of Baining songs.

> I sit here and hunger is killing me
> I sit here and hunger is killing me
> And I sit here and there is no one, and I am here
> Already they have gone down to Kavungum and Misseit
>   here.

> I sit here and cry, there is no one around
> Hunger is killing me
> And I sit here and cry
> For hunger is killing me
> For hunger is killing me
> And I think of him
> The dead man, the ghost [a ghost of a man who has died
>   a violent death].

> The *ambiowa* [a bird] cries for me
> The *ambiowa* cries for me
> She cries for me and hunger is killing me
> My parents and all of them, they went to Malasait.

Loneliness and hunger are closely related sentiments for the Baining,
but the affective state is usually expressed as hunger. People left alone
feel their loneliness as hunger. At such times, they recount hearing
birds sing since, when alone, it is so quiet that the bird calls stand out,
whereas at other times they are masked by human noise. The individual removed from his or her social milieu becomes acutely aware of
his or her natural surroundings. Being outside society brings one closer
to nature.

What is good and valued in social relations is based on using food as
a medium for creating social bonds. Since food is the primary cultural
medium of sociality, it is fitting that the absence of people is associated
with the absence of food (hunger). This concern with food is expressed
through social sentiments. The absence of both these elements is a
problematic state and is contrastively marked and mediated by sentiments. The person experiencing "hunger" is one whose expectations
are still oriented towards a complex social nexus but who is suddenly
without it. This transformation is expressed by sentiments.

When Baining travel they are severing their day-to-day social ties; they become social isolates. To assuage this isolation a visitor arriving in a Baining community is given food immediately. The social form that requires the giving of food is a response to the threat of "hunger" that the newcomer's alienation might evoke. The sentiment motivates behavior that has the effect of incorporating the guest into the social order. Presenting food to visitors also avoids another social dilemma, the shame Baining feel in asking for food. It is shameful to have to ask for food, and people who do ask for it are "shameless." This inhibition is so great that even when food is presented to a visitor, he or she might be too ashamed to accept it at first. Only after being coaxed to accept is sociality restored.

Awumbuk

The third sentiment in this set is *awumbuk. Awumbuk* is a lassitude that people feel after the departure of visitors, friends, or relatives who have co-resided with them (this sentiment is also experienced when co-residents leave to visit elsewhere). If people come to visit, sleep in one's house, and eat one's food, one will feel *awumbuk* on their departure. The experience is conceptualized as a physical indisposition, a heaviness. This "heaviness" is caused by the departing visitors, who go off lightly and leave this weight behind. The symptoms of *awumbuk* are tiredness, which includes sleeping late in the morning, an inability to get started on projects, a lack of success in activities (failure to find game or get a garden weeded), and some degree of boredom. *Awumbuk* lingers for three days. It is a "social hangover." I do not believe that it has an encompassing gloss in English, and therefore leave it untranslated.[2]

This peculiarly Baining sentiment negates the attributes that the Baining value most: industry and productivity. It is produced by a rupture of social boundaries. Communal social life and especially the sharing of food partially overcomes the barriers between individuals and connects them to one another. An individual's social persona is expanded to encompass the group. When the social group disbands, these connections are severed. The socially extended persona is ruptured and individuals must reconstitute their boundaries. A departure produces a loss of social vitality and those left behind feel relatively weakened and diminished. They experience this loss in the form of *awumbuk*, which is described as an additional weight or burden be-

2. *Awumbuk* is also experienced at the death of a person. It affects people before they begin the mortuary practices. I describe this more fully in chapter 7.

cause of the reduced vitality. The more people departing, the greater the *awumbuk*. Activities that require the greatest social energy, such as hunting and gardening, suffer most acutely from *awumbuk*.

Baining often seek to escape *awumbuk* by engaging in behaviors and activities that contrast with it. One antidote for those residents remaining in a household is to get up very early the morning after the departure and toss outside the house a dish (originally a coconut shell) of water that has been left out all night and which is believed to have absorbed the *awumbuk*. If this is properly done, life proceeds normally. It is *atlo*. A second remedy is for the remainder of the household also to leave home. In both of these cures the house (the epitome of social space) becomes identified as the locus of *awumbuk*. If people leave home, they typically spend several days living and sleeping in their garden houses, but they can also go visiting elsewhere. Both solutions have the indirect consequence of promoting the very characteristics that *awumbuk* undermines; by causing people to wake up early and take extended sojourns elsewhere, they encourage alertness, industrious productivity, and sociality.

Both *anaingi* and *awumbuk* are concerned with the creation and maintenance of sociality. They mediate and modify the boundaries of the person across different contexts. These boundaries are expanded or retracted through the giving and exchange of food. Food is both a model of and a model for the bonds that unite people in social relations. Food provides the individual with the natural vitality that underlies social production. Food is used to transform natural into social relations but this is a reversible process. Lack of food or the breaking of social relations is a social dilemma that the sentiments *anaingi* and *awumbuk* express and seek to control. *Anaingi* and *awumbuk* show clearly the points of tension in the system. In the normal order of events, social activity (work, exchange, food giving) predominates and cultural transformations are performed; this is the "good" state. When these processes are altered or reversed, people experience *awumbuk* and *anaingi*. These sentiments then motivate specific actions and practices, which start to alleviate these problems.

Sentiments are a manifestation of the interdependence between a social actor and his or her social environment. Not every situation needs to be mediated by sentiments. It is only in contexts where the boundaries between individuals and their social environment are problematic, where sets of expectations are in conflict, and where new roles are being negotiated or old relations are threatened or transformed, that sentiments are called upon to express and mediate the situation.

The set of sentiments described in this chapter are particularly salient for the Baining because they negotiate the transformations between the natural and the social. These transformations are usually implicit and unmarked. It is only by looking at the points where situations deviate from the normal or ideal pattern that these values and processes are made explicit. Sentiments are a means for bringing into focus and articulating important values of Baining society. The examination of shame, hunger, and *awumbuk* thus allows us to analyze both the normal social process and the means by which disturbances are adjusted to, and potential disturbances corrected. These sentiments inhere in the boundaries of the social and cultural system and come into play when it is threatened. Sentiments act not only as sanctions against behavior, but as vehicles to motivate acts with positive value, such as adoption, visiting, and food exchanges. They are part of the action schemas that produce the social person as they produce the social whole.

The Person in Social Action: The Person vs. the Individual

I have described the Baining as being person-oriented. By this I mean that their views of themselves, their experiences, and those around them are not predominantly individualistic. Informants do not readily speak or vouchsafe personal opinions about either their own actions or those of others. Evaluations of events do not invoke an internal, emotional explanation. The most common response to questions such as "Why did he do that?" is "I don't know about him." While not speculating on others' subjective attitudes is common in many non-Western societies, the Baining reluctance to utter even their own opinions seems extreme.

I have heard teachers, missionaries, and government officers comment upon the lack of individualism among the Baining. These range from comments about their lack of entrepreneurial motivation (compared with their neighbors, the Tolai, who have been called "primitive capitalists" [Epstein 1968]) to those regarding their lack of success in vocational or educational training. Students are increasingly leaving the Baining area to pursue secondary education in the neighboring towns under the auspices of church or government programs. Although I have no statistics, the number of Baining is said by administration sources to be quite low compared with other groups. The success rate has also been low. Almost all of the educated people have returned to the village and again taken up the life of subsistence gardeners. While an increasing number of Baining hold some sort of professional job in the communities, especially those trained in health skills, on the whole this employment remains secondary to their activities as subsistence gardeners. There are several Baining who are medical orderlies and nurses at Lassul, and one at Yalom.

For those who return home, acquired educational or vocational special skills and experiences are often unmentioned and are not displayed
in any way. It took me over nine months to learn that the son of my
adoptive parents in Lan, that is, my adoptive brother, had attended the
Administrative College in Port Moresby. He was trained as a "youth
officer," but had never done anything with his education. He, himself,
had a reputation as a shy retiring type, even among the Baining, and
was not an organizer or promoter. He acted as if he were ashamed of
his education and training.[3] His parents attributed his reticence to fac-
tions within the village, but it was not simple jealously or rivalry. The
pattern goes deeper than this; it permeates all relations throughout the
community. Individuality and inequality are antithetical to the values
of egalitarianism and reciprocity that the Baining work to achieve. The
attributes traditionally valued by the Baining are equally accessible to
every mature person. Everyone can attain social competence, and competition for prestige is minimal. It is not the new skills and new productive activities that the Baining object to, but their unequal distribution.
As these resources become more common, however, more Baining may
feel comfortable exhibiting them socially.[4] The situation may already
be changing.

Only two North Baining have attended the University of Papua New
Guinea. The first taught as a substitute teacher in mathematics at Kera-
vat Senior High School for a few months, but when he was frustrated
by a delay in his pay packet, he packed up and returned to his village.
He would have been content to settle down, but his return coincided
with the first Provincial Government elections, and he (as the most
eligible candidate) was nominated and elected as the Baining representative. He left politics as soon as there was someone who could take
his place.[5] The second college student had only just graduated in 1991
(fourteen years after the first), and it was unclear what he planned to
do. He spent most of his time driving the one vehicle the coastal Baining owned from Lassul to Rabaul, unable to settle in either the village
or the town.

3. One of the characteristics that evokes shame is that of being different from other
people.
4. The lack of competitiveness among the Baining contrasts with most known Melanesian societies, in which the person strives to enhance his or her prestige and value (see
for example, Munn 1986; Weiner 1976; A. Strathern 1971; Goodale 1995, to name just a
few).
5. The person who took his place was a dynamic and persistent entrepreneur. Herman
Kusak spent a number of years in the New Guinea Highlands and married a woman
from Goroka. When he returned to the Baining area, he initiated a number of business
projects and ran for the Provincial Government seat relinquished by John Landi. Unfortunately, Kusak died of a stroke in his mid-thirties.

My friend and assistant in Yalom, Tovi, was the first person from his village to attend high school (in this case, a vocational school). He had returned to the village and taken up bachelor life about a year before my arrival. He said he was unable to find a job in town and so returned home despite the fact that there was nothing he as a plumber could do in Yalom. After my stay he returned to school to train as a medical assistant, and now he lives in his natal village running the aid post in the morning and gardening in the afternoon.[6]

The other side to the Baining tendency to return to or remain in their community is that there are almost no Baining laborers or residents in Rabaul,[7] the nearest town and one filled with *wantok*[8] communities from virtually every other Papua New Guinean province. There have been very few Baining who migrated to town in search of wage labor.[9] When Baining go to town to sell their cocoa beans or garden produce, they stay for the day only. They avoid staying in town overnight because they have no *wantoks* with whom they can stay. As described above, they would be "ashamed" to visit or ask for food from people who are not kin. These patterns are in stark contrast to those of other Papua New Guinean peoples, where at least some youths, and often most, migrate to town for wage labor.

What emerges from these examples is that the Baining are unusually loathe to leave their communities, perhaps because their valued personality attributes lead to a dependence on being surrounded by members of their own group. Being bound by social ties to others is what defines and constitutes their category of person. This is why they have been relatively unable to step outside of the matrix of community roles and social expectations in order to succeed at or enjoy other endeavors.

6. Prior to his return to Yalom as medical orderly, Tovi had been posted to a number of different communities in East New Britain. He grew much happier when he returned to the Baining area.

7. In 1991 there was one Baining who had worked in Rabaul and had a house there. This house had indeed become a local "hang-out" for Baining (from Malasait and Raunsepna) who were visiting Rabaul. But considering that the Baining lived so close to Rabaul, it was remarkable that there was only this one house.

8. *Wantok* is a term used to describe speakers of the same language who see themselves as "tribal brothers" to others from that language/culture group, and often assist each other. This *wantok* relation becomes actualized only when participants are out of their tribal region.

9. In 1991 I was asked by the Department of Social Planning and Technical Development to estimate how many Baining lived and worked outside of the Baining area. I estimated not more than half a dozen, which shocked the Department as being incredibly low, but the local provincial member confirmed my estimate.

Personal Experiences and Individuality

Despite the emphasis on the social person described above, idiosyncratic behavior is fairly easily tolerated among the Baining. People's habits and styles are accepted, usually without comment. This is in keeping with the low tenor of gossip in the society. Everyone might know of someone's idiosyncracy, but few people seem to have the curiosity to ask about its origin. This was brought to my attention by the case of my adoptive father, who refused to eat pig. I asked him why this was, and he said that when his (adoptive) father died he had tabooed pig and never started eating it again. Putting a taboo on a foodstuff is a Baining custom at death (see chapter 7) and is not remarkable or surprising. What was surprising to me was that neither his wife nor his grown daughter had any idea why he did not eat pig. The wife simply answered that she did not know, while the daughter said, when asked separately, that maybe he did not like it—this in a culture where pig is the most valued foodstuff available! They showed no curiosity about his behavior.

In Yalom, the old woman Pinam (see chapter 5), was unique among my acquaintances because she neither chewed betel nor smoked, while virtually everyone else at least chewed betel. On one of my first evenings, while trying to create rapport, I asked why. She responded with a story from her youth:

> When I was young, I went with some women to the bush. We went to a certain tree [a tree with white sap which in times of scarcity was used as a substitute for betel nut]. We took this betel-like sap and chewed it with leaves [pepper leaves] and lime. We chewed and chewed and chewed. Then I vomited and vomited and vomited. I said I would never chew betel again. I left behind me a large packet of the sap, but the other women went back and fought over it.

Similarly she told why she does not smoke.

> Once when I was little, my parents went to the garden and left all the young girls and children at home. There was tobacco drying from the house rafters and the children took it all down and wrapped it in leaves, one after another, after another, after another. We smoked and spat balls of tobacco until the house was full. I got very, very dizzy and sat down and vomited and vomited. When my parents came back they scolded us because we had used up all the tobacco and leaf wrappers in the house.

These stories were told in a house occupied by three generations of Pinam's descendants. All of them knew well that she neither smoked nor chewed and said so whenever I offered her betel nut or tobacco. However, no one in the house had ever heard these stories before, even though everybody knew the tree she mentioned and had seen the cuts in the bark where the sap had been drained. People laughed and enjoyed the stories, but they had never arisen spontaneously.

These stories illustrate what seems obvious: that the Baining acknowledge that personal experiences may influence the later behavior of the person. Individuals retain memories of such experiences and can produce them in anecdotal form on certain occasions. Stories of this type, however, were rarely told spontaneously. The great majority of such incidents told to me were elicited by direct questions or produced for tape recording when I solicited stories.

The infrequent use of narrative for presenting personal experiences contrasts sharply to the use of song for the same purpose. Composing songs, about oneself or another, is the primary mode by which Baining (predominantly males) encode idiosyncratic experiences and behaviors. The song genre is relatively elliptical, and the referents are often obscure. Although this is a recognized forum for personal expression, songs are frequently performed and enjoyed by participants who lack any knowledge of the incident or person that they describe (I discuss the content of songs more fully in chapters 9 and 10). It is no accident that these idiosyncratic or personal experiences are relegated to a ritual genre and not daily discourse since like ritual they are outside the normative milieu.

Experiences Outside the Social Order

In contrast to the scarcity of narratives about the sorts of personal experiences described above, there is an abundant flow of accounts involving encounters with *aios* and other forest creatures. I was amused with stories of this sort in numerous contexts. Some stories were spontaneously told as I was sitting with an informant; some were elicited for tape recording; several were inserted into life histories; a few were included in the reminiscences of Pinam; and a number were recounted shortly after they occurred. These stories all allude to the ongoing negotiation between the natural and social milieu. Most of these encounters occur in the bush or forest, and the remainder occur at night, either in a house or the village. As a pattern, these experiences involve single men or small groups of women or children (women and children are more likely to travel in groups in the forest), who when walking through the forest, see creatures who look like real persons but who do not speak or behave socially. Sometimes these creatures chase the victims, but often they just lurk nearby. Occasionally the *aios* appear at a house at night, commonly when only children are at home, and chase the victims. In these cases, the *aios* disappear at dawn. Those who recount such stories always escape or keep the attackers at bay. Sudden deaths of young children are frequently attributed to *aios,* but not in these narrative contexts.

A more interesting and profound experience with *aios* is that of people who have run wild in some way (*kambain* [vb.]; *akambain* [n.]), or encountered spirits in illness. *Kambain* experience seems to span a range from intoxication (*ka surup ama ka kambain* [he drinks and he is crazy]), to disorientation due to being lost in the bush, to antisocial behavior. The effects of being *kambain* can be of very short duration or permanent. The one real idiot in the village was also described as *akambain pra ka* (the crazy one). The antihero in a whole series of stories, a man who does everything wrong, is called Kambainium, in which *kambain* is the first part of his name, which informants translated as "the crazy one."

In Lan there was an eighteen- or nineteen-year-old boy who was obviously mentally and physically disabled; he could barely walk or talk. He frequently fell into fires and was covered with burns. He was always surrounded by a swarm of flies, which were attracted to the sores on his body. Informants said he had once been normal and had even attended school and was said to have learned English. The onset of his craziness was attributed to a forest spirit of a type called *akumgi* (forest spirit; "masalai" in pidgin), which lived in a tree by a water hole. He encountered it when his family was clearing land for a garden. He became very sick and emerged *akambain* from his illness.[10]

In Yalom, there was a man in his forties named Ingi, whom a number of people treated as a crazy person. I was warned by Tovi early on to avoid frustrating or antagonizing him. His craziness had started when he was almost an adult: "He was almost married, but he became crazy and now all the women dislike him." He lived at some distance from the main village and only came in on Sundays to go to church and socialize. He was perhaps the most regular attendant at church. Despite his infirmity, he was still able to work and support himself; however, he grew no cash crops and did not work for wage labor. One informant speculated that maybe he did not pay council taxes because he had no money. He managed to acquire other store-bought goods by asking for them. Tovi explained,

---

10. He died about six weeks after my arrival in the field (although many years after being stricken) so most of my information is from informants.

> If you give him a new laplap, then he is all right until the
> laplap tears, then he might go crazy. People give him
> laplaps, tobacco, and betel nut so that he does not get frus-
> trated and go wild. You cannot scold him for anything
> wrong lest this set him off. If he gets violent he could kill a
> man; he runs around with a knife or axe. He hasn't killed
> yet, but he once attacked his father.

I think this latter incident, attacking his father, marked the initial onset
of his craziness. Nobody knew why he was crazy, but when questioned
and pressed for an answer most people mumbled something about
aioska.

I had a visit one weekend from the East New Britain regional psy-
chologist. He was curious about longlong (crazy) individuals in the
village and how the community cared for them. We talked to an older
man, a very good and open informant, who denied any knowledge of
"crazy" men in Yalom. At that time I knew of three instances of *akambain* behavior in the community (the other two will be discussed
shortly) and finally introduced them into the conversation. The old
man claimed to know nothing about two of these instances despite his
presence in the village on both occasions. At the mention of Ingi, he
registered a bit of recognition, but said he did not know the story. I
mentioned that I believed that he had tried to kill his father with an
axe, and Kusak nodded, but said that if I wanted to know the story I
should ask Ingi himself.

This incident affirms my belief that the Baining have little apparent
interest or curiosity about the behavior of others. They do not consider
it a proper subject for discourse. They do not gossip about others' behavior. As a consequence they are not prone to label events, even when
they know about them. Although the category of *akambain* exists, people do not readily apply it to others. Instead, it is a residual label for
behavior or experiences that deviate from the norm. *Akambain* behavior
represents an inversion of aspects of normal personhood. This is particularly evident when a person temporarily runs wild and does crazy
things.

A wild person might run off along a path out of the village or break
straight into the bush. When this occurs, others have to go after him to
restrain him. Once when Kangmani was dancing with an *akavuganan*, a
piece of dance regalia with a shield atop a pole (see chapter 9), he went
wild and started to run out of the village towards the cemetery. Somewhere en route, he grabbed a raw taro and started to eat it.[11] The men

---

11. Taro contains oxalic acid, which breaks down into a harmless substance during
cooking. Eating raw taro, however, produces an intense burning in the throat.

who pursued him did not know where he had obtained the taro; he said a "ghost" had given it to him. He held it by the stalk with the leaves pointing to the ground and started to eat it from the bottom. The men brought him back, took the taro from him, and threw it away, and carried him into his house. He recovered completely. During my stay we had another dance, and Kangmani decided to participate again. This time nothing happened to him.

After this dance,[12] all the dancers who had danced with *akipka* (a long spear tied to the back of the dancer by a rope that is sewn into the flesh of his lower spine) were laid low by the sores the rope caused. Inangaiyi was particularly sick. I went to see him and he told me that the ancestors sometimes died from these sores. His "father," Tapalat had died in this way. Many years before, when Inangaiyi was just a boy and Tapalat was sick with such an infection, he had sent Inangaiyi to the river to catch and kill an eel for him. Inangaiyi went and caught and killed one. Unbeknownst to him, however, it was not a real eel, but an *akumgi* (a forest spirit). He brought it to Tapalat, who cooked and ate it, and shortly afterwards died. Although others said the sore killed him, to Inangaiyi it was the spirit, *akumgi*, who had killed him. Several days after the dance I attended, but before Inangaiyi's sore had swelled up, he saw Tapalat in a dream. In the dream, Tapalat said "You are my younger brother, and now I am coming to get you." He showed Inangaiyi an eel in a small pool above the village water hole. The next day, Inangaiyi's sore swelled up, became infected, and his sickness worsened. Inangaiyi told me he was not going to send anyone to go and catch the eel, because it was really a "forest spirit" and not an eel. My young informant Tovi expressed relief at not being sent to get the eel for Inangaiyi since, having heard this story, he was sure it was a spirit. Inangaiyi was sure that he would die if he ate the eel, because Tapalat and the other *avungut* (bad ones) had marked him to die. He told me "I am finished now," and was afraid he would die from the sore even without eating the eel. Despite this fatalistic attitude, Inangaiyi accepted penicillin and recovered.

About six weeks after this, Inangaiyi ran wild *(akambain pra ka)*. This event followed a very tense period during which he had taken a second wife; his first wife Uras had left the village and gone down to the coast to live on the family cocoa block. After about six weeks Uras returned, and on the night in question she called on Inangaiyi and they talked. Uras said she wanted to give Inangaiyi some money, and then she would leave and go "wandering" or visiting on the coast. Inangaiyi said, "You can't give me any money," but Uras said she wanted to

---

12. This dance and regalia are fully described in chapter 9.

"shake hands over the money" (come to an agreement) while she went off and he stayed in the village with his other wife. While they were talking, Inangaiyi became "foggy" or "dizzy" and saw the "ghost" of his dead son, Supsis, through the door (which was closed). Supsis said "Come," so Inangaiyi said "All right." Suddenly, according to Inangaiyi, it was not night, but day. He and Supsis went into the bush and found some ripe bananas. Supsis gave him three and took two himself. Then they wandered into the village clearing where they met Tovi and another adolescent and exchanged greetings. Supsis said "Let's go," so they broke into a run and ran straight into the bush. Tovi followed them and suddenly Supsis disappeared and Tovi was holding Inangaiyi. Inangaiyi saw he was holding a hard, green banana, whereas before it had been soft and ripe. It was also night again.

Tovi described finding Inangaiyi standing in a soaking laplap alone on the green eating unripe bananas. When Tovi approached him, he ran off, and Tovi chased him for a while before finally catching him. He brought him to his brother's house, where they talked to him for at least ten minutes before he seemed to hear or could answer.

Inangaiyi recalled that Supsis said that he would return, and that when he did, he and his father would sleep in the bush for several days. He said he would draw his father to the place of the *aios*. Inangaiyi took this as an omen that he would die soon.

Both Inangaiyi and Tovi, when questioned, recognized the tension between Inangaiyi and his first wife Uras. Both thought that Supsis had appeared to try to resolve this problem. Neither of them suggested how he might do it. When I was recording life histories three months later, I tried to get Inangaiyi to reconstruct these two incidents.

> Inangaiyi: We danced with the spears, and they pierced the flesh of my back. When it was finished I was very sick, my back swelled up, and I was sick. I stayed with my two wives. One wife went to the cocoa block, and I stayed with the other, and she looked after me during the sores and the sickness. And Uvian [the anthropologist] used to come and she dressed the sore for me. She brought medicine and I drank it, and now I am all right. If it had not been so, I would have died. I danced with the dance spear [*akipka*], and I almost died after the *Asarai* [dance name] from the sickness.

> Anthropologist: What caused the sickness?

> Inangaiyi: The sickness came from the *aios*. I saw the *aios* and they said later I would die. My back swelled up, and they said I would

die from the sore on my back, just like Tapalat did. Then later I got better. Uvian gave me some medicine and the sore dried up.

Anthropologist: You saw another *aioska?*

Inangaiyi: Yes, after this one, I saw another *aioska,* who came with me and gave me some leaves. He said he would go with me and we would sleep somewhere together. I am afraid of *aios.* I saw him, and I was afraid since I had seen them bury him, the *aioska* [*aioska* here means corpse]. He made me eat leaves as if they were green vegetables. And later I saw they were just leaves. We talked to each other, and we ate food; we went to the bush, the *aioska* and I, and we ate food. We ate their food, their taro, and vegetables. It seemed like taro, but when I came up to the village it turned out to be just a seed pod. The seed was taro there, but when I came up to the place it was just a seed. The seed was not taro. I saw the *aios,* Tapalat, Misaigi, and Kariongi. I saw these three *aios.* They said that later they would get me; they would take me and I would stay with them [would die too].

Anthropologist: Had you seen *aios* before?

Inangaiyi: No, it was my first time. The second time I saw Supsis here.

Anthropologist: What caused this?

Inangaiyi: I don't know about these *aios.* I think they saw me making trouble like this [oblique reference to his two wives]. I don't know about them, I think only that I don't know. I made all this talk, this trouble. Yes, I think it was this, but I did not ask them enough, those *aios.*

Three months later Inangaiyi's memory of the experiences was quite detached. He failed to make any mention of the instances spontaneously, and only commented on them after direct questioning by me. The reality of the experiences, the fear of death, the personality and presence of the *aios* were all greatly diminished. What remained were the cultural remnants of the *akambain* experiences, the prediction of death, and the inversions from normal social behavior: eating raw food, night appearing as day, and the dead as alive.

My last example of *akambain* behavior is the least elaborated of this set, but it is the only one to which I was a witness. Several young men were having a song rehearsal, staged for my benefit so I could hear the song that had been composed about me, my stay, and my impending departure. In addition to this song, I was recording other songs recently composed by young men of my acquaintance. After several hours of very intense singing in a house turned over for the occasion, the group took a break. Tovi got up and asked to borrow my flashlight. He and several young men went outside. Next, we heard several whoops, rapidly getting further and further away. Tovi had started to run and whoop. He ran outside the village, past a clearing with one house in it, through another abandoned clearing, and fell down at the foot of some rocks on the path out of the village. Another boy was right behind him and a trail of others, including myself, followed. Tovi was lying face-down in the mud. He was trembling slightly. Marukawa told him to get up and he slowly stood up and walked back to the village, leaning on Marukawa.

Back at the house he lay down on the platform bed with his head half over the edge, and stayed there in a stupor for about fifteen minutes. Then he called for water and said his stomach was hot. Marukawa poured water over his stomach. People resisted my attempts to cover him, but agreed he should move over to a dry spot. When we told him to move he did, but otherwise he just continued to lie still. After another fifteen minutes, he started to snore. Then a few minutes later he sat up, took off his wet shorts, and wrapped himself in a blanket. After sitting for a few minutes he lay down again. During all this time, the young men sat silently. Tovi's mother and some girls came into the house and also sat silently. When his mother saw him sitting up, she said "He's gotten up," and she left. When Tovi lay down to sleep, people told me to leave. Shortly thereafter everyone became quiet and slept.

Tovi and all the other young men were up very early the next morning reroofing a neighboring house. After this work was done I questioned him, and he said he was all right. He certainly appeared normal. He said he did not know why he ran; he went crazy and ran without knowing why. It felt as if someone was holding his hair and pulling him up. He felt so light that he ran. When another boy held his arm he felt his touch, but it did not restrain him. This was the first time he had ever behaved like this. When asked, he said he thought it was connected to the singing, but then he lapsed into silence.

Despite a large number of witnesses, this incident was not widely discussed. Because of the low level of gossip and the readiness to forget such incidents, it is difficult to ascertain how common they are. All of my examples deal with men, but informants said it could happen to women too, and some mentioned a woman in another village as an example.

In these examples of *akambain* behavior and associated confrontations with *aios*, the Baining do not seem to see themselves as agents in their own right. In these contexts, their behavior is attributed to the influence of another force, which brings them under its direction. It thus seems that deeply emotional, idiosyncratic behavior is conceived as being outside the control of the person it affects. They do not see their emotional or antisocial behavior as caused by their own agency but displace it onto outside forces such as *aios*. *Akambain* behavior is alienated from Baining beliefs about self-production.

The emotions and behavior that erupt in these situations resemble Mauss's "l'emoi envahissant" (Mauss 1960: 385). These "invading emotions" (perhaps better translated as "encroaching emotional chaos") are seen as dangerous but potent forces, which pull the person away from his or her social milieu. As such, they are a threat to the social order and are therefore displaced by the Baining onto a force or being outside society. Individual emotions or desires can only be accepted and interpreted by displacing them from individual intentionality. Such an interpretation is what ultimately reasserts the dominance of the social order and erodes the potency of the emotional base. In the cases presented here, the actors regained control over their emotions and proceeded to reinterpret the experiences in ways compatible with social norms and expectations. People did this by attributing the events to outside agents, and not to internal desires or forces. This supports my hypothesis that the Baining devalue and de-emphasize interior states.

There are two notable aspects to the way in which *akambain* states relate to normal social activity. The first is that running amok or being *kambain* is clearly the marked state. It is differentiated from normal behavior and labeled as deviant. In contrast to the clear marking and labeling of *akambain*, the normal state is not explicitly named and categorized; it is all that is not marked. Terms such as *atlo* may be used to describe this state, but they do not denote it in the same way that the term *akambain* denotes the condition to which it refers. *Atlo* is not a category with a ready list of defining characteristics. It consists of traits that are implicit and assumed.

This brings us to the second point. Although the unmarked is implicit and consists of an array of accepted behaviors and perceptions, the marked state, *akambain*, is very stereotypically defined. It is a composite of traits that are symbolically meaningful as the antithesis of proper social behavior. On the occasions when people break from the social web, they express this departure in explicit ways. These ways are more accurately classified as antisocial than natural, since they are not raw or random nature but a set of characteristics that can be directly contrasted with their cultural counterparts. From a normal Baining perspective, reality is inverted during these experiences. People leave the social space of the village and head for the forest, but they think the forest is clear like the village; they see night as day; they see the dead as alive; they see unripe, raw, or inedible foodstuffs as good food; they fail to respond to social relationships or encounters. The marked state is a cultural construction of the social inverse. Their antisocial activities symbolize the disappearance or penetration of the barrier between the social person and the natural world. In this state they are temporarily on the other side.

This same perspective is advanced by the Baining explanation of their *akambain* behavior in terms of external agents. The victim deflects the origin of the feelings and subsequent acts outward onto external agents, such as *aios* and *akum*. It is as if the internal emotional aspects of the self are in some way continuous with external nature and can be located outside the body. These internal, emotional aspects are like the untransformed, unsocialized aspects of the Baining infant or elderly person. Socialization is the process of transforming the natural aspects of a person into social ones. This is most evident in the ways people learn to work and recognize themselves as productive agents.

The social aspects of the person mediate these two realms, and they are vulnerable to attack or penetration from both inside and out. This boundary, or social skin (T. Turner 1980: 112), is strengthened by its locus within the social order. In situations of marginality, which may be ritual, social, or spatial (such as the forest), the social persona is most vulnerable and the "invading emotions" most powerful.

In sum, sometimes people act in ways that are considered outside the normal order. Such deviant behavior is deemed to represent a collapse of social boundaries. This breakdown can be either permanent or transient. In either case, sentiments help define and rearticulate social relations. Among the Baining, deviance—like conformity—is socially stereotyped, and an examination of deviant patterns reveals major values and structures of the system.

The Baining tend to minimize this sort of experience. Although they recognize its occurrence, they do not give it any permanent or transforming place in the social order. For example, there is no specialist role or status, such as shaman or warrior, that is assumed as a result of such experiences.

In this chapter I have analyzed Baining behavior and orientations ranging from the normal to the deviant. Normal, socially approved Baining behavior is characterized by a belief in a person's agency. By participating in certain key activities and relationships, notably working, food giving and food taking, actors are a key part of the productive and reproductive cycles in the society. These behaviors and activities are opposed to a range of natural forces. Nature and society are ideally kept separate through continuous productive activity on the part of the actors in the system. Occasionally, however, situations arise in which such activity is insufficient to maintain their separation. When these situations are external to the actor, the actor experiences the ambiguity of the situation as his or her own vulnerability to the elements of nature, barriers that are normally maintained socially. These experiences are mediated through a culturally meaningful set of sentiments, of which I have discussed shame, hunger, and *awumbuk*.

When situations lead to conflicts in the internal emotions of the actor, perhaps anger, jealousy, frustration, or fear, which are not socially transformed by work, food, reciprocity, or which are aroused by conflicting social relations, the actor falls victim to these conflicting values and experiences *akambain* disorientation. *Akambain* is also a product of the opposition of natural and social forces. In this case, nature is manifested either as the untransformed aspects of the individual or as the dissociated and thus alienated aspects or fragments of his or her persona and relations. Through the *akambain* experience these disruptive elements are transformed into "antisocial" elements—inversions of normal life. In most cases the victim of *akambain* returns to his or her former role and status in the society. Only very occasionally is someone unable to readjust to the normal activities and associations of the group. Sometimes, as in the case of Ingi, a person can sustain certain activities, such as subsistence production, while being unable to engage in more intensive transformative activities, such as marriage and child rearing.

This range of personal and psychological behavior cannot be represented through a static classificatory schema, but is rather the product of a dynamic range of situations and responses across a variety of contexts. People do not consistently fall into one category or another, but move between them as situations change.

7   Death and Social Reproduction

Death is the occasion for the most important rite of passage for the Baining. It is a culturally important transition both for the individual and the society. Mortuary rituals are concerned with the passing of an individual and with reconstituting the social world after a death. Death disrupts individual and collective relations and is a major threat to social life.

Death

The first response people have upon learning of a death is *awumbuk*. *Awumbuk* is the "tiredness one feels after another has left one." Survivors feel *awumbuk* because the deceased has left them. *Awumbuk* gives way to *arum* (sadness) once the mourning begins.[1]

When a death occurs, people are sent out to inform the community and neighboring villages. Lan informants stated that people should be notified and given a chance to come and "pay respects" to the dead person before the burial. If those taking responsibility for the burial do not wait for distant friends and relatives to come, the mourners will be angry and challenge them to a fight. This fight might be fought as a whipping match using a particular type of vine or wild ginger from the forest. The two sides would alternate in whipping one another.

While waiting for more distant mourners to arrive, those already present engage in preparations. The mood is solemn during this time, but there is no continuous crying or wailing. As newcomers arrive, they approach the body, and standing over it, weep or wail. This might provoke some of the other mourners to weep or wail, but the display is not prolonged. Meanwhile, the body is prepared for burial. This usu-

---

1. My field notes mention three occasions during my year in Lan when news was brought to me and my neighbors that a death had occurred, and my companions immediately concurred that this was the reason for our great lassitude that day. On these three occasions it did seem that little had occurred, but there were many boring days among the Baining when there was no death to explain the monotony.

ally entails dressing the corpse in his or her best clothes: a shirt and laplap for a man and a good "meri" blouse and laplap for a woman.

If the wait before burial is expected to be long, some people present might go off to the deceased's gardens, where they will cut and slash the plants, roughly harvest the foodstuffs and bring some of the food back to the hamlet where the person died. On their return they will halve and drop taro corms at the junctions of all paths between the garden and hamlet. This severed taro will inform passers-by that a death has occurred. It also symbolically severs the medium of exchange, food, which is used to create social pathways or networks between people.

While sitting with the body, people do not eat; but cooking might begin for a meal after the burial. If food is gathered and prepared at this time, it cannot be treated properly. When such food is brought into the hamlet, it is dumped unceremoniously on the ground. Some of it is trampled, stolen by pigs, or left lying around. The taro stalks are not properly cut from the tubers and therefore they cannot be replanted. Cooking is done perfunctorily; the taro might be badly scraped or slightly underdone.[2] There is a general sense that people should not eat well in the face of death. However, this does not mean that food is unimportant to the occasion; on the contrary, food is symbolically important in a number of stages of the events and serves as a mediator throughout the cycle.

Burial happens relatively soon after a death. A group of youths or young men prepares a grave in the cemetery. At the graveside, the mood intensifies dramatically and there is an outburst of crying, wailing, and moaning. This surges to a crescendo and lasts several minutes. Many people step forward and throw flowers onto the corpse (in the past it might have been feathers [see Rascher 1909]). Then the men begin to throw dirt down and fill up the hole. This is done quite rapidly. At the end, the dirt is mounded over the grave and several decorative plants are planted on it. Later, betel nut trees (areca nut palms) may be planted on the grave.

When the burial is over, most of the mourners slacken their mourning, sit back, and begin to chew betel and chat. A few, however, keep wailing and crying at full pitch. They may huddle by the grave or lie prostrate on the ground. In and among these distraught mourners

2. Taro stalks need a bit of the corm attached in order to regenerate. Cutting the stalks this way kills them, a death that is parallel to the death being celebrated. Badly scraped taro is still partly charred. It is thus "dirty." Although it has been transformed through cooking, the transformation has almost gone too far, turning the substance into ashes, not food. When taro is raw or undercooked, it is slightly poisonous and causes burning and itching in the throat. This unpleasant quality disappears upon cooking.

weaves a group of people, each member carrying a large bunch of areca nuts and long vines of pepper leaves. They approach the remaining mourners and hand them several nuts and leaves in the traditional gesture of greeting. The mourners continue to ignore, or pretend to ignore, the betel givers for varying periods of time, but the givers will eventually either thrust their prestation into their hands, or the mourners will eventually hold out their hands (often without looking up) and take the gift. After this the wailing and crying taper off. The betel nut givers then go on and give betel to everyone present. After people chew, the gathering breaks up. Most mourners go home, but those who sat with the body might go back to the deceased's hamlet and prepare a communal meal.

The ceremony of giving betel at the end of the burial is a richly symbolic one for the Baining. Betel nut is a token of social intercourse; it is given in greeting, and chewed at social gatherings. At death certain channels of social intercourse are definitively cut off, but the gift of betel is symbolic of the opening of new social encounters and relations. Givers are the close consanguineal kin of the deceased: brothers, daughters, sons, etc., while affines and adopted children are the most desolated mourners. The consanguineal relatives of the dead person are said to give the betel nut to "cut" or stop the mourning. As one informant explained, "We should not be too sorry for this woman [the dead person], so they give us betel nut, and we can no longer be too sad." Those who are grief-stricken do not want to accept the prestation and thereby terminate their mourning; they have to be urged or forced to take the offering. The consanguines of the dead give betel to affines (and adopted kin) linked to them through the dead person in order to renew and continue the social tie that has been severed by the death. Affines' intense mourning asserts the closeness and strength of their social tie to the deceased, which consanguines do not need to demonstrate because their ties are "natural" and unbreakable.[3]

3. This is one of the usages that show that the Baining believe that natural ties endure beneath and beyond social ties. They persist after death and in realms beyond the socially constructed Baining society. Baining informants in Lan said that adoption does not hold in the eyes of the church and government. They believe that children go back to their natural parents in heaven after death. When the government comes to take the census, kinship is often reshuffled to maintain the groups noted on the previous census. Baining-constructed kinship is embedded in Baining society and is not easily or necessarily projected into domains outside their communities.

John Landi, a highly educated Baining from the mountains, had not thought about the persistence or transformation of adopted ties in these other realms. When I asked him about this, he was very interested but did not have any opinions of his own on the subject.

Mortuary Sequence

Different phases of the mortuary ritual are directed towards different aspects of closing off thought and sorrow for the dead person. In the first phase, immediately following a death, peoples' responses are primarily what we would recognize as emotional; their sadness is expressed by crying and wailing and is provoked by the sight of the corpse, the grave, etc. This phase is ended by burial, when the dead person is put out of sight and the first phase of putting him or her out of mind is also accomplished. The symbolism of burial seems very important at this stage. I do not know how important it was in precontact times, when at least the inland communities did not bury their corpses but left them to rot on platforms outside their houses. As we saw in chapter 5, people frequently express their fear of dying as "fear of the hole." "I don't want to die; I am afraid of the hole. I want to stay as I am now" (Pinam [elderly woman], life history). The complete disappearance of even the corporeal reminder of the dead makes death appear as the kind of oblivion that the Baining fear it is. Although the contemporary pattern is burial of the corpse, in parts of the Baining region this has not always been the case. People in Lan claimed that burial was their ancestral custom,[4] but they told me about the different traditional pattern up in the mountains (in places such as Yalom, Raunsepna, and Wiliambempki). Later, when I was in Yalom, people confirmed the Lan accounts of their ancestors' customs. Before contact, corpses used to be laid out on a platform built outside the house of the deceased, and left to rot. This platform was built several feet off the ground, similar to those built outside houses today to store taro off the ground and out of the way of pigs. When considerable decomposition had occurred, and liquids were running from the body, the household would begin to store taro underneath the platform. According to informants, the juices from the corpse were absorbed by the taro, which was then cooked and eaten. Only when the stench became unbearable would the corpse be transported out of the hamlet and transferred to an above-ground burial in a tree or some such place. This type of burial vastly prolonged the phase of separation from the corpse.

Nowadays, the emotional reactions to death, such as crying and wailing, are cut off and soothed through prestations of betel nut, which begins the phase of adjustment and reasserts the continuity of social life and patterns of intercourse against its disruption by the natural

4. I don't know if this is true or they have just lost any knowledge of what they had before.

force of death. The giving of betel to extend, create, or initiate ties with the living is contrasted to the tradition of using food to break ties with the dead. When a person dies, his or her garden and sometimes coconut and betel nut trees are destroyed.[5] The products of a person's labor should "die together with their owner."

The First Feast

Food consumption, exchange, and abstention are important aspects of the entire mortuary process. Immediately following the burial, those who sat with the corpse might partake of a communal meal. Occasionally this communal meal is expanded into a mortuary feast. If the mourners have not already done so, they go out to the gardens of the deceased and simultaneously harvest food and symbolically destroy the plots. They will pull out quantities of the predominant root crops: taro, Singapore taro, sweet potato, and manioc, and also pick some greens and bananas. Some plants will remain after this harvesting and the mourners will slash, uproot (but not take), and otherwise damage the garden. Destroying the garden destroys the social products of the deceased. These products were what defined his or her social persona. When a person dies he or she returns to nature, and the Baining deem it proper for the fruits of that person's labor to die along with him or her. Informants say that sometimes the *aioska* of the dead accompanies this group to the gardens, as if the ghost did not yet realize its own death. When it sees the wanton destruction of the garden it is heartbroken and weeps, asking "Why do you damage my gardens? I am not dead yet." The sight is, however, effective in bringing home to the *aioska* its true status as a dead person, both psychologically (in the Baining sense) and sociologically.

On the way back to the hamlet from the gardens, the mourners leave severed taro or bananas as markers where paths cross or diverge. Where they have broken the taro on the roads, people are afraid to walk at night for fear of meeting the ghost. If they are out at night they walk very quickly.

The food is taken to the hamlet where the deceased died, and is dumped unceremoniously on the ground. If there are pigs, the men suffocate, butcher, and cook the pigs. People prepare a variety of vegetable foods for a mortuary feast in order to accommodate those who

5. Nowadays people have begun to supplant the traditional practice with a more moderate version. Instead of chopping down the trees, they will merely climb the trees and knock down large bunches of green coconuts. This leaves the trees basically intact for surviving kin to inherit (see chapter 2 for changes in inheritance patterns).

will now assume food taboos. Food taboos undertaken after a death are called *ahis* (pl.) (*ahiska* [sing.]) and can assume many forms. People taboo a certain food to express their sorrow over the death of a loved one. Despite the emotional and individual nature of the taboos (no one is forced or required to taboo anything after a death) not just anybody can taboo a food after a particular death. While informants said that in general it was a good thing *(amuris* or *atlo)*, to express sorrow through *ahis*, there are certain categories of people for whom such an act would be "shameful." This category includes the members of the natural nuclear family of the deceased.

The occasion of the feast becomes the occasion for publicly informing everyone else of these private vows. Portions of food are distributed to all present and various members of the gathering make it known (by refusing to eat one or another of the foodstuffs presented) that they are avoiding certain foods. It is considered unmannerly and impolite to inquire beforehand who will taboo food. I was chastised both for asking individuals whether they were going to assume a taboo and asking a group of informants casually who in the community they thought might do such a thing. Both times I was told to wait and see, people adding that only the individuals involved could know. From this I infer that there are no absolute social expectations for who ought to taboo foods.

If the death was unproblematic, if it was an old person who died from "old age," or if there had been a lengthy sickness that led gradually to death, the feast breaks up soon after eating. There is sometimes a final distribution of food, pieces of meat and taro that people are meant to carry home with them. The meat given out in this context is called *amerika*, which is the Baining word for areca nut. Here, and only here, is pig called betel nut. We will come back to this puzzle when we discuss final death feasts.

If the death was problematic in some way, if a young and seemingly healthy person suddenly sickened and died, or if the illness or accident causing the death seems aberrant or mysterious, then the community might decide to perform a divination called *amungom*.

Divination

An *amungom* is held to help determine the cause of death where that may not be immediately evident. The *amungom* is an accepted practice for ferreting out the truth in unclear events. It is not intended as a stimulus to action, such as revenge, but merely as a means of discovering the cause of the death (e.g., sorcery, a bush spirit, etc.).

Preparations

There are two basic preparations for the divination. First a long log, about eight to ten feet long and about nine to twelve inches thick, is chopped. This log comes from the *anuska* tree.[6] The log is stripped of its bark for half its length, and the bark is left intact for the other half. The bark half is the "human" half, and the stripped half is that belonging to the *aios*.[7] After preparation, the log is carried to the cemetery and laid on the grave of the deceased in question. It is left there for several hours absorbing the spirits of the dead, and is not retrieved until after dark.

The second step is the construction of a small hut, about the size of a latrine. The hut does not need a roof, but the walls are roughly covered with coconut fronds to hide the interior. The hut should be situated right on the edge of the hamlet clearing with a small opening facing into the clearing. At this opening a forked stick is planted that will be used as a fulcrum for the log when the seance begins.

Amungom

After dark a group of men retrieve the log. They return carrying it. As the carriers approach the clearing everyone falls silent. The log is carried to the hut and slid onto the forked stick. Half the log is inside the hut and half extrudes into the clearing. The extruded half, that with the bark, is held by a group of men, averaging eight when I saw it, but the composition and number altered as the evening wore on. There is no restriction on the age or sex of the participants, but men always seem to initiate the proceedings.

The divination routine consists of the men sliding the log back and forth over the fulcrum. As they do this they ask questions. The regular motion of the log should be an even glide. If the log suddenly rotates in their hands, the answer to the question is "No." If the log is suddenly lifted and slammed down on the fulcrum, the answer is "Yes." The participants claim they are not pushing and pulling the log, but that the *aios* are gathered at the opposite end of the log and are pushing it into their hands. The Baining believe that they represent only half of the participants "playing" with this log. Playing is the Baining word for this activity. They call out to the *aios*, "*ngun ndin, ngun talak, di urat talak* [you (pl.) come, you (pl.) play, we will play]."

6. The only other use for this tree that I could discover is that the leaves are used in making coconut cream (they are shredded and mixed with the cream, imparting a pastel green shade to the dish and supposedly acting as a preserving agent to prevent rapid spoilage).

7. There may be some idea that the stripped log is like bones stripped of flesh.

After the rhythm is established and the game begun, the men try to determine which *aioska* is predominating on the other side of the log. They ask directly, "Who is there? Is it Sawilki [Balu, Garideran, Lumuan, Dauwit, etc.]?" They seem to call the roll of all the recently deceased people in the community. The participants are prepared to bandy with other spirits for a while, playing with them in the hope that eventually the newly deceased will appear.

On the occasion I witnessed, the group was never able to establish the identity of any of the *aios* on the other end of the log. The shoving and sliding of the log continued for over an hour without any response on the part of the *aios*. Numerous participants came forth to ask questions or suggest names, but to no avail.

When it became evident that the *amungom* was a failure, the participants prepared to terminate it. The final act of the divination is when the humans heave the log into the hut of the *aios*, thereby ending the game and supposedly scattering the *aios*. People believe this act has to be done quickly, quietly, and secretly so that the *aios* do not get wind of the impending finale, or they would turn the tables and heave the log out onto the ground outside. In order to avoid alerting the *aios*, the message to end is passed tactilely, by tapping or scratching the others. At the appointed moment, the whole group lets out a whoop and sends the log flying into the hut. The *amungom* is now finished.

People speculated on the reasons for the failure of the *amungom*, blaming it variously on the deceased's shame, on a bush spirit, and on other *aios;* someone even said it was because there was a full moon and the *aios* were afraid to appear when it was so bright. In addition to "explaining" the cause of death, the *amungom* has a secondary purpose as a rite of passage. It is the definitive transformation of the deceased into the other. The deceased is no longer a contemporary or consociate of the living population. He or she is now only called up in the company of the whole mass of *aios* and is not easily differentiated from them.

Food Taboos and Their Termination

After the immediate funerary rites have been completed, the community returns to normal life, with the exception of those who undertook food taboos. These taboos are generally followed for between two and four months, although some people maintain such taboos for life.[8] In the past the taboo period was brought to a close by a death feast, similar

---

8. In such cases the taboos seem to involve foodstuffs like pig, and not staples such as taro.

in many ways to the description of the immediate postfuneral meal, but bigger, more elaborate, and with several extra events. Recent elaboration of this feast has meant that it is usually delayed for over a year to give people time to breed larger pigs, perhaps plant extra gardens, and amass a sum of money for rice and tinned fish purchases. The food taboos are generally ended before this feast is held.

In the past, there was a whole range of taboos people could adopt,[9] but the only ones I saw or heard about in the contemporary context were avoidances of pig, taro, singapu, and shaving. The choice of a taboo is an individual and personal matter. Despite the variety and diversity of the choices, what they have in common is that they restrict the sociability of the abstainer. Mortuary taboos negate the role of food as a medium of exchange and the act of eating as a social event. Food taboos are private acts and occasionally people keep them secret. Included among the range are these special taboos my informants remembered.

Men's Taboos

1. A man wanting a different kind of taboo might taboo food and water for a day and a night. He can smoke or chew betel nuts but has to be careful that no liquid from the betel nut is swallowed. He is expected to feel hunger pains and suffer.

2. A man can build a platform on the edge of the hamlet clearing. Every afternoon his wife will come and put some food on the platform. Later, when no one is watching and all is quiet, the man will approach the platform and eat. He ought not to eat well, and if when he takes some of the food a piece falls to the ground he has to leave it there. As soon as he hears a noise or movement he runs away, even if he has not yet eaten anything. This man's behavior is said to be analogous to a parrot's, since a parrot is startled and flies away whenever a person passes near it.[10]

3. A man who is a close in-law of the deceased is not supposed to enter the house in which his relative died. He might decide to generalize this taboo and thus refuse to enter any house but his own for the duration of the mourning period. He will sit outside the houses in which others are gathered.

4. Another type of *ahis* is when a man eats taro in an odd way. To follow this taboo, he must select another person, man or child, to ac-

9. Some of these did not even involve food (e.g., a taboo on shaving or entering other people's houses).

10. It is this characteristic that the Baining emphasize. In some stories the startling of a parrot serves as a warning to people that raiders are nearby.

company him everywhere. This person is his *anyimga* (the watcher), the one who looks out for him. When someone gives the man taro, his *anyimga* must cut the taro into tiny pieces; then he must "put his teeth around each piece." He surrounds it completely with his mouth and bites off each corner, then he gives each piece to the man keeping the taboo, who can then eat it. Only the *anyimga* can do this. If the *anyimga* is not present, the man must go hungry or carry the taro back home.

5. Another food taboo involves eating only the scraps left over from the preparation of taro (the holes cut out of taro, analogous to potato eyes, or the scrapings of the charred skin). These scraps are thrown onto a limbung spathe (the bark of a limbung tree), mixed with dirt and fed to the man. This food is comparable to that given to pigs. This taboo is called *misandum* (bad taro).

6. There is a taboo called *asuamga* (thief). When other people eat, this man does not. No one (not even his wife) knows where he gets his food. No one should see him cooking or eating. The man goes into gardens (not necessarily his own) and breaks off a few bananas and then he hides and cooks for himself.

Women's Taboos

Women's taboos are not as elaborate as men's. The men's explanation for this was that women should not get so weak as to be unable to care for the children or work in the gardens. Women had no explanation for the discrepancy. They, nevertheless, have a range of taboos.

1. Some eat only bananas without any of the common side dishes: greens, pig, or fish.

2. Another taboo restricts eating or drinking during the day. A woman must wait for the first star to appear (the evening star, called *ning harup*) before she can eat. Since she can eat until the morning star *(ta nindemga)* fades, such a woman wakes up very early and begins to cook. If she is slow and it gets light before she eats, she must wait until night. This is called *ta tis ama aweldanga* (they eat with the star).

3. A woman might gather all the immature taro, even those the size of an areca nut, and cut them even smaller, and then roast and scrape each tiny piece of taro over the fire. She can eat these pieces only at night.

Roughly the same procedure is used to terminate any or all of these taboos. The consanguineal kin of the deceased prepare a special taro and coconut cream dish called *ahindumgi* and approach the person who has been under the taboo. When he or she becomes aware of their intentions, he or she tries to run away (supposedly still sorry about the death and not ready to give up the taboo). When the person is caught he or she is led inside the house (forcibly, if the taboo has been against entering houses). Then one of the deceased's kin takes a large piece of taro and breaks it in half, giving half to the abstainer. Both participants begin to wail and talk of their sorrow. Then they eat the shared taro. After this they are supposed to stop thinking about the deceased.

The Symbolism of Food Taboos

The set of taboos helps us to constitute a picture of a complex but integrated set of Baining customs and values about food. These values are implicit and uncommented upon in daily life but are made explicit through the process of symbolic inversion that these taboos present. Since food giving and food taking are the basis of the most important social relationships in the society and the means of transforming asocial, or natural, ties into social ones, the denial of food is, essentially, the denial of such bonds. Food taboos are an appropriate means of symbolically severing the social ties that have connected the living with the dead. By denying the bonds that have constituted one's ties with the deceased, however, one is also alienating oneself from ongoing society as well. *Awumbuk* occurs when the socially extended persona contracts or collapses because relations are broken; this is much more powerfully the case at a death. A person who gives up food for a period of mourning is simultaneously abdicating his or her social connections to the rest of society. He or she becomes a marginal person.

Food taboos both negate and reflect upon relations and activities of normal daily life. These taboos delineate a world beyond the simple denial of certain foodstuffs or the symbolic severing of ties to the dead. The set of taboos reveals an order antithetical to normal social life—a realm where people are prevented from engaging in social intercourse by being unable to enter houses where people are eating, talking, or drinking, or from eating in the presence of others. Instead, they are forced to the margins of social space to eat like animals, fed as if they were parrots or pigs, and given only food fit for animals. Eating is severed from any sort of interaction or exchange involving others. The participants get their food by stealing or scavenging, behaviors considered animalistic and reprehensible by the Baining (see chapter 5). Others regress to the point where they are not capable of feeding themselves, but must have another to cut, nibble, and then deliver the food. This procedure is reminiscent of the way mothers prepare food for their babies (they masticate the food into a pulp and then feed it to the child) and indicates a pre-social state where one has to be tended by another. Women's taboos especially invert the normal order of events, which includes social mealtimes, by restricting the taboo holder to eating only at night and by herself. Although no one taboo inverts the entire social norm, the sum total of all these discrete behaviors is an illustration of the Baining view of "man in nature": a person who is too immature to eat properly; who eats alone and outside of social time (day) and space (house, hamlet, garden); who steals food without properly working or exchanging for it; or who eats bad, immature, or rotten food. By engaging in such activities the participants are demonstrating their alienation from society, an alienation that has been caused by the ultimate triumph of entropic nature over society, that of death.

Mourners, however, cannot be allowed to wallow permanently on the margins of society, since this would ultimately undermine the basis of the rest of the social order in a way analogous to the death that was the original occasion of the taboo. The reintegration of these marginalized people is thus an act of resocialization. It is differentiated from normal socialization by being performed as a collective act. Although this is no longer a part of the final death feast, it is, nevertheless, a rite undertaken by a group of people (the consanguineal kin of the deceased). In this ceremony, they collectively reincorporate the taboo holder into the social nexus by sharing and exchanging food. After this ceremony, the parties concerned are supposed to "forget" about the deceased and focus on their ongoing lives and social concerns, including such social relations as those initiated by this little ceremony.

The Death Feast

At the time of a person's death, nowadays, his or her co-household members take the person's *aratki* (basket), or *asiengi* (string bag) and set it aside, usually in the rafters of the house. This basket holds the few personal or private possessions of a Baining individual. It is used to carry betel nut, lime and pepper leaves, tobacco, and newspaper for rolling cigarettes. In addition to these essential consumables, one finds a wide range of *awubung* (belongings), which includes some of the following: a comb, a mirror or piece of mirror (only men carry mirrors, which they use to shave with; women would be ashamed to be caught looking in a mirror), a cigarette lighter, shotgun cartridges, a change purse with a bit of money, a slingshot or catapult (mostly carried by bachelors and used to shoot at birds), a taro scraper (often carried by both sexes although primarily used by women), a small- to medium-sized knife, and sometimes a spoon or clam shell used as a spoon.

With the basket safely stowed, the relatives undertake plans for an *aioska ama asmasini* (death feast) to occur some time between three months and two years after the death. To this end, they begin (or continue) to look after pigs, plant larger gardens, and accumulate money. Whatever money was left by the deceased is also put into this fund. At this feast, one of the opening acts is to burn the basket of the deceased (at one such occasion that I witnessed a lot of other goods, presumably possessions of the deceased, were also burned). As long as the basket remains in the rafters of the kin's house, the memory of the dead person remains, but once that basket is destroyed, so too, supposedly, is any thought of the dead.[11]

During the wait before the final mortuary feast, the natural, adoptive, and affinal kin share the responsibility of selecting one or more pigs to contribute to the feast. When the pigs are mature and food is relatively abundant in the gardens, talk of the feast might begin again. During the early stages this talk is very low-key and secret, so that if contributions, labor, and emotions do not consolidate, the subject can be dropped temporarily.

Preparations

During the early negotiations for one such feast, I was chastised by some informants for inquiring too openly about the proceedings. But an increasing number of signs convinced people around me that preparations were really under way. These included the stockpiling of firewood and a communal hike down the mountain to the river below to carry up lots of stones to use in the earth ovens.[12] Shortly after this event, one of the organizers took several bags of cocoa to Rabaul to sell and returned with a load of cargo: rice, tinned fish, tinned meat, tobacco, laplaps, etc. Some of this stock was sold in the community store, thus confusing me as to whether or not this was a stage in the mortuary preparations. Enough, however, was set aside for the feast and my confusion simply proved the success of the lengths that people go to, to disguise their actions at this point. Finally, the preparations came out into the open. About a month after the covert preparations began I found two taro cut in half on the road between the water hole

11. Langerkan said that the burning of the basket is a relatively new custom. It had started with a death about nine or ten years previously. Before that they just made a feast to end the food taboos. Nowadays, they say that when the basket is burned, people must stop thinking of (mourning) the dead person. In the past this same injunction was applied after the ending of the food taboos. Quite obviously the period of mourning has been considerably extended, and as death feasts tend to be delayed for longer after the burial than was previously the case, this process continues.

12. There are very few rivers in the Lan area since it is mostly limestone, and good cooking stones have to be fetched from quite some distance away.

and the path to the gardens. These taro were a sign of the impending event.

When the date for the feast is finally arranged, everybody in the community becomes aware of it. On this occasion the event was announced at the community meeting after church a week before the scheduled date. This general announcement also served as an invitation. Following this collective meeting, the Kolkiaring and Raunit sections each adjourned to separate meeting places. The Raunit group agreed to prepare a large basket of *ahindumgi*, the taro and coconut cream dish. At Kolkiaring, the meeting generated a schedule of events for the following week.

On Monday all the women of Kolkiaring went to their gardens to gather bundles of taro to carry to the hamlet of Kavais, the deceased's widower. The people of Kolkiaring were all involved because there was a sense of kinship among them. The deceased woman was the adoptive mother of many of the current older generation, a generation that had come of age during the dysentery epidemics of the 1930s, followed by World War II, when many people were left orphaned. Garideran had taken care of a large number of people and she was remembered for her special food-providing attributes: "She bossed all the crayfish and fish from the mangrove. She'd go and get them, mumu them, and then distribute them to everyone. She was also a good one for pounding large amounts of galip nuts into a nut paste" (Langerkan [elderly woman], life history).

When the women came back from the gardens, they fabricated special bundles out of the taro. When all the bundles, called *amruawa*, were prepared, a long procession of neighbors set out for the deceased's hamlet. On arrival everyone unloaded his or her bundle, and the taro was added to a large food display. This display was erected on a platform. The taro was laid between several vertical posts. The tubers were all placed facing the door of the house in which the woman had lived, and the stalks faced the bush beyond the clearing. As the taro was added to the display, it was stacked neatly and tightly, although in the several days before it was taken down to cook, the whole display settled, slipped, and fell askew. This shifting was attributed to the *aios*.

After delivering the food, everyone was seated while delegations from other hamlets presented their contributions. The hosts cooked rice and tinned fish to feed all those who had come (they could also have cooked more traditional food such as taro and bananas). After eating this food communally, the group broke up, and everyone returned home. It was by then dark.

On the way home, Langerkan, who was in the lead, sighted an *aioska*. She turned and called out to me, "What is this?" but by the time she

Plate 7.1   Death feast

turned back it was gone. She described it as being just like a person from the village, but only one and a half feet tall. Her daughter and daughter's husband, seated in their house about fifteen yards ahead, said they had heard a "person" walk by. After discussion of this event, the consensus was that it was an *aioska* who had seen our preparations for the feast: "This feast is something for them. We cook for them." When the ghosts had seen us carrying all this taro, they began migrating to the place. *Aios* always gather in and around large food displays. Since *aios* are "ahuman" their actions are the inverse of social productive ones. *Aios* are forces of entropy. Rauniram said that the *aios* often try to interfere with the cooking process so that when one mumus a pig one half will be well cooked, while the other half will not. If this happens during a death feast, they simply recook the pig and eat it, but they say that "the *aios* have taken our pig."

The *aios* inhabit the taro in the platform too, and that is why, according to informants, the taro begins to slip and fall from the wall. Before the taro can be removed from the platform display, the *aios* must be dispelled. The relation that the *aios* have to food is the inverse of the human relationship. The *aios* "go inside" the food displays, instead of having the food going inside them. Social persons do not share substance with raw food at all, but rather act upon it and transform it by harvesting and cooking it prior to taking it inside themselves. The food displays seem to retain their form and substance despite the incorporation of the *aios*, whereas human beings incorporate food but retain their own size and shape. Humans act on and transform their food internally while the *aios* cannot do this. The *aios* can also be separated from their food homes; once people have eaten food it becomes inseparable from themselves.

The taro on display takes on the attributes of the *aios* in yet another way as it is prepared for cooking. Normally the taro stalk is cut from the tuber so that a small section of tuber remains attached to the stalk. This stalk can then be replanted and will generate a new tuber. The taro that is brought to a death feast, however, is permanently destroyed. At the appropriate moment, the men climb up on the platform, grab each plant, and cut the stalk off above the tuber so there is no point of regeneration. They throw the taro tuber down into the clearing and let the stalks drop down on the other side of the platform (not coincidently, this is the side facing the bush). The Baining explicitly say this practice is to "kill them now," to "cut the neck of the taro." They throw away the stalks of the deceased. The stalks die and rot like the deceased. The regenerative part is left to rot, and this rotting part is the *aios'* portion.

After the taro was contributed, the men began to butcher the pigs. A large group of men gathered to work, watch, and supervise. Each pig was butchered sequentially, although there were more than enough men to do several at once. While the butchering was going on, some of the taro fell off the display platform. One man saw a connection between these events and said that the *aios* had knocked it down. Another informant, however, said it was just the sun drying out the tubers. In any case, the *aios* are thought to be present and even mischievously active during the preparations.

The day before the feast, the women from each of the hamlets in Kolkiaring arrived to get their share of taro to cook. The taro, which they had amassed earlier in the week, was now redistributed and each woman took a supply back to her own home to cook. Of the large quantities of taro each woman was given, some was to be cooked and mixed with coconut cream to make *ahindumgi*, a feast food, some was to be cooked and brought plain to accompany the pig, and some was to be left at home to accompany the pig that each would bring home with her.

While the women were coming and going, the men were again building fires and heating stones to mumu the pigs. The last pig was killed, but not cut up. Its entrails were removed and the carcass split, but it was left whole. It was mumued in one piece, and would be served at the beginning of the feast. This is called *aravetdumga*.

The Feast

The actual feast got under way after church on Sunday; it was before 11:00 A.M. The people from Kolkiaring arrived in dribs and drabs, while those from Raunit and Akarum (hamlets) came in a procession carrying their contributions.

The women and children all sat down in one area. The men sat separately. The event began, as do all large Baining gatherings, with lots of people going around exchanging betel. Then Suabem made a fire with a large bundle of twigs tied up and lit with kerosene. This made a big blaze onto which they put the deceased's basket, wrapped in a new cloth laplap. The widower came and knelt by the fire and cried into the crook of his arm. As the basket burned, several women started to wail. This wailing died down with the fire, which was a short burst of intense flames crumbling into ashes. Almost immediately the organizers decapitated the top knots of the large baskets of *ahindumgi*, coconut cream taro. This act is called "cutting the neck of the food," and is analogous to cutting the neck of the taro done earlier.

The first men at the baskets threw the top pieces from each basket onto the ground. These pieces are said to be thrown to the *aios* (but are swiftly eaten by the dogs). The pervasive idea at this feast is that one is not supposed to be careful and parsimonious with food, but quite the opposite: one is supposed to take a bite out of a piece of taro, throw the rest down, and then take another piece. This is in direct contrast with normal behavior when food is consumed carefully and the left-overs carefully put away and saved. Despite the ideology of waste and the initial gestures, I saw very little conspicuous consumption or waste being practiced. The women all gathered around two of the baskets (the third was low to the ground for the children) and began wrapping up quantities of the food to take home. The men obviously considered themselves above this mad hustle and were served smaller packages of the taro and coconut cream mixture where they sat. They did not make up packages to save, but ate it on the spot.

When people were seated again, groups of workers served out portions of cooked pork and roasted taro. Before this stage was even finished several young men came out bearing the whole cooked pig on a piece of bark. There were six men carrying it, and it was still steaming hot. Immediately the crowds surrounded it. This pig is supposed to be eaten without using one's hands or any utensils, simply by leaning down and biting into it—"putting their teeth into it," like a dog. While some actually bit into it, the rest just tore out hunks of the meat (albeit in a relatively barbaric manner). The whole pig had disappeared in ten minutes.[13]

While people ate and chatted, groups of workers passed through the crowd, giving out tobacco, rice, and pieces of pork. They gave a piece of pork to each and every woman saying *"ani, giamerika* [here is your betel nut]." This portion of meat was meant to be taken home, and this act essentially marked the end of the feast.[14]

Death Ritual in Its Social Context

Mortuary ritual has an important place in many Melanesian societies. Extensive analyses of rituals surrounding death have described how the social persona of the deceased is deconstructed into renewable or reusable social parts and distributed or exchanged among the survivors (Weiner 1976). Others have discussed how memory is constructed or captured in a variety of media: songs, sculptures, names, and ceremonial objects (Battaglia 1990; Foster 1995; Maschio 1994; Schieffelin 1976; Wagner 1986). In this and other ways the Baining differ from other Melanesian peoples. In contrast to classic cases of secondary burial and the initiation of the deceased into the world of the dead (Hertz 1960), the Baining emphasis is almost entirely on the world of the living. Although many of the broad outlines of Hertz's ritual model are paralleled in the Baining case (burial, then a period of liminality ended by a great feast), this is not, as Hertz would suggest, merely a survival from a custom of secondary burial and initiation into the world of the dead. It is my impression that the world of the dead holds

13. At Raunsepna, the same idea was performed somewhat differently. There, men started grabbing pieces of pig fat, taking large bites out of them, and pushing them into the faces of other men. Most men were not feeding themselves but were taking bites out of pieces held by other men. The men said they ate the slabs of fat like this out of sorrow for the dead man. They said that women could do it too, but I never saw a woman do this. In Yalom, Pinam had described this custom as *arakinggi* (tooth). She said it was like *amerika* (when I described the Lan custom of *amerika*), since it was given to people but they could not eat it all at once. Thus, they would eat half of it and their teeth marks remained on the piece. Then they took the rest home with them. With such pieces one cannot hold them oneself and eat them; rather, another person (brother, sister, etc.) has to hold them for you and you eat out of their hands. Then your mother or sister has to come and take this piece of meat for you, wrap it up, and take it home. This step did not seem to be done at Raunsepna. The practice of putting one's teeth into the meat without using one's hands corresponded to the custom of eating the whole pig that I saw in Lan.

14. During my fieldwork in 1991, I was surprised to find that the entire feasting cycle described here was repeated twice over two successive days. Informants said this was a return to a traditional practice, but I am not sure.

very little interest for the Baining, and what feelings and emotions they do have are based on fear and anxiety. The Baining emphasis is on the here and now, and the rituals that surround death emphasize this aspect. Baining mortuary ritual is almost entirely focused on relations in this world, and on the reintegration and maintenance of social ties in the face of disruptions such as death.

Despite token references to the *aios* at these rituals (the idea that the memory of the dead remains as long as the basket does, or that some of the food is discarded for the *aios*), in general, the ghosts, corpse, and afterlife play little role in the activities. The main focus of these events is upon food and its means of exchange and consumption. I have argued that food giving and sharing is one of the main media of social relations in the society. This argument relied, in part, on the negation of such bonds at death. This interpretation can now be substantiated in terms of the data reviewed above.

The Roles of Food in the Mortuary Process

The main funerary events focus not on disposal of the body, or on purification of the dead or those associated with the dead, although all of these do occur, but on the preparation of food in various contexts. The use of food progresses through a series of phases.

At death, food is associated with the deceased. The fruits of the dead person's labor—his or her gardens, pigs, coconuts, and betel nut—are either completely or symbolically destroyed. The creation and production of these goods epitomized the person's sociality. With death, the productive capacity of the person is stripped away, and these artifacts of sociality are also destroyed. It is in keeping with the Baining conception of the relations between nature and society, and the lack of an ideology of descent or inheritance that nothing survives this cycle; rather than bequeathing gardens, trees, or possessions to one's descendants as is frequently done in other societies, the Baining terminate them with the owner/producer. Nowadays, this is not done with all of the belongings of a person. For example, some commercially valuable trees are spared and are claimed by descendants.

It is not just the deceased's individual achievement of sociality that is destroyed at death, but the intertwining networks of sociality that the person had created with others. This extension of a person's persona beyond the skin into social space to others is particularly strong when people share food. The severing of these bonds at a death thus diminishes not just the deceased, but all those engaged with him or her. This is *awumbuk* (the diminution of self due to the loss of others) to the highest degree. As with *awumbuk*, people feel a lassitude at death.

This is not a temporary collapse of the extended social boundaries of the person, but a permanent one. In order to seal the rents in their social boundaries, the Baining taboo those foodstuffs which originally extended the boundaries. The fact that it is often the deceased's own food (i.e., the produce of the deceased's destroyed garden) that is avoided makes this act all the more potently symbolic.

As the period of abstinence progresses, however, the refusal of food becomes less associated with the deceased and more a negation of the processes that continuously interrelate people in the society. Abstinence from food becomes equated with the absence of sociality, and the person who holds a taboo becomes socially marginalized. This state is transformed during the last stage of the mortuary rites, when food is further transformed. Food is now disassociated both from its connections with the *aioska* and its negation of social relations, and is used specifically for the purpose of reestablishing social relations through consumption and exchange. Food has by this time regained its role as the essential medium of socialization and the means of bond formation.

Kinship and Relations through Food

We have already observed that quite different roles are performed by naturally and socially related persons in the mortuary process. The roles and motives behind the actions of social kin have been discussed and analyzed, but those of consanguineal relatives are not yet clear. Natural kin are proscribed from tabooing food at the death. They are also less likely to mourn overtly or wail at the various points where such actions are appropriate. All of these acts are cultural expressions of sentiments of sorrow and bereavement, and they are fitting only for those whose relationship is defined in social terms. By contrast, because the natural kin share their natural substance with the deceased, they are substantively affected by the death. It is not a social bond that has been severed but a natural tie, which in some sense is never severed. Thus, at the death of a kinsperson, the natural relative is threatened by nature or entropy encroaching on his or her social persona. It is as if the mourner fears the contagion of nature and therefore goes to extraordinary lengths to express his or her hypersociality. Starting at the graveside, it is the natural kin of the deceased who distribute betel and pepper to the mourners. This, as we have seen before, is the quintessential social act. It always occurs at the initiation of social encounters, when people visit or meet on the road. By giving betel, the natural kin reinitiate social relations.

The reason the consanguineal kin need to do this is that death disrupts the cultural order between nature and society. It is nature turning against and destroying important social achievements. The solution to this is not to reassert the social at the expense and denial of the entropic aspects of nature, but rather to reassert the proper positive and complementary relations between them. In the early part of the mortuary ritual, each party overreacts in opposite directions. The social kin completely strip themselves of their sociality to mourn this destructive act of nature. The natural kin act hypersocially to differentiate themselves from that natural being, the deceased.

In line with this we might now reinterpret aspects of the practice of eating the decomposed fluids of the corpse. The corpse and its processes of decomposition are the essence of death and thus of nature in its most negative and antisocial aspect. By transforming this matter into food, the medium of social relations, the deceased's kin are transforming this natural force into a social substance. By incorporating this social matter into themselves by eating it, they are also transforming themselves. This is one step towards restoring the proper balance between the natural and the social.

The role played by the natural kin in terminating the food taboos of the social kin continues this theme of restoring proper social relations. Not eating (taboo) is the negation not only of a social activity (eating food), but of the proper and positive relation one should have towards nature (transforming nature into food, which creates social relations and thus society). Food taboos inhibit this process. The natural kin struggle to overcome death by specific social behaviors. Initially, they are inhibited by the negative behavior of the social kin, but eventually they succeed in reestablishing social relations between the groups, and the proper relations to nature. Through the termination of food taboos, the natural kin become socializers and initiate new social relations through food. This act reasserts the balance within society. This reintegration is symbolized by the distribution of pig called *amerika* (betel nut) at the end of the ritual.

Food Symbolism

The final death feast begins with the consumption of taro (symbolic of the termination of the food taboo), moves through the consumption of pig, and ends with the distribution of pieces of pig that are ritually called *amerika*. This final distribution echoes the presentation of real betel nut at the graveside. Although no informant spontaneously associated these two events, when I brought up the two uses of *amerika* in a single question to Langerkan, a big smile crossed her face and she said, "The two are the same thing." Thus, it seems that the death feast ends on a note of initiation. People are given an item that signals the start of social and reciprocal exchange. This makes sense if we think of *amerika* as an item used to initiate social relations. But why is it pig and not betel nut that is exchanged in this instance?

To explain this, we have to look further into the symbolism of food; space; nature and culture; life and death; and humans and animals. Mortuary rituals confront the opposition between life and death, but for the Baining death also forces a confrontation between nature and society. *Aios* represent death and decay; they are the embodiment of entropy, the inverse of work and production. *Aios* are not translatable as ghosts, ancestors, or spirits, but rather stand for processes of decomposition and desocialization. They are opposed to social processes of transformation such as food production, cooking, and exchange. Food is produced and food displays are constructed to express social values and intentions, but these constructive processes are shadowed by their opposites. *Aios* stand for the specter of death and destruction, and are thought to appear when social processes are most at risk. At death people say they taboo certain foods out of "sorrow" for the dead, but this act might be more aptly seen as an expression of their own social loss due to the death. Those engaged in taboos act in ways considered less than human. As such, they are analogous to animals and people who are marginal to society: in particular, pigs, birds, dogs, thieves, and spirits. At certain other stages of their lives, especially when very young and very old, people may again be seen to be analogous to animals, especially pigs. Pigs are an apt symbol for people on the margins of society, since they live part of their life with humans and part foraging in the bush. Although they are given a portion of their food by their owners, they must find the rest themselves and pigs are responsible for most of the damage and theft in gardens. They are born wild but are domesticated.[15] As Leach (1979: 162) suggests, Europeans feel a special guilt about pigs since they do not provide any assets (such as milk or wool) while they are living. They are raised only to be killed and eaten. "Besides which, under English rural conditions, the pig in his backyard pigsty was, until very recently much more nearly a member of the household than any of the other edible animals" (1979: 162). Leach suggests that this makes eating the pig almost a sacrilege. Although circumstances are similar among the Baining and pigs are almost family, I suggest that the symbolism of eating pig is much more complex, and the ambiguities of a pig's qualities make it ritually powerful rather than problematic. Pigs do not reciprocate food in life, but are eaten in

15. The Baining do not breed domesticated pigs. All boars are castrated, and females are inseminated by wild boars. Wild piglets are found in the bush and domesticated. In this sense they are analogous to adopted children.

death. In this sense the Baining pig resembles the Lele pangolin rather than the English rural swine (Douglas 1966). Douglas suggests that the pangolin is spoken of as a "voluntary victim." It does not fight or run away, but allows itself to be caught and eaten in a sacred ritual (1966: 169). The role of the pig in Baining mortuary feasts parallels this, but goes beyond just this one attribute. Pigs in the death feast undergo transformation and the pig comes to instantiate a number of Baining values.

In this context we can begin to see how pigs fit into the mortuary feast. The mortuary feast is aimed at reintegrating key mourners into the social order. It begins with the eating of taro, and in this phase, those who were abstaining from a food are given it to eat, and the bonds of sociality are reintroduced. Prior to this moment, however, they have been living as marginal, that is piglike, beings, and this aspect of their persona is expressed and destroyed by the next event, which is the bringing in and eating of the whole pig. In this event, the pig is still in its whole, recognizable shape. It might be said to be reciprocating the food and care it has received throughout its life, and in so doing it is symbolically a medium of sociality. It is, however, consumed in a bestial way; people act like animals, especially dogs, biting directly into it. When this pig is consumed, so too is this natural, animalistic side of peoples' behavior. The pig has transformed its naturalness into sociality through reciprocation, and the people have given up their bestiality by incorporating the pig.

Pigs are not the only marginal foodstuffs. Coconuts and betel nuts are too, because they grow on the edges of hamlets and are planted on placentas and graves. The symbolism of marginality and the manipulation of the boundaries of both person and community go on throughout social life. People are always extending the boundaries of themselves through the sharing of food and the exchange of betel nut. Social beings are constantly engaged in transforming nature into social space through the creation of gardens and hamlets. It is on the margins of these spaces that betel nut is grown. By giving pig but calling it "betel nut," the Baining combine all these aspects of the opposition between society and nature: the transition from relative naturalness to relative sociality during the life cycle; the transformations produced in nature through social activity, particularly gardening; and the interrelations between people based in large part on the products of other transformations, such as food, children, households, and communities. Pig sometimes appears as a symbol of the natural qualities that are more negatively valued, but in this final act of the mortuary ritual it is transformed into betel nut, which has only good social connotations.

Pigs and betel nut are mediators between place and forest, human and *aios*, culture and nature.

The Ritual Process

In Baining mortuary ritual, the deceased is disposed of quite quickly, but it takes much longer to deal with the living. The giving of betel nut at the graveside is essentially the finale of the funeral per se, but it is just the beginning of the ritual cycle for the survivors. The burial and giving of betel closes the deceased's life. The only other act oriented towards the dead person is the *amungom* (divination). Even this act does not really impact on the dead person, but tries to explain the death in terms of some act of carelessness or malevolence in the past. The *amungom* does not stimulate any further activity, such as revenge or sanctions. What the divination really does is relegate the deceased, the corpse *aioska*, to the realm of the dead (*arimbab* [home of *aios*]).

The rest of the mortuary ritual becomes a rite of passage for the living. There is a ritual of segregation when the survivors break with their normal social milieu by tabooing food. This is followed by a period of liminality in which the participants are marginal to normal social life and interaction and behave in ways that are symbolically antistructural and natural. This antistructure is not, however, equatable with V. Turner's concept of communitas ("a feeling of common humanity" [1967]). The participants in these rites are not engaged in communitas; rather, they are peripheralized by the very individuality of their experience, their separation from social intercourse, their isolation and association with nature. Nor do Baining mourners experience transcendent liminality (T. Turner 1979). While T. Turner sees the liminality as offering a perspective that encompasses all of the phases and aspects of the normative world, the Baining experience a fragmentation of their world. Liminality for each Baining consists of inverting one aspect of the normal system. Each of the taboos described above picks an aspect, attribute, or phase of normal Baining social life, and negates it. Seen as a whole, the composite set of mortuary taboos denotes an inversion of the entire system. No individual subject ever sees the whole, but instead each individual's perspective is of a single event or action in isolation. The ritual reduces the actor's perception of his or her world rather than broadens it. It is subscendent rather than transcendent (T. Turner 1979). It is the integration of these pieces into a whole that must be achieved during the rites of aggregation. The rites of incorporation are specific reenactments of the rites of social intercourse: the exchange of food and betel nut. Although the fate of the survivors might not appear as a transition or a *rite de passage*, death is nevertheless a disruption of the social fabric and social order. Death threatens everyone by destroying the fragile bonds that maintain what the Baining perceive as order. It thus requires rituals of reintegration.

Aios

The Baining concept of death is most readily constructed in its opposition to life. Some have described the world of the dead as the inverse of the living, social world (see Hesse and Aerts 1978); this, however, is a more formal and consistent picture than my informants produced. Baining notions of death, the dead, and nature are not so much a consistent system as a residual category, a catchall for many ideas and elements, which share aspects but are not coherently connected. These ideas emerge in response to particular social contexts and events and not as an internalized descriptive domain. The concept of *aios* is a perfect example of this residual nature.

For the Baining the term *aios* refers to many things: (1) corpses; (2) bush spirits who live in the forest and scare, tease, befuddle, and sometimes steal food from people; (3) spirits that inhabit certain lianas and trees in the bush; (4) fireflies; (5) creatures one talks to in seances, the ancestors of those now living; (6) creatures who inhabit food displays; (7) the names of certain dancers during *Amambua*. From an outside or etic perspective one could say that there are many shared attributes between these categories, or even a continuity among them. This, however, does not emerge as the cultural perspective of any Baining. My informants did not conceive of these concepts as continuous or similar in any way. They see them all as separate entities that just happen to be homonyms. Neither in elicitation nor in spontaneous usages did people perceive a continuity between the *aioska* of a corpse, and the spirits who walk in the bush (ghosts) or those called up during divinations. In answer to direct questioning, people said they were not the same.

While Baining do not see connections among these groups of beings, from an analytic perspective shared attributes are abundant. Each of these creatures is in some way opposed to normal human life and social values. These oppositions range across such qualities as life-death; place-bush; productive-unproductive (stealing); social products–natural materials; visible and spatially located–invisible and diffuse; unmasked person (i.e., normal social identity)–masked being (i.e., extrasocial identity); producing food–inhabiting food displays (or stealing food). All of the attributes that I have placed first in these oppositions are those of normal Baining existence and are socially valued.

Those listed second, however, do not describe a state or domain of relationships and emerge only in these oppositions.

The beliefs about the natural and supernatural domains are not a coherent, ordered set, but consist of elements that are relegated to these domains by virtue of their exclusion from the sociocultural realm. In this sense, the domain of the natural and supernatural is a residual category; it is created by a series of inversions each of which is meaningful in a particular context, but does not join with others to make an "alternative" world or domain. The Baining see human society as relatedness; to be unconnected or isolated is to be outside of society. *Aios*, by definition, are outside society and structure. The world of the dead should not be as coordinated and ordered as that of the living. It should reflect the isolation and disconnection of the deceased.

From an emic perspective, it appears that the Baining deny the continuities and connections between the different referents of *aios* because they are defined as disconnected, even though outsiders and analysts recognize similarities and continuities among them. Despite this denial, however, the Baining do occasionally assume continuities between these referents. This happens when an *aioska*, a recently deceased and buried corpse, is called forth during a seance; or when the *aios* are called during a divination and the audience then equates their presence with the proliferation of fireflies in the area; or when a bush spirit is encountered on the path, and its presence is associated with an impending mortuary feast. Such continuities are potentially unifiable into a coherent belief system about life after death; the Baining, nevertheless, do not consciously hold with such a coherent system.

Although nature and society are constantly used in opposition to one another in this analysis, it should be clear by now that they are not equally systematic and coherent domains. As seen in the discussions of the concepts of *aios* and death, the category of nature is fragmented and chaotic in keeping with its residual status. In contrast to the ongoing social system, death and nature appear as mere unsystematic chaos rather than a "mirror-image" of a system of structure and classes.

This chapter has focused on the role that death plays in the Baining social order and cultural system. The Baining system is built up and maintained through a variety of action schemas: adoption, food production, exchange, and reciprocity. Through these acts people continuously transform nature into society. This process is not unidirectional; it is reversible. The whole Baining life cycle is constructed of the progressive and regressive transformations of these relations. Death, however, is the ultimate reversal. Death does not just reverse/close the individual life cycle; it affects the larger society. Death, like adoption, affects not just the individual involved, but the matrix of relations that encompasses him or her. Death and adoption are the major processes that affect the continuity of Baining life.

Baining society is not manifest in any corporate institution or set of institutions. It is entirely constituted out of a series of productive activities, which build a pattern of relations and interconnections between people, places, and things. Its continuity is based on the maintenance of these bonds. When a death removes a person from this web, it destroys the patterns and connections that have evolved around that person, and the social order as such is directly threatened. Even a single death becomes, under such circumstances, a crisis for society. For this reason, death is extraordinarily important, and mortuary ritual emerges as the most elaborated ritual sequence. Mortuary rituals are simultaneously individual rites of passage and collective rituals of social cohesion. Death, the only life crisis that poses a threat to the structure of the society as a whole, is thus the occasion for rituals that evoke collective participation.

On the ritual level, we have seen that Baining mortuary rituals focus only briefly on the fate of the deceased and his or her passage into death. This may be because the dead person is now part of the chaotic, residual, and therefore unknowable, domain beyond all systematicity. Far more elaborated are the socially and culturally structured means of reintegrating the society. This process is accomplished through a series of rituals designed to reconstruct social relations. These rites function on both a symbolic level and one of concrete social action to weave together the elements into a coherent whole. Nowhere is the logic of the Baining system made manifest so clearly as it is when it threatens to fall apart. It is only when social bonds are severed and individual parts fail to maintain their sociality that the true foundations of Baining sociality are revealed as it strives to reassert and reconstruct itself.

Part Two

Play

8   Baining Dances

Continuity and Variation

The dances the Baining perform have been their most noted cultural attribute in general reports and the one most remarked upon in the anthropological literature (Read 1931–32; Bateson 1931–32; Poole 1941–42). The "Fire Dance" (chapter 10) is what the wider national culture knows about the Baining. Anthropologists and others have focused on the dances, both because of their intrinsic color, style, and flamboyance, and because in these respects they contrast so vividly to the rest of Baining social life:

> The whole artistic energy of the people is exerted in the songs and dances, and especially in the design and decoration of the masks. If as a result of European contact, these dances should cease to be held we shall have destroyed the only patch of colour in the otherwise drab existence of the Baining people. (Bateson 1931–32: 341)

Despite their noteworthiness, the dances were prohibited by early missionaries, and have survived mostly in the inland communities, which were missionized much later. Nowadays, they are usually performed in conjunction with mission or national cultural events, such as a building dedication or national holiday. Such events have, in fact, become the principal pretexts for the performances, which otherwise appear to have no indigenous occasions.

Several different dance complexes coexist among the Baining. Within a community dances are classified according to whether they are performed during the day or night. The three main complexes are *Amambua*, primarily a night dance held in the Lan/Puktas area near the coast;[1] *Asarai (Asaraigi)*, a day dance performed by the inland people;[2]

---

1. I have given an account of *Amambua* elsewhere (Fajans 1985). *Amambua* is only very occasionally performed. I was fortunate to witness two performances of it in 1976–77.
2. The Lan term *Aharaigi* (Rascher 1909; Parkinson 1907) is cognate with the mountain name *Asarai*. The sounds "s" and "h" are allophones for the Baining. This event was

and *Atut*, which is a night dance among the mountain people. To some extent the dance forms are distributed geographically, so that different communities perform different dances. There are, however, similarities among all these complexes, since there seems to have been considerable adoption, substitution, exchange, and invention across communities.

Without ignoring the content and individuality of the present-day dances, it is important also to see them from the perspective of their interchangeability. The people of Lan say that the *Asarai*, which is now performed by the mountain people, was borrowed from them. The mountain people acknowledge this, while claiming that they used to perform a dance called *Asingal*, which is now lost except in the memories of the oldest inhabitants. There is a dance performed on the coast called *Asingal*, which is probably (but not necessarily) related.[3] The Lan version itself was very nearly lost, but it was resurrected several years ago by a few old men. In the mountains the principal night dance, *Atut* (the Fire Dance that has made the Baining famous throughout Papua New Guinea) is believed to be a recent introduction into the North Baining area from the Central Baining, where it might have originated and is referred to in ethnographic accounts as the "Snake Dance" (see Read 1931–32; Bateson 1931–32). Older people vaguely remember that the dance was borrowed and adopted by their "parents," but young people think of it as indigenous. In more recent memory, a dance called *Akurikuruk* has been incorporated into the *Asarai* complex. Pool (1969–70) traces this dance to the Central Baining and says that its performance has been slowly moving across the North Baining area. According to Pool, it was first performed in Wiliambempki during his field stay in 1970, at which time members of his community traveled specially to Raunsepna to watch the dance preparations and learn the procedures. They then returned to their own village and taught the others. In Yalom, this dance has been performed for over a generation, but its introduction is still within people's memory, and I was able to elicit the names of some of those responsible for its introduction and

described by missionaries but is no longer performed. Some of the oldest Lan residents remember seeing the *Aharaigi* performed when they were five to eight years old, but none was old enough to participate. The myths that currently proliferate about the dance make it the biggest and most elaborate of the dances (descriptions of men's seclusion during the preparations for *Aharai* suggest parallels with *rites de passage* such as initiation). It is hard to know how much of this elaboration is glorification of the past ("nowadays people only take two months to prepare for a dance, but our fathers took two years," Peni told me). Enormous and very elaborate masks from this dance are housed in the collection of the Hamburg Museum in Hamburg, Germany.

3. I saw this dance performed in Lan, but since I could get no descriptions of the mountain version, I am not sure if the two dances are related.

those who composed the accompanying songs. The variation and sub-stitutability of many of the symbolic elements of these complexes raise questions about their interpretation. There is a flexibility to the con-struction of Baining ceremonies at this level that seems not altogether in keeping with anthropological concepts of ritual as symbolic commu-nication.

The dances are, indeed, spectacular. The dancers perform with gi-gantic and frequently grotesque masks, and other bizarre constructions made of bamboo, bark cloth, feathers, and paint. Although these regalia are the product of months of intensive labor at special sites in the bush, they are destroyed at the end of each performance. In addition to the preparation and parading of these regalia, the participants engage in extraordinary activities, such as dancing on fire, whipping one another with lashes made of vines, and piercing the flesh of the lower back in order to fasten cumbersome fifteen-feet-high spears to their backs with ropes tied through their flesh.

Although aspects of these activities are not dissimilar from ordeals known from other parts of the world, the Baining variants seem excep-tional in that they, like the total dance events of which they form a part, are without ostensible pretexts, functions, purposes, or explicit meanings of any kind. They are not appeals to the gods or ancestors; they are not a kind of initiation; they are not done for harvests or fertil-ity; they do not bestow courage or beauty; they are not means to ritual power, shamanic vision, curing, or secular leadership.[4] No one needs to participate, and although most members of the society take part at some point in their lives, there are a few who have no interest in doing so and never have.[5] These individuals are not socially sanctioned in any way.

For all these reasons, the dances cannot be regarded as ancestral rel-ics passed down unchanged by the guardians of tradition. They are not rigidly prescribed performances from which deviation is impossi-ble. Their lack of explicit purpose or exegesis notwithstanding, it is virtually unthinkable to anyone who has ever seen Baining dances that they are not in some way meaningful and centrally important constit-

4. The one instance in which I can tie a ritual to some related event is when *Atut* is performed the evening before an *asmus ama aioska* (mortuary feast), as was done in Raunsepna during my stay. Although I saw this done, I asked frequently if dances were regularly or traditionally performed in conjunction with mortuary feasts and got mostly negative replies. The few positive replies seemed motivated more by a desire to please me by responding affirmatively than by a real association.

5. This lack of interest extends to women as well as men, so that Pinam claimed never to have sung at, or even watched, the dances that occurred outside her door, despite the fact that they were often organized by her deceased husband.

uents of Baining culture. They are simply too spectacular, complex, and take too much time and energy to be without any significance. I therefore persistently inquired about them. The most frequent answer I got, however, to my increasingly frustrated questions about their "meaning," was "We just do it—it's play."

Play

What was going on here? Why were these ceremonies considered "play"? Once I asked this question, I became aware of the fact that the Baining have some unusual ideas about play, and in order to understand the meaning of Baining dance, I would have to understand what the Baining mean by the term "play." One way to do this was to analyze the range of meanings signified by the Baining word for play. In Baining as in English there is both a noun and a verb form of the word: *talak* (to play) and *atalak* (the play). As in our own society, children's play is not the only activity to which the word refers. We have already seen that it is also used to refer to the dances. In this and other instances, the noun form of the word seems to suggest not only the behavior of play, but an event as an encompassing performance, like a theatrical play.

The Baining, as I explained in chapter 5, regard children's play as the antithesis of proper social activity. It stands outside the realm of social behavior. This is why, although Baining children are not treated harshly, the Baining suppress spontaneous play by children. In the Baining view, children are characterized by their initial asociality. This "naturalness" is expressed in their lack of control over bodily functions, their inability to hear (and therefore understand) what is told them, their inability to work (which results in playing instead), and their stealing of food (which illustrates their fundamental ignorance of important social relations). The play of children is contrasted to the work of adults, especially the activities of gardening, cooking, and giving food to others. Play is not considered the work of children; eating and learning to work are.

In addition to children's play and dances, there are two other referents for the term. One of these is the divination described in chapter 7. In this context, the Baining say that they "play" with the *aios*. In this activity they mediate the boundaries between life and death and between the social and the natural. The "play" consists of shuttling a log back and forth across a fulcrum from the "bush" to the "hamlet" while asking the *aios* questions. The *aios* are not conceptualized as a collectivity on other occasions, but in this "play" the Baining create the groups "us" and "them" by relegating each group to an end of the

Plate 8.1   Children playing at *atut*.

log. Here, play is a collective activity, which sets human actors against forces outside of society.

The other referent of "play" is sorcery. In sorcery, "play" is the term used for the sorcerer's activity. The Baining do not appear to have sorcerers in their own culture, but they are acquainted with them through their interactions with plantation laborers from other parts of Papua New Guinea. Sorcery is an antisocial activity in Baining terms because it undermines the processes that the Baining value most highly: socialization and work. It is thus an inversion of normative social behavior. Since it is also performed by agents from outside the community, the whole activity appears from the Baining perspective as deriving from outside their social domain. Sorcery differs from the divination seance in that it is an individual activity and not a collective one.

By looking at the whole set of activities referred to as play, we can begin to see some underlying consistencies in the meaning of this term for the Baining. In two of these examples, the seance and sorcery, play invokes "natural" or supernatural forces or behaviors, which are usually excluded from society. In the other two examples, play refers to abnormal behavior enacted by the Baining themselves, which seems to have asocial or natural/supernatural aspects. In both instances, play transgresses the norms and margins of Baining sociocultural life, and becomes a context for delineating or reflecting on social boundaries. Implicit in this idea is the principle that only actors who have attained full sociality are strong enough to engage (i.e., play) with asocial forces without getting hurt. It is consistent with this principle that the Baining feel children ought not to play, since they are not strong enough or firmly enough rooted in society to confront these forces. It also follows from the same premise that the Baining regard the rituals in which they collectively engage the powers of extrasocial reality as the supreme form of play.

Work and Play

Although the Baining have little in the way of institutional structure beyond the household level, the dances are a partial exception to this rule. They have the effect of integrating, albeit only temporarily and partially, all the people of a community. The preparation for the dances requires the cooperation of men from a large number of households. They associate in this venture more on the basis of region and proximity than on that of kinship. In this work there may be acknowledged ritual leaders who take charge of the preparations. These leaders may perform as such for one or several dance events. Their influence during the preparations, however, is not transferred outside this realm. In addition to the cooperation of community members, the dance event becomes a focus for an even wider gathering, since people from the surrounding districts are usually invited to attend. Communities invited to one group's dances reciprocate at a later date with return invitations. In this way, the dances integrate a community as a unit, and present it as such to an even wider range of people. The social groupings defined here are in contrast to those of daily life, even to those units most prevalent when raiding occurred, since although raiding tended to take place between districts, the participants usually acted as individuals or as family members, and raids and battles did not occur on any larger scale. Baining dances thus involve, albeit on a rudimentary basis, a higher level of community planning, participation and feeling than any other social activity.

Because of the paucity of interpretable symbols, structural referents, and exegesis, an analysis of these dances had to wait until the analysis of Baining life had been completed. The dances must be understood in the wider social and cultural framework developed in the earlier chapters. The rituals initiate a set of transformations that reverse those current in daily life. They provide energy and renewal through a cycle of transformations in which the domains of everyday life are polarized and then recombined: first the social is transformed into the natural and male into female, then this process is reversed. The dances end with an expression of empowerment and social unity.

Although the Baining speak of the dances in general as play, there are really two distinct levels connoted by this term. In its more general sense, "play" *(atalak)* is a relatively "unmarked" term, which refers to the event as a whole.[6] Within this whole there are three distinct phases: the preparatory work, the performance, and a residual third phase that terminates the cycle. It is the second, the performance phase, to which the more "marked" sense of the term "play" applies. The first phase, that of the preparations, has no single label, but is referred to by several phrases (e.g., *ta takmut banas* [they make themselves], and *ut matna ama asleng* [we work in the garden]). It is therefore essentially contrasted to the performance phase as "work" to "play." The relationship between work and play thus emerges as the underlying dichotomy between the first two phases of the dance cycle. In addition to the contrast between work and play, the contrast between the natural and the social, and the dynamic and the static are also manifest in the dances. The final phase is virtually unmarked, and I did not elicit any term for it.

Work

The first phase requires lengthy preparation. Nowadays it can take up to two months of intensive labor, and in the past, according to informants, it could take considerably longer. What motivated the start of ritual preparations in precontact times is vague. Informants specifically deny any association with harvest,[7] ancestors, initiation, or other *rites de passage* such as mortuary or birth rites. They said that when an *akusa-kaiginaka* (ritual leader) saw that gardens were plentiful and the weather was good, he would decide it was time for an *atalak* or "play." The association between an abundance of food and a dance turned out to rest on the fact that abundant food gave people freedom to engage in alternative activities. It had no causative effect on the ritual, nor was the ritual thought to have the effect of increasing fertility or production, thus enlarging the food supply. As far as either Pool (1971) or I could tell, these rituals are not deemed to be efficacious in any particular way. They are, however, seen as good fun, and thus good for the soul or spirit. The Baining do seem to see the rituals as something they do for themselves, and something they do as themselves. This attitude is reflected in the expression used for ritual preparations *ta takmut banas*

6. I use the terms "marked" and "unmarked" following Greenberg (1966).

7. Corbin (1976), and Hesse and Aerts (1978) suggest that there are cyclical, fertility-oriented associations with the ceremonies, but neither Pool nor I elicited such an aspect despite repeated attempts.

(they do for themselves, or they make themselves) (*ta* [they]; *takmut* [to do, or to make]; *banas* [reflexive marker]).

Although this phrase is aptly expressive of the collective nature of the work, the process is nevertheless initiated by a single person. I was told that the preparations must be initiated by an elder who knows the magic that has to be said over the water used for washing at the end of the day.[8] The prerogatives of the leader lie principally in initiating preparations, saying the magic, and perhaps marking the actual day of the event, when he perceives that the preparations are almost complete. He does not in any way boss or direct the preparations. The wife of the leader should be the one who calls the first song rehearsal, and who introduces particular songs in a schedule that coincides with the work in the bush. If a man has no wife, or if she does not care to lead the song rehearsals, he can ask his sister, mother, or some other female relative.

Bush Preparations

Once the timing and site have been decided upon by the leader, much of his influence recedes, and people begin to work on tasks of their own choosing. As I have mentioned before, nobody is required to work on the dance preparations. People participate for their own reasons of skill and enjoyment. When we started preparations for the *Asarai* I witnessed in November 1977, there were only five or six men going to the bush each morning, but gradually the number increased and the energy and excitement seemed to draw more and more people in. Towards the end of the preparations there were ten to fifteen men gathering every day, and people had been steadily trickling into Yalom from the coast to participate. Even so, these preparations and the dance in Yalom were on quite a small scale by Baining standards.

In addition to the men, there is a special category of women who are also able to participate in the bush preparations. These women are called *anepkusakta* (*anepkusaki* [sing.]), which means "in the bush house" (with a feminine ending in the singular). The *anepkusakta* work alongside the men as if they were men; in fact, a second term for such a woman is *awatki* ("man" with a feminine ending). The *anepkusakta* are often chosen in childhood, frequently because they accompany their mother, another *anepkusaki*, to the bush, and thus see the work in progress. They hold this title and privilege through numerous events, and

8. Inangaiyi was the initiator of the bush work in the proceedings I witnessed. This was somewhat aberrant since he was not, at the start, an *anguraman* who knew the magic. He learned the magic from Kusak during the preparations.

their status is not dependent on age or marital status. Eventually, a woman may be retired from this position, in which case she is symboli- cally stripped of her status by crawling through a split banana tree trunk (Pool 1971: 72). The presence of these women further serves to dismantle the stereotypic picture of the men working in isolation and secrecy in the bush.[9]

The preparations are made in a clearing in the bush, called *akusak,* which makes it situationally similar to Baining garden work. The men joke about how they go off to the "gardens" each morning, but nobody is fooled. This is one of the few occasions on which I heard joking. The ritual preparations, as collective work produced by a sizeable group of a single sex, differ from daily gardening, which is done by a small group of mixed sex (the household). Most of a community's men spend some time in the bush site, and many of them spend long hours there day after day. While the men's work is secluded, it is not secret. The women know both where the men are going and what they are doing there. They know where, because they are often invited to the site prior to the preparations in order to carry kunai grass for the hut roof. After this visit they are expected to avoid the spot. They know what is being made and when, because when each new class of object is started the leader comes back to the hamlet and tells his wife to begin rehearsing the songs for that object. Meanwhile, the women are engaged in their own preparations in the village. The most important of these are the song rehearsals, which increase in content and intensity as the work in the bush nears completion.

In the bush, the men produce a whole range of regalia, many differ- ent pieces for each of the three different dances. Despite this prolifera- tion, there are structural similarities in the composition of the pieces. They are all made out of bush materials, and a considerable amount of preparation time is spent foraging in the forest for the appropriate substances. The predominant materials are bamboo, reeds, various leaves, bark cloth, tree sap and berries for dye, vines for lashing, and bird feathers. These materials are brought "raw" into the bush site and then transformed into finished products. Thus, although the product in the bush site is not "food," the work done there transforms natural

---

9. In Yalom, where I did my primary research, there were no *anepkusakta.* This came as a surprise and disappointment to me since I had read about them in Pool's (1971) report. I had envisaged being appointed to this status and gaining access to the bush in this manner. Although there were no *anepkusakta* in Yalom, people there knew of the custom. They simply supposed they had once had *anepkusakta* and had lost the custom. After much persuasion and cajoling, I managed to convince the men, particularly the ritual leader, that I should be allowed to accompany the men as an *anepkusaki,* and that I would take all responsibility for my own health and safety.

vegetal matter into socialized objects, and is in this sense analogous to what occurs in a swidden garden. This analogy is explicit in the way the Baining refer to the bush site as a garden.

For the most part, the ritual objects are not attempts at realistic representations of objects or beings; they are remarkably abstract. A few have names that can be meaningfully interpreted but most do not. Even those that do, do not seem to represent a thing or concept. During the preparatory phase, the essence and value of the objects seem to be derived from and embodied in the process of their creation. As raw materials they are analogous to babies or growing garden plants, but through productive work they are transformed into social products analogous to the Baining adult. In this light, the phrase "they do / make themselves," which the Baining use for the preparatory phase, makes sense. The bush phase is a process of social production. The ritual objects are thus analogous to the Baining themselves, as products of creative socialization.

The bush site and the objects in it are considered dangerous to women. Although the men are not themselves vulnerable to the power and danger of the bush site, they are potential carriers of the danger, and for that reason they undergo a ritual purification at the end of each day's work in the bush. It is in order to accomplish this rite more easily that the *akusak* is located near a stream. In this ritual purification the ritual leader's special knowledge becomes paramount, because it is the essence of his role to know the magic that has to be said over the leaves. The leader takes a small branch or twig of *asagang* leaves and says a spell over it. Pool (1971: 70) says most men do not understand this spell, implying that it is in "archaic" language, but that "it calls for washing away the harmful 'breath' of the ritual work." The spell that I recorded was in ordinary, comprehensible language. It talks of rotting and decomposition.

> Now I speak the talk [spell]
> Of the *ananbil* [a tree] which rots
> And the *auvunga* [a bush] which rots.
> Now these two will rot with us away from
> The *akip* [spears]
> And *asarai* that we have been working on.
> Today these both will rot with us, away from these
>   things,
> With all these new things.
> Today both will rot away from us,
> And from the knots on them
> And from the *akip*
> And from the *asarai*

And from the *aramariki*
Today they will rot away from us, from everything.
Today again, we come up good this day.

Both the *ananbil* and *auwung* are plants that rot very quickly. The bark of the *ananbil* tree rots and falls off rapidly, while the leaf of the *auwung* is also quick to disintegrate. The best interpretation of this spell and the use of these materials that I could arrive at with my informants was that it is important to wash with something that is rotting because it suggests that bad attributes, such as sickness, will fall away as easily as these leaves and bark do. The pollution of the bush will fall from the men's skins like the bark of the tree.

After the spell is said over the leaves, they are placed in water, often held in place by a rock. The men then purify themselves, first by drinking and spitting out water that has run over these leaves, then by sprinkling the water clinging to the leaves over themselves, their clothes, and their belongings, including their baskets, knives, tobacco, and betel nut. In some cases (Pool 1971: 70; Hesse and Aerts 1978: 10) they then wash themselves more thoroughly, and may wash every individual item in their basket. Even after taking this precaution, a man would not give a woman food or betel from his basket, since it might still be harmful.

Culture and Two Natures

Each day as the workers head towards the bush site, they pick up some token of the bush around them—a stick, a branch of leaves, or a bit of vine. This they deposit on a heap just outside the site before they enter it. This heap is called the "heap of the women." At the end of the day as people are leaving to wash and return to the village, each worker is supposed to pick up some detritus from the floor of the bush site— a snippet of bark cloth, a vine or feather discarded in the act of making the regalia—and deposit it on a second heap just outside the site. This second pile is called the "heap of the men" (Hesse and Aerts 1978: 10; Pool 1971: 87). These heaps grow as the work progresses. These two heaps symbolize in significant ways the whole process of creation in the bush site. The Baining had no exegesis for these heaps, but I would suggest that the two heaps represent two contrastive aspects of nature. These two aspects I shall call "raw" nature and "entropic" nature. "Raw" nature consists of things that are potentially social and can be transformed into social people or products by activities such as work. The first heap, then, is that of raw nature; it consists of materials that are potentially transformable by human productive action.

"Entropic" nature, by contrast, is essentially a residual category, composed of elements constituted through the negation or decomposition of some aspect of normal Baining social life: death, spirits, and the waste products of work, for example. Such phenomena are products of the dissolution of social form. The second heap represents entropic nature; it consists of the residue from these social transformations of work and nurturing, the bits and pieces that have dropped out and been lost in the course of these processes.

It is significant that the Baining do not explicitly conceive or recognize any connection between the categories I have called "raw" and "entropic" nature. There is no general category of "nature" that encompasses both. Neither are there any recognized "natural" transformations that link the two realms, such as the reincarnation of the dead, or the growth of new plants from rotting waste material. The Baining do not use the ashes of their swidden fires as fertilizer, and they make no attempt to scatter it over the gardens. "Raw" and "entropic" nature are thus in effect connected only through the action of human workers. Society, in other words, is the central link in a linear sequence of which these domains constitute the beginning and end, respectively. The direction of movement is from "raw" nature to society and from society to "entropic" nature. This flow is renewed or maintained only through the continual replication of work at the social center. The relations between the bush site and these two middens are analogous to those between the Baining social world and the nature that surrounds it. These relations are radically altered at the end of the work phase.

From Work to Play

The day before the performance, when the bush preparations are completed, there is an event that changes the prevailing pattern of relations. On this day, all the women from the village are invited back to the bush site to view the artifacts. Before being allowed into the clearing, however, the women ritually destroy the two rubbish heaps built up over the months of preparation. The women delve into these piles and hack the pieces into bits with their machetes. They then scatter the piles across the forest floor. Only after these piles have been destroyed do they enter the bush site. Here their job is to untie the knots that have "rooted" the masks to the spot. These knots, arsong (called in pidgin "pasim tambu") are believed to have the power to protect that to which they are fastened.[10] During the preparatory phase of the ritual, the

10. People tie knots on betel or coconut trees to protect the nuts from theft, or they may put a knot in a package of food to prevent the aios from stealing the food's essence.

workers make sure that each object they have made in the bush site is protected each night with an *arsong* knot. When asked why, they say it makes the objects *atlo* and protects them. I was never told what it protected them from, but Pool elicited a statement that it protected them from spirits. This is in keeping with implicit Baining attitudes about the efficacy of the knots. In addition, I suggest, there is a symbolic analogy between these knots and umbilical cords. The knots connect the objects to the place where they are formed into social products. In this case, the agents of this gestation are men, an inversion of the normative female role of gestation. In this context, it is the men who gestate the masks, but the women who cut them loose. The women both untie the knots and destroy the rubbish heaps. These heaps may be further interpreted as symbolic placentas, the first one symbolizing the placenta in its role as nurturer to the fetus, and the second, the placenta as residual afterbirth.

The preparatory phase consists of the transformation of natural substances through human work into more highly structured forms. It is through such processes as these that the Baining see themselves as makers of their social world. The expression *ta takmut banas* (they make themselves) indicates that this process is semiconsciously acknowledged. These productive processes are in distinct contrast, however, to the patterns of relations that come into force on the day of the dance itself.

The rite of untying the knots marks the symbolic completion of the work phase, which is analogous to the life cycle phases of gestation and socialization. At this point the ritual regalia are considered complete. By Baining standards they have attained adulthood, and are thus able to engage in "play." The play phase of the dance, in this way, corresponds to that of adulthood in the social life cycle.

How is the transition from work to play expressed in the ritual performance? First and foremost, there is a change of locale. The setting of the action is now transferred from the bush to the "place," the village. This marks a shift from work done in seclusion to open and public performance. The nature of the activity changes from construction to dance, or from socialization to action. There is also an inversion in the temporal arrangements; what was relegated to the night (e.g., the rehearsals), is replaced by a daytime performance. What was a predominantly single-sex activity now needs the cooperation of both sexes. Up to this point, all the participants have been members of the same community, but now the performance needs an audience, and those who are invited to watch are usually from different settlements. Participants in the ritual "play" are thus segmented into performers and spectators; hosts and guests; us and them.

Along with the changes in the spatial and temporal position of the ritual objects as they move from bush camp in towards the "place," there occur subtle but important changes in the people's relations to the dance objects. The social groups of musicians, women and children dancers, and spectators, on the one hand, and the ritual regalia on the other, take on new meanings as the regalia are paraded into the dance plaza, held on high, carried around by swarms of people, combined with other items of regalia, and danced to the accompanying songs.

The exotic beings that have been constructed by the playful work of the men and given symbolic birth by the women have no referents or counterparts in either nature or society, but they partake of aspects of both domains. They embody, on the one hand, a process of social work analogous to that through which the Baining "make themselves." This process, on the other hand, is performed by only one sex, carried out in a special ritual domain set apart from society, and located in the natural domain of the bush. While the masks embody the creative process of Baining production, they stand outside society as quasi-social, quasi-natural beings. By defining them as "outsiders," the Baining simultaneously define themselves as "insiders," and in so doing become a collectivity. The power latent in the masks is essentially the power to make the Baining into a unified social group. The social processes achieved in this ritual go beyond the production of social actors to the production of society. The power of this process is displaced upon the masks as potent beings, but is really produced in the whole dance event. Although both the masks themselves and the collective integration of the performance are produced by human action, consciousness of this social power is fetishized as the power of the masks. By performing collectively on the day of the dance the Baining appropriate the masks' power to themselves as a community.

Instead of being isolated objects, the masks are now brought into relation with collective social groups of men and women. This relation of collective confrontation continues as the essence of the "dance" phase as a whole. Throughout the entire day of the dance, the women hold forth on the dance plaza, both as chorus and as dancers. A group of women sits on the edge of the plaza and sings from before dawn until dusk. Another group of women, many carrying children on their shoulders, dance monotonously around in a circle all day. Periodically this scene is interrupted by lines or groups of male dancers who enter wearing or carrying the regalia. They costume themselves in the bush on the edge of the village. In these regalia, they then leave the bush and enter the plaza. Here they join the dance for a while, strutting their "individuality." After a short time the dancers return to the edge of the village, dump the masks and other ritual regalia, and return as male dancers to the plaza, where they join the collective group. The dancers with their entrances and exits seem analogous to individuals who are born, mature, and die, while the chorus and the circle of dancers can be seen as society itself, continually accepting and losing individuals but persisting nonetheless.

Despite, or perhaps because of, all the work and preparation that have gone into the event, the dance itself appears anticlimactic to the observer. The months of preparation are traded for minutes of display. All of the elaborately created masks and pieces are brought into the central plaza, danced around for a couple of minutes (usually not even five), and then discarded on the periphery of the clearing, to be salvaged for materials by any who want them and otherwise left to rot. This is, in fact, their final and essential task, which completes the homologue of the social life cycle. Having performed their metasocial function of playful "work," they must now go through the third phase of their own life cycle, in which they lose their powers and return to the bush from whence they came, through the entropic transformations of symbolic death and decomposition. This entropic transformation, then, constitutes the third and final phase of the dance as a total performance.

We now see that the dance cycle parallels the life cycle. I want to take this one step further and show how the dance cycle parallels the socialization cycle. In the life cycle, the achievement of the role of socializer represents the apex of the life cycle; in dance, the "play" phase is the apex of the ritual. Just as the socializer is the creator of a social person, the ritual participants constitute society itself as a collective domain of meaning. The creation of society is socialization in its most encompassing sense. Play and work ultimately merge in a performative drama of social reproduction.

9

Ta Takmut Banas:
The *Asarai* Dance

When dance preparations start, the atmosphere in a Baining community subtly changes. The normal emphasis on subsistence activities and household cooperation shifts towards bush preparations, interhousehold activity, and a more marked division of labor. Accompanying these changes in orientations is a change in mood. People are caught up in their own activity, and it spills over into their interactions with others. There is an increase in excitement with an air of barely concealed secrecy. Although the men's work is supposed to be a secret from the women, there is no way that this can be sustained; in fact, the men do not actually expect secrecy. They foster, rather, a sense of exclusion, which promotes an increase in the differentiation between the activities of each sex. Although work in the bush is metaphorically alluded to as work in the "garden" *(asleng)*, it is analogous to garden labor only in certain respects. It is no secret that a man's contributions to household maintenance drop to virtually nothing, and that the sexes now go separate ways each morning. If these clues are not enough, the women are asked to carry thatch to roof the hut in the bush site, then they are told to begin song rehearsals in the place. As each new type of paraphernalia is begun in the bush, the men return and tell their wives to begin the songs associated with that piece. Thus, women not only know that the ritual work is in progress, they have a fairly accurate idea of the stages of progression. As a result, the intensity and excitement of the activities pervade the whole community.

Work in the Bush

Asarai is not a unified "play." It is a composite of a series of different acts. Each act has a separate type of paraphernalia and adornment. There are at least eight different kinds of regalia, or more if the variations within categories are counted as types in their own right.[1] The work that goes on in the bush site itself is extremely varied.

1. Not all of these are performed at every occasion; in fact, some of these acts are seen as regional specializations of one group or another, and are only done if that community is involved. Others are included as time and materials permit.

Akip

The preparations in Yalom began with the construction of part of the *akip*—these are wood and feather poles worn in a harness sewn into the flesh of the dancer's back. *Akip* means spear. The whole day dance is sometimes called *Akip* after these pieces. The spears consist of four separate components. The first is the base into which the long spear is fitted. This base, called *akusak* (pl.) (*akusakaigi* [sing.]), is cone-shaped. The cone is itself carried in a cradle or harness, which fits between the legs of the dancers and is called *akavalka* (testicle). Decorating this cradle front and back are two rosettes made of cassowary feathers. These rosettes are called *anis* (literally, "bird's tail" or "grass skirt"), *aravat*, or *amunirang*. The last part is the shaft itself, which is a long, thin, and flexible pole, ten to fifteen feet or longer. The very tip of this spear is frequently a separate piece of wood lashed onto the first, and it is called *avilanga* (tail). Some spears have an inset that looks like a shield of bark cloth; this special feature is called *akavuganan*, and it often gives its name to the whole apparatus that contains it.

The main work on the cone bases is the painstaking application of thousands of tiny feathers. These feathers are lashed to the cone by wrapping a thin vine or strip of bark over the lower half of the feather; the rope is then masked by the top of the next row of feathers, and so on, all the way down the cone. Commonly feathers of one color are applied in rings one to two inches wide. The end result is a cone of rings of alternating colors. Red, yellow, maroon, green, blue, black, and white are the most common colors. It is strikingly beautiful. The fact that the Baining too see this object as beautiful is evidenced by their desire to display it as much as possible. On fine days the men in the bush unwrap the completed *akusak* and array them in the sun around the work site; they call this the "line," analogous to the dance line on the day of performance. The color and beauty of the displays of these and other paraphernalia around the bush site contrasts markedly with the drab and colorless appearance of Baining villages and houses. It is undoubtedly a strong element in the altered mood of these ritual preparations.

Although the work on these *akusak* is painstaking, it is not particularly difficult or complicated; anybody watching for half a day could pick up the knowledge necessary to do it, as I did myself. Nevertheless, several of the men confided to me that they did not know how to make *akusak* and that if they were to try they would probably turn out naked (meaning that all the feathers would fall off).

After the *akusak* cones are completed, work begins on the long shafts, called *akaseul* (also the name for a variety of small parrot). These are

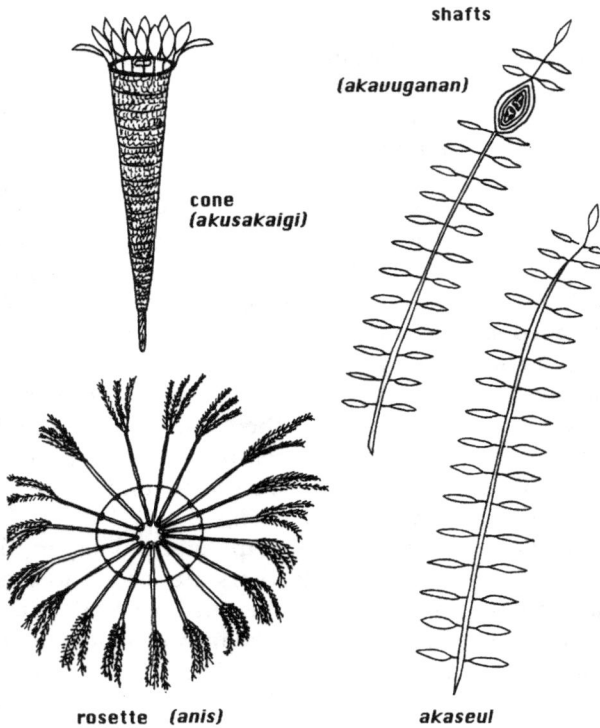

Figure 9.1   *Akip*

basically very long, thin saplings of a number of tree types. Their length and slenderness give the pole a great springiness, which is the desired quality. It is considered beautiful for the spear to bounce and sway as the dancer moves. These long shafts are decorated with large feathers (mostly wing-tip or tail feathers), which are affixed in matched pairs on either side of the pole about every six inches.[2]

Each *akip* dancer wears two cassowary feather rosettes, differentiated primarily in that the one in the rear is larger than the one in the front.

2. The spears described above are the commonest and also the simplest type. As mentioned in the text, some poles carry an additional feature built into the middle of their length, the small oval or kite-shaped frame covered with painted bark cloth called *akavuganan*. Occasionally a more complex variant is constructed. Instead of just a single tall pole, a pole flanked by lateral supports is made. This is generally constructed by lashing several cross-pieces to the main pole, and then rigging ropes or vines down these horizontal supports. They are subsequently decorated with feathers.

The rosettes are made by fastening cassowary feathers to each end of a thin piece of wood. Later, these sticks, with feathers at either end, are folded in half and attached to a ring about two inches in diameter. The sticks and feathers can be splayed out to form the rosette, or folded inward, like an umbrella, for storage.

The final part of the *akip* dancer's paraphernalia is a U-shaped cradle, which is held between the legs and into which the base and lance are fitted. This piece is made of a light wood frame covered with unpainted bark cloth. It usually has a prong extending from the frame in front and in back, over which the *anis* rosettes are fitted. The tip of this prong in front is usually further decorated with an object impaled on the prong; this object can be anything, but it is often a bird's head (a male hornbill or parrot's head), or sometimes a cucumber or banana flower (see fig. 9.8).

This cradle is sometimes called *akavalka* (testicle). The appellation may stem from its position between the dancer's legs, or from the fact that before the dancers took to wearing shorts as part of their costume, it served to contain their genitals. The name might also symbolically refer to the fact that the cradle is at the base of the long penis-like spear. Informants would not say or speculate on why the object had this name; nevertheless, discussion around this work site became significantly bawdier, as jokes using the term abounded (e.g., "Inangaiyi's balls are bigger than Kwanukndum's").

The frame of this cradle is made out of a light, flexible wood. Over the frame are lain large leaves to pad the frame, and bark cloth is sewn over this padding. The prongs, front and back, pierce through the bark cloth and remain as bare wood. The front prong is usually grasped in the dancer's hand as he tries to counterbalance the weight of the base and spear behind.

In addition to all this paraphernalia, the spear dancer also wears ankle rattles, *anis* or grass skirts on his neck or arms, and a hat or scarf on his head. These decorations will be described in detail later. The dancer's body is painted with black paint, the preparation of which is part of the bush preparations. The paint is made by burning the wood of certain trees until it is ash. The ashes are stored until the day of the dance, when they are mixed with water to constitute a dark black paint called *awalsaing*.

Aramariki

Although I began my description with the *akip* because that was the way preparations began in Yalom, Pool (1971: 73) suggests that the

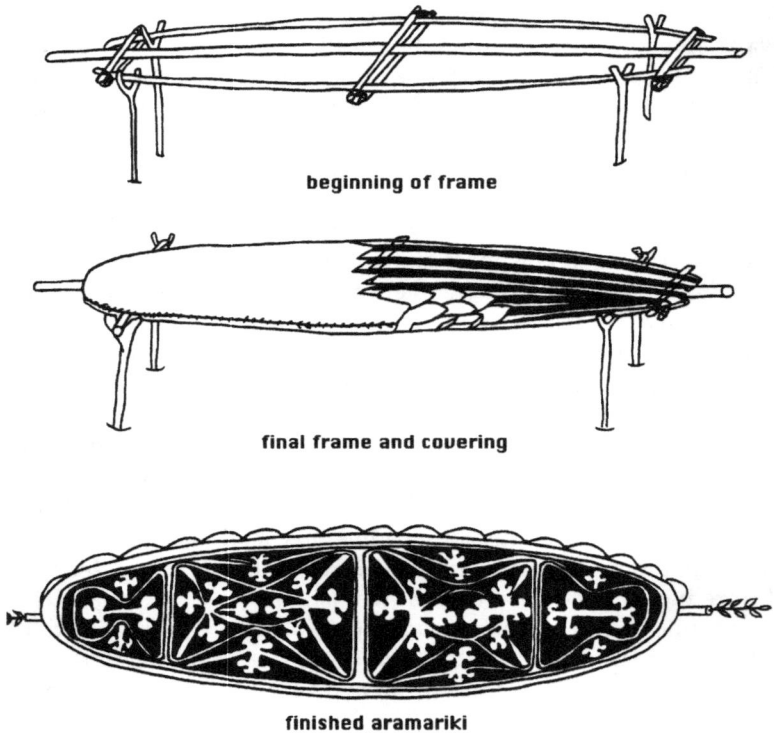

beginning of frame

final frame and covering

finished aramariki

Figure 9.2   *Aramariki*

large masks, *aramariki* or *aisingaigi,* should be the first constructed. This
order of construction would parallel the order in which the masks appear on the dance ground.

The *aramariki* is a very long and relatively flat object, somewhat resembling a shield held sideways (see fig. 9.2). The one in Yalom was
about eleven or twelve feet long. The frame was made out of bamboo
and flexible wood. Long, thin bamboos were laid across forked sticks.
The bamboo poles were joined by shorter sticks laid in pairs perpendic-
ularly between these poles and lashed to them. The longest of these
pairs of sticks were bound to the middle of the rods; they got progressively shorter towards the ends, so the two rods curved to meet at their

extremities to form a shield shape. The basic frame was then covered by long strips of split bamboo. This constituted the basic skeleton. Over this was placed a layer of leaves. Finally, the whole thing was covered with bark cloth.

Bark cloth is gathered from any one of a number of species of trees. The most preferred type, because it is the whitest, is found in the lower altitudes near the coast. The bark cloth is extracted from the tree by pounding it loose from the underlying wood. It can then be slipped off like a sock or legging. Once off the wood, the cloth may be further beaten.[3] After the bark cloth has been pounded, it is washed in the stream and stretched out to dry. When the time comes to use the cloth, it is wet once again so it will conform to the contours of the frame. The cloth is cut to make a tight fit for the frame and then it is sewn into place. Although the Baining now use metal needles, they still use vines and strips of bark as thread (see fig. 9.2).

After the *aramariki* had been dried and bleached, Sugunaigi decided to paint it. This required making the paint. To do this, Sugunaigi took down a small leaf bundle that had been hanging from the rafters of the *akusak*. This bundle contained the sap of a particular tree, which had been previously tapped. The sap was now a congealed rubbery mass. The men cut off pieces of this lump and wrapped them in bits of bark cloth, which they then chewed. After thoroughly masticating the wad, they spat out their saliva mixed with dye into a cup made from a length of bamboo. Informants said that the dye only adhered to the bark cloth if it was mixed with saliva rather than water. Thus they chew it despite its sharp and bitter taste. Once the paint had been mixed, Sugunaigi blocked out the design using pieces of wood as markers. He then began drawing the outline of his design, using a long thin piece of wood as a stylus; this he dipped into the paint and then laid it across the bark cloth.

The predominant Baining design (*awuringdang*), is composed of two elements, which are variously arranged: the first consists of sets of parallel lines (usually four), which are called *asis;* the second is a trefoil pattern, which fills the areas outlined by the *asis.* This design is called *avutik* (see fig. 9.3). *Avutik* is the name of a plant found in the forest; the design is said to resemble its leaf, but there is no other association of this plant with the pictures drawn. On the *aramariki* the *asis* or paral-

3. Traditionally the beating implement was a fossilized scallop shell hammer. The Baining area is a region of limestone in which fossil shells are occasionally found. These rocks, for such they are, made good hammers since the ridges on the shells helped to raise the bark. The shell is hafted onto a stick with some sort of resin (from descriptions it may also have been beeswax).

Figure 9.3 *Avutik*

lel lines were painted in a series of zigzags across the length of the shield, enclosing hourglass-like shapes. These shapes were later filled in with *avutik*.

Although Pool (1971: 86) says that the painting of red lines on the big masks was the last work executed in the bush site (on the very last morning) so that the construction of the big masks initiated and ended the preparations, this was not the case when I participated. On this first day of painting, in the middle of the bush period, Sugunaigi applied the red paint. He used it to outline the black lines he had already drawn, and applied it in a very thin line. Possibly in the days before store-bought red paint was used, they saved the red paint job for last because both the red dye *alasaka* and human blood that were used for the job fade very rapidly. With the advent of store paint, however, the Yalom Baining no longer had to delay this task.

After all the outlines had been finished, it was time to start the *avutik*. At this stage the painting became a communal project as several men joined in. Each man was allocated an interior space, which he proceeded to fill. Although all of the designs are called *avutik* and are basically similar, there is some individual variation in execution. Pool said that the composite work of painting by different men produced a piece with a multiplicity of patterns; "the overall effect is one of patchwork" (1971: 75). I have never seen a North Baining piece that looked so varied. In my experience, the pieces look remarkably uniform in composition, and are very striking in form, color, and execution.

The painting of *avutik* takes some skill and concentration, since one is essentially composing a negative design. What shows as the pattern upon completion is the unpainted portion. The application of black is merely background for the foregrounded figures formed by white (unpainted) areas of cloth. The black paint is applied to the cloth by means of an asparagus-like stalk (this stalk is also eaten as a vegetable), which has a round bottom. This base is dipped into the paint and used as a stipple brush to cover the area with overlapping dots. There is an effort to cover the cloth as neatly and uniformly as possible given the irregularities of its surface.

Although I asked about the meaning of the designs and the symbolism of the colors, the answers were mostly vague. Many but by no means all of the designs have names—*angalipki* (galip nut tree); *avrang* (grub); *alaskuka* (tree); *anguangi* (owl); *anatdiknuk* (taro bulb); *akutikput* (to draw or write)—but they are not particularly representative of these things. These designs are remembered by a few men and occasionally executed. The rest of the designs, probably the majority, are the inventions of their executors, combining on the spot the basic elements of *asis* and *avutik*. Hesse and Aerts say that all the designs are mythically stored; "there is, for instance, a stone called Ngaringpemki, near Raunsepna village, which is said to carry all the patterns used on the masks. The culture hero Sirini, who dwells in this stone, is the author of the masks one can observe" (1978: 17). None of my informants had any idea of this sort.

When I asked about the use of particular colors, I got no response; nobody gave me any reason for red vs. yellow, black vs. brown, etc. When I explicitly asked if the red could be symbolic of blood, Kusak looked at me with surprise and answered, "Yes, blood here." A few minutes later, after more attempts at questioning him, he said, "It would be bad for the women to hear us." Although I got no more explicit statement than these two about blood or women, I feel that although he did not himself produce the association with blood, it was implicitly there, and that it was also implicitly an association with menstrual blood. When I asked, all I got in response were raised eyebrows. Corbin (1976: 43) says both the red and black pigment are referred to as blood and that "the red lines represent the blood flowing through the display piece." As far as I know, neither pigment is referred to as blood, and in fact the only corporeal referent I ever heard for black paint was when it was spoken of as the "feces of the *aranigi* tree." I can only conclude that color symbolism is less important for the Baining than it is for the Ndembu (V. Turner 1967).

Aisingaigi

Aisingaigi is a very large object which like the *aramariki* often opens the day dance. It is also carried into the dance plaza by a large number of

men, far more than are needed to support its weight. That its entrance
assumes the form of a collective effort is clearly an integral part of its
role in the ritual. Both *aisingaigi* and *aramariki* are supposed to sweep
clean the dance ground *(ki suwup ama aluwupki)* by their circuit of the
arena. This cleaning is metaphorical; my informants, however, could
not specify what was in fact swept away. We speculated together that
it might be *aios,* based on my analogy with what happens in Lan at
the beginning of *Amambua.* My informants did not deny this interpretation, but the specific suggestion was my own. Hesse and Aerts (1978:
25) just say it chases away all the "evil influences."

Aisingaigi is the name for either python or eel. "Python" is almost
always given as the translation for this ritual object, but I add eel because the word is the same and I believe the play on this second meaning is significant for its interpretation. The object given this name, however, bears little resemblance to either of these creatures, except
possibly in the most abstract way. Pool says "the masks which have
been referred to as *aising* [plural] are also considered to be eels, rather
than pythons, and go by another name meaning eel" (1969–70). I received only the translation of python and Hesse and Aerts, Pool, and
Corbin all refer in their written accounts to the *aisingaigi* as "python."
Nevertheless, when I asked informants whether it could really refer to
an eel, being suddenly inspired to associate eels and foam (see below,
angwarumgi [fig. 9.6]) they got excited and said "Yes," they thought
so.[4]

The reason the *aisingaigi* looks so little like an eel or python is that
it is not long and thin (see fig. 9.4). Rather it is composed of a large
and bulbous head about eight to ten feet long and three to four feet
high, which has a large mouth in front, pierced eyes, and a tail, which
ranges in size from about two feet to twelve feet long. This tail juts out
directly behind the head.[5] This creature is constructed out of a light
wood frame, a leaf covering, bark cloth, and paint.

Aisingaigi, in contrast to *aramariki,* never enters the dance ground
alone. It is always accompanied by at least one *anaruga* (pole mask)
and often by two or three. Yet another piece, *angwarumgi,* invariably
appears together with it and is only found in this context (see fig. 9.6).
Angwarumgi has several referents. The first is to an insect that has a
long plumelike appendage sticking out of its rear end (Pool 1971: 80)
and whose other characteristic is that it sits in trees and produces little
drops of spittle, which rain down on those who pass beneath. Its spittle

4. I am heartened by the discovery in Pool's field notes that he was actually told of
this double meaning.
5. The shape of this creature is almost identical, except for the mouth and size, to that
of a cucumber as depicted in the pole mask design.

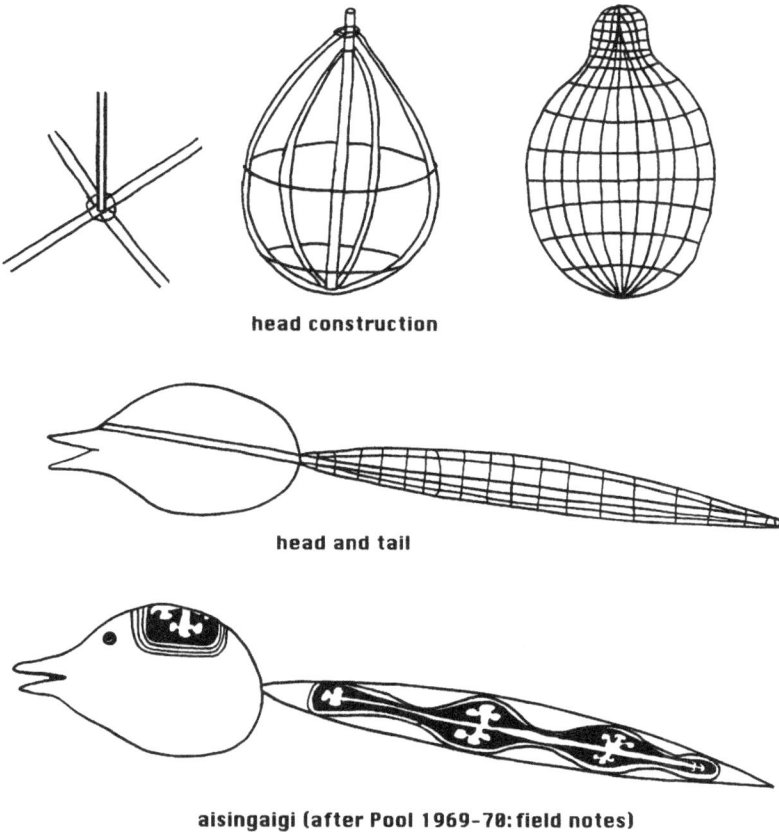

head construction

head and tail

aisingaigi (after Pool 1969-70: field notes)

Figure 9.4   *Aisingaigi*

is said to be used by *aios* to make rain. However, informants denied that this mask might be some sort of magic to prevent rain. A second, related, meaning of the word *angwarumgi* refers to foam or spume on water. The Baining say that *angwarumgi* appears when the rivers are flooded, and that this foam is the food eaten by freshwater eels. This association between *angwarumgi* and *aisingaigi,* foam and eels, parallels the convergence of these two masks on the dance ground during the opening act. When I suggested this idea to Kusak he got very excited and said "Yes, yes," as if he had had an insight, but even his recognition of such an association did not lead him to make any additional interpretations, nor was any other informant able to articulate this further.

The *angwarumgi* piece is made of a wood frame and bark cloth, in the same manner as the *anaru* described below. It is carried atop a long (fifteen to twenty foot) bamboo pole, which is steadied by two long ropes attached at the top and held taut in each of the dancer's hands. The shape of the piece resembles a canoe with a cone inside, about three feet in length and one foot high. The outside hull of the piece and the cone are both painted with *asis* and *avutik*.

Akurikuruk

One day while we were at work in the bush, Kusak looked around at all the paraphernalia prepared to that point and remarked that there were "three plays" represented there: *Akip, Aramariki,* and *Akurikuruk.* This comment points up the vaudevillian character of Baining dances, which develop from a process of accretion of many different ones.

The newest of these adoptions, *Akurikuruk,* is now an accepted part of the festivities and one which arouses a good deal of attention and admiration, the latter because those who have been appointed to dance with the masks must undergo a strenuous fast. They are expected to fast (or rather to eat only a few mouthfuls of food) from the time they are nominated to wear the mask until after the dance. The dancers should have "stomachs that go inside," that is, are hollow, from weight loss. The dance step emphasizes this characteristic by having the dancers suck in their stomachs as they move. The display of this hollow stomach is proof that the dancer has kept to his fast.

The *akurikuruk* masks are the most spectacular constructions made for this dance (see fig. 9.5). They are basically composed of two sections: a lower head and face, which resembles the *atut* or *anguangi* masks of the night dance (see chapter 10), and a long cone, which protrudes from this head at about a 45-degree angle from the vertical. From the top of this cone, two ropes are hung, which are held in the dancer's hands and help to balance the mask.

The face helmet is constructed first. It is built around two wicker-work circles (see fig. 9.5). These circles form the basic helmet; from this core, the mask is created. It usually consists of a snout projecting from the front of the helmet and a superstructure of eyes and ears rising from it. The mouths of these creatures protrude from the face, and the lips are curved and open. The eyes and ears section, also made of light wood, is often an exaggerated heart shape, with an eye located in each lobe. The eyes are created by a method resembling an embroidery hoop, the same way as those of the *anguangi* (described in chapter 10).

The cone, which extends to the rear of this mask, is built out of bam-

stages of head construction

cone construction

cloth covering

finished akurikuruk

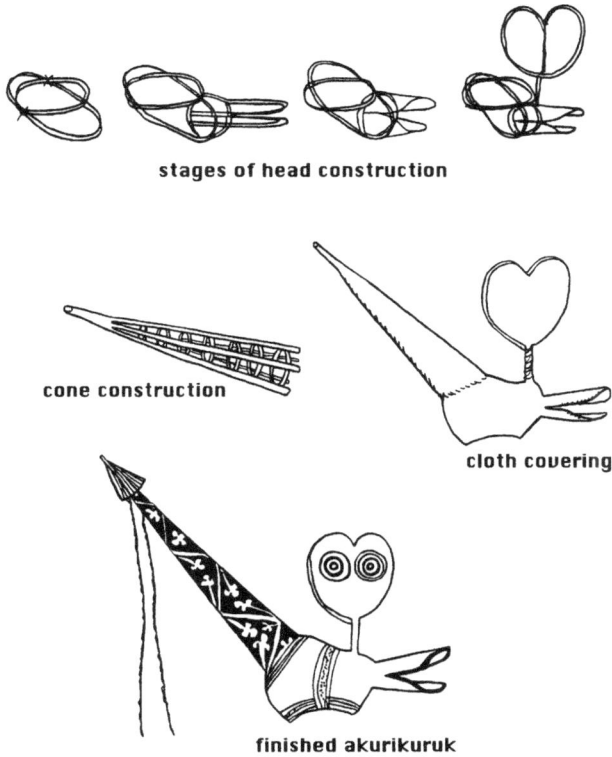

Figure 9.5   *Akurikuruk*

boo and light wood. A long bamboo is split in quarters almost to its end. These quarters are then forced apart by inserting circles of wood every five or six inches. The circles, of course, get steadily larger as one descends. The whole cone is then lashed to the crown of the helmet. Once the frame has been completed, it is covered with leaves over which the bark cloth is carefully and tightly fitted and sewn on; even the inside of the mouth is covered.

The masks are then painted. By far the greatest area of decoration is the cone. This is completely covered with the *asis* and *avutik* motifs. Parts of the head are also painted; the eyes are always painted in concentric circles, and the ears, snout, and lips may also be decorated. There is a generous use of red paint on these pieces, and a general feeling that they should be as dramatic and beautiful as possible. On the top of the cone, where the bamboo rod emerges, two long ropes

Plate 9.1   *Akurikuruk* in preparation

or vines are affixed. This peak is then hidden under a conical hat or cap made either of bark cloth or of cordyline leaves sewn together.

The *akurikuruk* dancers wear very little besides these masks. Their only clothing is a penis-covering and a flap or tail in the rear. This covering used to be sewn or tied onto the dancer's pubic hairs, but nowadays it may be tied around the hips with a thong. The most striking thing about the dancers' bodies, however, is the way they are painted. They are decorated with two colors of paint or clay, a reddish brown and a white. These two colors alternate in a curvilinear design, which highlights the dancer's movements.

Anaru

The pole "masks" are not really masks at all. They are three-dimensional constructions, which are worn atop a long bamboo pole, fifteen to twenty feet long, the base of which has been split and flared to make a conical structure. This cone is worn on the head of the dancer. The whole structure is tenuously balanced by two ropes, which extend from the top of the pole to the dancer's hands. Outwardly these pieces seem the most playful and the simplest of all the "masks." They are made in the images of common Baining flora and fauna, and their performance demands none of the rigors of fasting or piercing of flesh that many of the other dances do. Despite this simplicity, there is an aura of potency and taboo around their construction, which was nonetheless powerful for being left inexplicit. There are two main classes of pole "mask": *avuganan*, and pole "masks" of flora and fauna referred to above (see fig. 9.6).

The *avuganan* accompany the *akip* dancers. These pieces resemble the *aramariki* in that they are small shields (see fig. 9.6). They are built to "fly" horizontally, with the flat painted surface facing downwards. They have, thus, not a smooth, uninterrupted painted surface, but one that is pierced by a hole in which a bamboo cylinder is inserted. Into this "shaft" the long bamboo pole is fitted, and the *avuganan* is said to "fly."

On the day that construction of the *avuganan* began in Yalom, nobody passed by my house to accompany me to the bush, nor did I see others heading that way. It did not occur to me that this was intentional. I saw it as an accident and consequently I betook myself to the bush site. The men there were quite surprised at my arrival, having been under the impression that I had been forbidden to come. I had no inkling this injunction had been issued, the implicit suggestion having obviously gone over my head. I was surprised by this attitude, but took it as another attempt to discourage my participation. It was only later that I realized their unease on that morning was due to the construction of the *avuganan* in particular, and not my presence in general. After intuiting this motive for their reaction, I then tried to find out why this piece was different from the others.

I failed in this endeavor. Although there was a definite air of mystery around this particular project, it seemed more like a mood than a specific secret. For example, when I asked the name of the piece that they were working on, Kariangi immediately told me *"avuganan."* Kusak, who was working alongside, told him to be quiet. While one might interpret this as an expression of a desire to keep the name a secret,

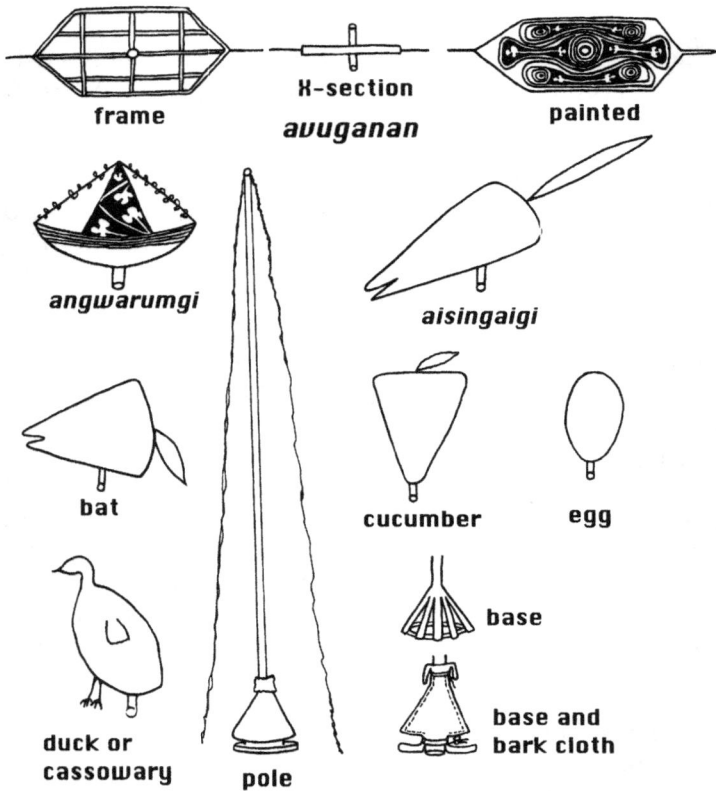

Figure 9.6   Pole masks

somehow it appeared to me more like a more diffuse caution against irreverence. This piece was treated with more respect than the others, and calling its name seemed to be asking for trouble; thus, Kusak referred to it as *asaraigi*, which is the singular term for the whole dance event, *Asarai*. Anything within the dance event could be called *asaraigi*, but it is possible that the use of the term for this piece somehow indicated it could be symbolic of the whole. Kusak mentioned that the ancestors had called this piece *aioskakumgi* (ghost/bush spirit), but again it was not clear if this term referred to just this piece or to any piece. This name lumped as one word both of the potent supernatural entities the Baining recognize, so I tried to elicit a connection. I asked what kind of connection these spirits had to this piece: if, for example, they lived in it or danced with it. Although some of the men vaguely

shrugged affirmatively, they said that *aioskakumgi* had the same association with all the bush paraphernalia, which is why they put *arsong*
knots on everything. People reiterated that these things were taboo and
dangerous to women, but they confessed they had no idea what would
happen if women saw them. In short, I could not elicit in what way,
or how, the danger and potency were manifested, or whether this piece
differed from other ones in the bush. Hesse and Aerts also refer to the
potency of these pieces.

> One builds his mask in the name of his place of the dead
> *(arimbab)*; this relationship gives the mask its own proper
> name. During the construction of this mask, it is left at night
> under the custody of the spirits by performing the *arsonga*
> rite. Finally before leaving the forest a special rite is per-
> formed with ginger or chalk powder in order that the pow-
> ers connected with the mask might not harm any of those
> attending the festival. (1978: 39–40)

None of these characteristics definitely differentiates this type of
piece from the others constructed in the bush. Although my informants
did not specify that the masks were named after places of the dead
(arimbab), they did impute special significance to the name of this piece.
The reference to *aioskakumgi* might be seen as a variant of this practice.
The practice of saying magic over the pieces before bringing them out
of the forest is also done for the *aramariki* and *aisingaigi*, which are also
believed to have especially strong powers (Pool 1971: 95). In short,
there was nothing about the *avuganan* (except possibly naming it after
one's place of the dead, which was not practiced in Yalom) that really
differentiated it from the other pieces; nonetheless, it seemed to be a
focus for the fear of danger and overall anxiety associated with the
preparations.

The other kind of pole mask, *anaru*, is made in a variety of shapes.
Aisingaigi, a snake or eel form, is identical in shape but smaller than
the big mask of the same name. *Avunarupka* is a small bat; the mask
has a shape like an early space capsule, conical with curved edges. It
is also about three feet long, and it can be affixed to its pole either
horizontally or vertically; it might also have a tail that projects at an
angle from its point. *Aunsimgi* is a cassowary; it has an egg-shaped
body with a head (the head may optionally have a beak), and two legs
coming out the bottom. The *apatagi*, which is a duck, is similar to the
cassowary but squatter, the egg shape running horizontally and not
vertically; it has shorter legs. The *alauruska* is a cucumber, although it
can also denote a sea urchin. It looks just like a snake *(aisingaigi)* but
without the mouth. Finally, the *aluaka* is an egg—specifically a casso-

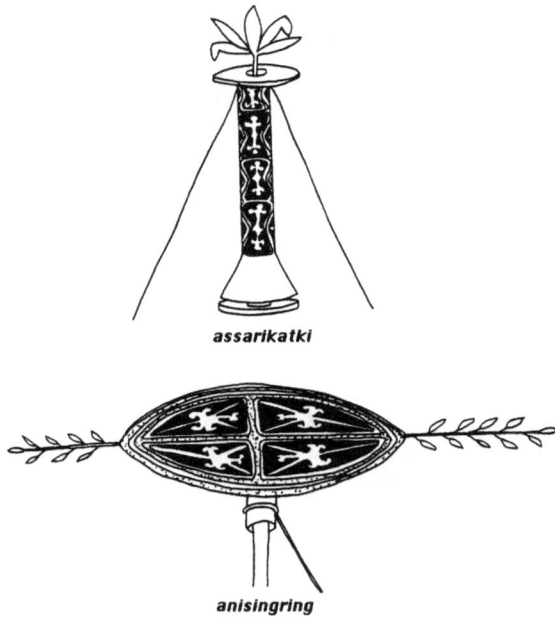

assarikatki

anisingring

Figure 9.7   *Assarikatiki*

wary egg. This mask looks very much like a balloon. It is carried on a much shorter pole than the others (six to ten feet) by a child or youth. Every dance will display at least one of each kind of mask, since there are special songs that refer to the different forms, and if one style is absent, that song can not be sung.

Assarikatki

This is a type of headdress, which appears to be made only by Komgi and Yalom villages, and appears in dance events only if people from these communities are participating. *Assarikat* (pl.) are of a very simple construction (see fig. 9.7). The basic structure is a length (about five or six feet) of a broad type of bamboo. The bottom of this bamboo is flared outward to make a headpiece similar to those at the base of the pole masks. At the top of the bamboo a brim is constructed of double circles of wood and bark cloth. The long cylinder of the bamboo is then padded with leaves and the whole thing is covered with bark cloth. The effect is somewhat similar to a long spool or bobbin, except that the bottom brim is conical and not flat. The *assarikat* headdresses are balanced on the head by means of two ropes hanging from the top of the headdress, as are the pole masks and *akurikuruk*. The bark cloth on this headdress is then covered with typical Baining designs of *asis* and *avutik*, although one headdress was covered with a very different pattern, a checkered pattern in which each square was divided diagonally and half of it was painted black. This design was called *angalipki* (galip nut tree). Sticking out of the top of this piece is either a long stick decorated with cockatoo feathers or a branch or sprig of cordyline leaves. The *assarikatki* adorned with cordyline is called *alangungi*. Special songs refer to seeing the *alangungi* amidst a line of *assarikat* dancers and for that reason at least one *alangungi* is always constructed.

Anisingring

These constructions are frequently referred to as the women's pieces although they are neither made exclusively, or carried, by women; nonetheless, they are associated with women, especially the *anepkusakta* (who are the "female men," the women who accompany the men at the mask construction site). They were not made in Yalom because, so the explanation went, there were no *anepkusakta*. I saw them performed but not made in Raunsepna. From informants' accounts, and written descriptions (Pool 1971: 76–83; Corbin 1976; Hesse and Aerts 1978: 36), their composition is very like that of a smaller version of the *aramariki*, similar to the *avuganan*, except that their flat surface is oriented vertically and not horizontally (see fig. 9.7). The plane of the shield is painted on at least one side and sometimes on both. It is decorated with feathered sticks at each horizontal end. These shields are held aloft by means of a pole passed through the plane of the shield. These poles are not quite as tall as those used for the pole masks and are not balanced on the head. A man holds the pole upright in his hands, while a woman, an *anepkusaki*, holds onto a rope attached to the top. According to Hesse and Aerts "the reason why women do not carry the poles themselves is, according to the Bainings, that they are not strong enough to do so" (1978: 36); since the weight is minimal, and traditionally Baining women carry enormous loads, I do not believe this is the reason. The *anisingring* pieces never appear alone on the dance ground, but accompany other masks, frequently *akip* and *akurikuruk*, and less frequently *aramariki* and *aisingaigi*.

The name of this piece of paraphernalia, *anisingring*, has the word *anis* (tail) as its root. Pool says the suffix *-ingring* means flat object (1971: 78), although I think it means the several sections that make up a whole, like the segments of an orange making up the whole. The singular ending *-ingel* often refers to a part of a thing. In addition to the root *anis* in the name, there are several other *anis* associated with the appearance of this piece. The women who hold the ropes wear two kinds of *anis:* the first is the ordinary *anis,* which makes up part of the woman's grass skirt, although here somewhat more decorated than normally (this skirt will be described shortly); the second is a piece of oval bark cloth, painted with *asis* and *avutik* designs, which is worn on top of the grass *anis* and flutters in the breeze like a kite tail. The recurring motif of the *anis* will be elaborated as we proceed through the discussion of this dance.

Preparations in the Village

While all these preparations are happening in the bush, there are also preparations going on in the villages. Most of these activities are performed by women, although the men participate increasingly as the day of the dance approaches. The women's involvement takes two forms. First they begin rehearsing the songs that are sung at the day dances. These rehearsals grow in intensity until the last one, which is almost a dress rehearsal in scale and participation, although not in the literal meaning of dress or costume. The second activity is preparing grass skirts or *anis* for the dance costumes.

   The fact that preparations are happening in the bush is, as we have seen, no secret. Although the women are excluded, they are in fact cognizant of the progress of the preparations. In Yalom, the women knew the preparations had started when Inangaiyi, who was presiding over them, came home and told his wife Uras to begin song sessions. Uras had never led song sessions before, so she asked two older women (both classificatory mothers to her), Pelas and Suvanan, to assist her.

Song Rehearsals

The song rehearsals begin relatively casually. The women gather shortly after sundown and sing through the night. At first it is mostly adolescent girls who attend these sessions, with a few older women from whom they say they are learning the songs, but as the weeks go by, more and more women join in, and the median age rises considerably. The young girls who formed such a significant force in the beginning are now relegated to the periphery and sometimes stop participating altogether, saying that they have not yet mastered the songs. These events are not just rehearsals in our sense, as the work in the bush is not merely preparation in the eyes of the men; both activities are ends in themselves. Because of the value attributed to these activities, the ritual can be said to have begun with these preparations. As time goes on, the intensity of people's involvement in the activities increases.

Plate 9.2   Song rehearsal

The first song rehearsals center around what might be called the general *Asarai* songs. These are the songs that are sung in between events on the day of the dance. These songs are often of recent composition and may refer to events and people in the community. Songs of this type may be composed by both men and women, although those in my sample are predominantly by men. Songs are learned through being sung; there is no other educative method. Originally the composer of the song attends one of the rehearsals and teaches the others the song, but several of the women in the composer's household may have learned the song in advance and help with the instruction. There is no rule against men accompanying the women, and in Raunsepna and Wiliambempki they routinely do. On several informal occasions in Yalom they joined in, showing both knowledge of the song repertoire and an enjoyment of the process. In Yalom, however, no men consistently sang with the women during rehearsals, and the chorus on the day of the dance was exclusively female.

As the work in the bush proceeds, the ritual leader comes back and informs his wife (or sister, etc.) of the men's progress by saying "now sing of the *akip* [or *akavuganan,* or *akurikuruk,* etc.]." This indicates the projects being undertaken in the bush, since each type of song can only

be sung after its subject's construction has begun. The men think of
the women and their songs as they work in the bush, and thus they
construct *akavuganan* and *alangungi* for the women to sing about. Songs
that accompany these marked pieces are generally of less recent composition, although they are not "traditional" in the sense of being
passed down from immemorial ancestral generations. The composers
of most of them could still be named, although many of them are now
dead. By the end of the months of preparations, there is a full mix of
general and specific songs in each rehearsal session. Each rehearsal also
recapitulates the dance sequence through the order in which the songs
are sung.

The same musical instrument is used by men and women. It is a
long bamboo tube, which is rhythmically pounded against a horizontal
log that serves as a striking board. In addition, the women have two
further accompaniments. The most important of these is the *anirka*,
which is a small slit drum. It is made of an enclosed section of wide
bamboo, about one and a half feet long and five or six inches in diameter, into which a slit has been cut. This drum is struck with a thin stick,
about the thickness of a pencil but a little bit longer. The mode of striking this instrument is unique and takes a lot of skill. The stick is encir-
cled loosely by the fingers of one hand, while it is joggled up and down
by the rapid maneuvering of the fingers of the other hand. This hand
holds the stick very loosely, somewhat in the manner of a pencil, between thumb and forefinger, while the other fingers run staccato taps
along the stick. The stick dances along the surface of the drum, making
a very rapid, staccato rhythm, which forms a variant melody against
the slower pounding of the long bamboos. There is generally only one
anirka being played in an orchestra, although women may take turns
playing it. The last instrument, which occasionally accompanies the
women's chorus, is an *asingi* (mouth harp). This is made of a section
of bamboo, part of which is slit, with a string extending from one end.
The slit end of the bamboo is placed across the mouth and the string
is pulled causing the bamboo to vibrate and echo in the mouth cavity.

The women's rehearsals are held in one of the village houses. As the
women sing inside, men, boys, and other women may dance around
the house. Although a few women dance regularly at every rehearsal,
more and more people join in as the day of the dance draws nigh.

Anis

The women's preparations include making grass skirts for the day
dance. These grass skirts, *anis,* have two uses. In the first place, they
form part of the costume or decoration of many of the male dancers.

These men are adorned with *anis* around their necks and arms (occasionally around the waist), which they wear on entering the dance ground, but which may be removed from them by any one present who wants a new grass skirt. In the second, they are used as attire for the women, who adorn themselves in new *anis* for the festivities. This latter use is becoming less important as fewer and fewer women wear the traditional female garb, but it is still true that many women return to the traditional attire for the dance.

The women's traditional clothing consists of three parts: (1) a cane "belt" (*aravakpum*); (2) a "grass" tail (*anis*), which covers part of the buttocks of the women; and (3) a small apron of ferns (*asil*), which hangs from the belt in front over the pubic region and is tucked between the thighs. Only the preparation of the *anis* is routinely done as a stage of the dance proceedings, but the whole manufacturing process will be discussed here since the preparation of the cane belt is often cited by informants as being women's work analogous to the men's work in the bush.

The belt consists of long thin strands of cane that have been dyed red. This cane is wrapped around the hips and buttocks of the woman. They wrap many strands of the cane around the body until it forms a thick mass, tying together the first and last piece. I did not see the preparation of the cane since it was not done while I was in the field, but I gathered accounts of the process. The cane is prepared in two steps. The first step comprises cutting the cane, heating it, and then splitting it into sections. The cane is then soaked overnight. When it is pliable, it is folded by coiling it and then tying a string around the middle of the coil so that it looks a little like the way lengths of ribbon are packaged. The cane is always carried and stored in this form. The second stage is that of dying the cane. The stages are often done consecutively, but need not be. The phase of dying is the part that is considered analogous to the men's work in the bush. The women, often in groups, go out into the forest where they pass one or several nights boiling the cane in the dye.

The women gather a certain type of berry that is found in the deep forest. They crush this berry and boil it in water. Once the dye is prepared, the cane is submerged in it and the dye is left to take. This is supposed to occur overnight, during which time the women sit and tend the fire in the forest (this is a situation in which several informants claimed to have had encounters with *aios*). After the cane is dyed, it is hung to dry and then recoiled. The women now return to the village. The cane thus prepared might be saved for a considerable time until it is used or needed; this procedure does not seem to be performed very often.

The second part of the *aniski* is the tail. This differs from that of the stereotypic grass skirt in that it covers only a small section of the anatomy and does not encircle the body. In fact it is only about five or six inches wide and relatively thick. It is made in two lengths, a relatively long layer (about twelve to fourteen inches) that hangs down against the body, covering an area about five inches in the middle of the buttocks, and a shorter layer that flaps over the belt and hangs on top of this longer layer like a bun. Pool (1971: 76) describes this bun as a pillow since "when a woman sits down she shoves this pillow underneath her legs, and she sits on it." Pool speculates (and I think he might be right) that

> the association between the grass skirt and a bird's tail is based on the image of a cassowary. A cassowary's long thin plumes hang down in back as a short tail which has a remarkable resemblance to a woman's grass skirt. This resemblance is most noticeable, though, when women are seen in one of their most common positions: bent over at the waist. (Pool 1971: 76)

This skirt is made from leaves. In the several weeks before a dance, these leaves are gathered in the forest and brought back to the village. They are shredded and then laid out to dry in the sun, often on the thatch roof of the house. For festive occasions two types of leaf may be used. The most common form dries to a straw color, while the special one, made of cane leaves, dries to a white color. These are used to set off the center of the *aniski*.

After the leaves are dry, the strands are fastened to a rope, so that they are only five to six inches long on one side, but ten to twelve inches on the other. When the *aniski* is worn over the cane belt, the long strands go underneath the belt against the skin, and the short strands hang over it.

The final part of the women's attire is the easiest to prepare. It consists of fern leaves, which hang down from the front of the belt over the pubic region and are tucked back between the legs. Common ferns found in many areas of both bush and forest are used. These fronds are not secured in any special way, just tucked in; they appear to the outsider as a rather scanty covering although they do cover the genitals. While watching Alangurik don an *aniski* the night before the dance (she had always worn a laplap in my presence before), I was amused to watch her put in some ferns; then, some minutes later, she added a few more; shortly after that, she added another bunch. She was obviously feeling self-conscious.

The night before the dance in Yalom, women in many households

Plate 9.3   Making *anis*

were lifting down baskets that had hung in the rafters for months, maybe years, and they were taking out bundles of *aravakpum* to make belts to hold their new *anis*. On the day of the dance, three times as many women were wearing *anis* as normally wore the traditional dress in the village. Many of these women continued to wear the *anis* for weeks, even months, after the dance until some event, like getting drenched in a storm, caused them to change back to their laplaps.

In addition to making the *anis* to adorn the male dancers, some women also sew necklaces of colored cordyline leaves, which are worn by the men carrying the *akavuganan* and *assarikatki* pieces. Neither these nor the *anis* have to be made by women in any particular relationship to the dancers, but they seem to be made by women of the same household. Women are also responsible for making the knee rattles worn by the men (Pool 1969–70).

Conjunction of Bush and Place

One or two days before the dance is to take place, the final rite is performed. By now the men have finished all the dance regalia and the women have completed the song rehearsals, culminating in the dress rehearsal, which has perhaps taken place the night before. This last rite is designed to end the segregation of tasks that has predominated until this point. To do this, the women penetrate the bush site and untie the *arsong* knots.

On the morning of the day this is to occur, the men hurry to the bush site to get it ready. For the most part, this means arranging all the spears, masks, shields, and pole constructions in a display around the *akusak* clearing. In Raunsepna and Wiliambempki it is enough that each piece of paraphernalia has a knot affixed to it; in Yalom these knots are augmented by bushes of cordyline plants stuck into the ground in front of each piece with every leaf on the plant knotted. The men then clean up the rubbish from the bush site and burn it. Finally, they cut large palm fronds, tree branches, and fern leaves, which they stack across the opening of the bush house.

Meanwhile, the women and children leave the village and go to bathe. After washing, they anoint themselves with lime powder on the temples, forehead, neck, elbows, wrists, stomach, knees, and toes. When the men are ready, they blow a trumpet of conch or bamboo. Then several of the men go out to meet the women and say a spell over them (identical to the one said over the water). Traditionally the women go first to the large heap of rubbish that the men built up on their departure from the bush site each evening. They first drink water from a filled bamboo next to the heap and spit this water over the debris and each other. Then they go to the water next to the other heap, the one built up as the men approached the bush site each morning. Here they drink and swallow a bit of the water and may sprinkle it on themselves (Pool 1971: 88). After this purification, the women, armed with bush knives, set about dismantling and destroying both heaps; each piece is chopped or broken, and everything is dispersed. "This is done with a great deal of boisterousness and enjoyment" (Pool 1971: 88).

After scattering the heaps, the women arrive on the periphery of the clearing. The majority of the men, those who have not been accompanying the women, have been hiding in the bush house behind the screen of ferns and branches. With a whoop, they all burst out of the enclosure now and line up inside the clearing. As the women enter the clearing, they pass along a reception line of men, each of whom shakes their hand and murmurs "*Atlo*" (hello). Reaching the end of the line, each woman sets about untying knots. Every knot must be untied, and each woman must untie at least one knot; any knots left untouched are pointed out and duly untied. When this is completed, the women stand back while the ritual leader(s) display(s) each piece of work. At each piece, the leader informs them of who will wear the piece during the dance. If the making of a piece was the special responsibility of one man (or woman), the leader names this worker. After the tour through all of the paraphernalia at which I was present, Kusak called Pelas forward and pointed out the presence of the *akavuganan*, so that she, as song leader, would be sure to recognize them and sing their special songs.

After this event, all taboos on food from the bush are effectively ended and the men no longer need to wash when they leave the *akusak*, nor do they fasten knots on any of the pieces. They said that now that the women had seen everything, there was no further need for precaution. A further explanation could be that the pieces were now complete and independent.

Ritual Process

The dance preparations create a situation in which the normal Baining world is progressively fragmented. The domains of bush and place, male and female, hot and cold, night and day, up and down, work and play are increasingly separated both spatially and temporally, and the processes that usually mediate between them are temporarily suspended.

The usual pattern of daily cooperation between men and women is superseded by the men's bush activity. The women continue to sustain the normal subsistence tasks, transforming nature by means of fire and sweat, but the locus of the men's activities becomes the bush. These changes produce a male-female, bush-garden opposition. In the bush, the men work with materials gathered from all parts of the forest. Although worked on, these materials retain natural qualities associated with decomposition. The men constantly have to wash away this naturalness or coldness before returning to the village. The preparations are viewed as "work," a term which is consciously contrasted with the idea that the day of the dance is "play." The men work, during the day, but in the bush; the women sing, at night, but in the place. There are thus oppositions: cold-hot, bush-place, raw-cooked-decomposed, night-day, and work-play. All of the activities are out of order in at least one dimension, and it is not until the day of the dance that they get properly realigned.

Work Phase

This period is not just a time of seclusion and isolation; it is also a period of creation. This creativity is analogous to the fundamental reproductive processes of the Baining world: principally the production of garden crops and the socialization of persons. The men refer to their work metaphorically as their garden work. As in garden work, they clear a site in the bush within which they transform natural material into social products through their own labor.

Throughout this process, the men interact with nature in two forms. The first is the realm of the bush and forest and all its contents, that domain which is opposed to "place." This aspect of nature is represented by the heap of twigs, leaves, etc. that the men build up on their approach to the bush site; it represents nature as the *raw material* for social processes (or "raw" nature as we have termed it). The second aspect of nature is that which remains after the processes of production and socialization have occurred. It is the *residue* of social processes. This aspect is represented by the second heap, which the men create on their departure each day from the site, when they pick up any old piece of debris around the work site and deposit it on the pile. This heap represents "entropic" nature.

The products of the bush site are thus contrasted with both these heaps just as the Baining people and society are to the two aspects of nature in their system. During the preparations the ritual pieces are not yet completed and have to be guarded from the powerful transformational processes that surround them. They are therefore protected with *arsong* knots. The knots iconically hold things together.

According to informants, these knots protect against vague destructive powers often glossed as *aios*. As we have seen, the men's work is analogous to gardening and socialization. The ritual regalia are analogous to food and their manufacture out of raw goods is analogous to cooking. As Lévi-Strauss (1965: 19–29) has pointed out, food can undergo two possible processes of transformation: cooking or decomposition. The real threats to the work the men are engaged in are actually the processes that invert work and socialization. These are rotting and social disintegration. If not properly protected, the ritual regalia could undergo the natural or reverse transformation of decomposition or deconstruction that the *aios* embody.

In the act of creation, the men use heat and sweat as agents of transformation. Parts of the materials are heated or singed to remove bark or pith, to make leaves soft and pliable, or to bend pieces of wood. Later they use lime, ginger, and sugar juice to symbolize aspects of heat. Their bush magic, however, speaks of the other side of the transformational triangle, that of decomposition. The spell seeks to divert the process of rotting away from the men's products and to focus it entirely on materials provided specifically for that purpose, the *asagang* leaves. These materials, through doing what they do best, which is to decay, serve as decoys or alternative foci for the inverse transformation.

Contact with nature and these processes of decomposition makes people cold (see chapter 5), and the Baining believe that heat can best be restored through washing. The ritual of washing condenses both these aspects of pollution. At the end of each day the men rid themselves of the polluting aspects of contact with nature and natural decay by washing themselves and all their belongings before heading back to the village. They also subordinate the decaying process to that of the purifying one by submerging the decaying leaves in the purifying agent, water. We can now see that the Baining notion of pollution is strongly tied up with beliefs about decomposition, and that this is inextricably tied up with ideas about death and *aios*.

It is this aspect of *aios* which lurks on the edges of all Baining ritual preparations. *Aios* here represent death and decay. In *Asarai* there is a vague idea that *aios* might come and inhabit the paraphernalia when the men are away. To chase off the *aios*, the first man to the bush site each morning throws a stick into the clearing (Hesse and Aerts 1982: 44). The role of the *aios* here is analogous to that in the mortuary feasts. The *aios* reside in both food and ritual regalia not as the embodiment of ghosts, ancestors, or spirits, but as representatives of the forces of decomposition, which are opposed to the social processes of transformation through work and heat (e.g., cooking). The food displays and the manufacture of ritual regalia in the bush are both unstinted processes of social production, but activities of such positive value inevitably raise the specter of their opposites embodied by *aios*. The decay threatened by the *aios* would not only destroy the artifacts, it would also rob the workers of their ability to exert their transforming powers and thus to remain potent beings. Such an outcome would mean that death would win over life.

The creations made in the bush are both products of and metaphors for the Baining's ability to transform nature. While these abilities can result in products of almost any size or shape, the metaphorical properties of the bush creations might be expected to lead to at least some symbolic resemblance to other socially transformed items, which in Baining terms means food or people. With the exception of the *anaru* pole pieces, however, the pieces manufactured for the dances do not have any iconic resemblance or linguistic reference to either of these categories of normal social products. These creations are, nevertheless, symbolic in a number of ways. Despite their lack of overt resemblance to people, Corbin (1976) describes them as metaphorical human beings. He sees the wood frames as analogous to skeletons; the layer of leaves covering the frame as analogous to a layer of muscles; the bark cloth on top as the creature's skin; and the red and black paints as blood and sweat circulating through the pieces. The effect of human-ness is enhanced through the act of painting. Just as body painting is a principal means of transforming an individual into a social person (T. Turner 1980) so too is the painting of these pieces the final act that transforms them from natural to social creatures.

Once the work (or transformation) is completed the threat of deconstruction diminishes and the knots become less important. They become completely unnecessary after the women arrive and destroy the antecedent forms and residue of the completed products, as embodied in the two rubbish heaps. With these destroyed, the masks are now completely disengaged from their natural aspects and are full social products. This liberation is represented by the women's untying of the knots. The women represent the completed, transformed state of society in this act. The act of untying knots has multiple referents, however, and at this point it is also symbolic of women's reproductive powers. Untying the knots is like cutting the umbilical cord after a birth. The masks can now enter society as independent actors. The heaps analogously become the placenta: the first heap representing the placenta in its nurturing phase, which supports growth; and the second heap, the "afterbirth" or residual by-product of gestation. The activities up to this point represent the liminal phase of the ritual, which the women's rite now closes.

Although these masks are metaphorical humans, they are not unambiguously so. They do not look like humans, and this ambiguity is part of their function. They contain elements from a number of natural domains and refer back to those domains. They are thus good mediators. The vegetal materials can be seen to refer back to the trees of the forest of their origin; the feathers are still associated with the birds that produced them; and the same is true for the cassowary bones and feathers.

The dance itself functions as a rite of reintegration, because it is the phase in which all the segmented domains are brought back together again. The bush work is brought to the "place"; what was done at night is now performed during the day; what was hidden is now open, etc. The dance reconstitutes the articulation of Baining society.

The masks and regalia change their meanings and roles as the phases change. Up to this point, they existed primarily as canvases for the men's productive labor; their shape, colors, and forms did not really matter; the productive processes and the simple fact of their creation were what mattered. On the day of the dance, however, they finally become not only finished but animated products and, as such, symbolic mediators of a number of different Baining domains. They physically and symbolically mediate bush and place. As males dressed up as female creatures *akipki, assarikatki, akurikuruki, aniski*, etc., they metaphorically mediate male and female. As birds and strange creatures, they mediate between animals and humans, and humans and supernatural beings. As long poles that reach to the clouds (the *avuganan* is equated with clouds in songs), as cones that are equated with trees, and dancers who are identified with birds, they mediate earth and sky. All these attributes implicit during their construction emerge as active qualities only at the point of performance.

This performative transformation coincides with the change in the Baining classification of the ritual activity from "work" to "play." Work is transformative and productive. Play does not make persons or products, but brings them into relation with one another. It articulates the different domains which I gloss as nature, society, and the supernatural. In situations which the Baining define as play, these domains are brought into conjunction with one another. Things are no longer being transformed from one domain to another (by work) as they are in the preparatory phase. Rather, the danced pieces actively mediate between the different domains simultaneously because they share attributes with each.

There is another difference between the dance and the preparations. In the performance of the ritual, the masks and regalia are no longer passive entities being produced, but become instead the active embodiment of the work that went into them, now transformed into a capacity for action in their own right. The pieces thus now convey meanings that until this moment they have not conveyed. They now both instantiate and enact the transcendence of anomalies and the process of mediation.

Although the day-dance paraphernalia taken by themselves appear as a series of bizarre and abstract forms, in context one can see that the particular symbolic attributes contained in each piece together form an articulated picture of Baining culture and society.

The Day of the Dance

Very early in the morning of the day of the dance, between 3:30 and 4:30 A.M., the men begin to ferry the pole "masks" from the bush to the plaza, and to lean them against the scaffold, often tying them to the cross-bars so they cannot blow over. According to informants in Raunsepna, as soon as these pieces appear on the dance ground the women should start singing, and often they do start singing around 3:00 or 4:00 A.M. They are then said to be "singing under the *anaru*." Once they begin, their musical accompaniment continues virtually unbroken until sundown. As soon as the singing begins, people begin to dance. For the most part the early dancers are all women, who dance a slow shuffle step around in a circle. The step is very simple, 1–2–3 pause, 1–2–3 pause; it is performed relatively slowly and sedately with very little movement of the upper body.

The women dancers are decked out in new *anis* or laplaps, and may have red and white on their faces. In addition to these adornments, all of the dancers wear a new laplap around their shoulders, like a shawl. This is a modern adaptation of the older custom of wearing a piece of bark cloth around the shoulders. Many women carry young children on their shoulders as they dance, and in this case, they wrap the laplap round both the child and themselves.[6] Many of these dancers also shine with sugar cane juice, which has been spat over their bodies and this effect is often renewed during the day as they retire to the bush to help the male dancers adorn themselves.

Alambakka

The songs that are sung during this early-morning period are similar to the *Atut* songs (see chapter 10) in that they are generally of relatively recent composition and tend to be about events in the lives of the composers and the community around them. Composition is attributed to the author and not to any outside source of inspiration. "If you see someone doing something, you watch and then a song comes up in your head about this thing." There are two important facts about Baining songs. The first is that songs are constantly composed, and they tend to have as their subject matter incidents from daily life. These incidents are frequently, but not necessarily, scandalous in nature. Song composition is, for the Baining, a form of gossiping. The songs can be about animals, people, or ghosts, but they are often about people being like animals, or animals like people. The second fact is that songs are intricately bound to geography. Every song must mention a place-name in its text, and there is a whole set of songs in which a fixed sequence of mountains is used. In these songs, only a single line of text interspersed between the mountain names differentiates one song from the next. The use of place-names here differs from that in other Melanesian societies, where the names are used to evoke affect and memories of a particular place or event (Feld 1982; Schieffelin 1976). The list of mountains in Baining songs remains constant from one song to the next and becomes the frame for the song.

This form made it quite easy for people to join in songs they did not know, by simply singing along with the chorus. During a dance, when

---

6. Corbin mentions that the children carried are supposed to be those born since the last day dance. By his account, then, being carried is some sort of initiation. Although I was told constantly that the women would / did carry children on their shoulders, no reference was made to this "initiation." I believe that women carry children on their shoulders because they represent the socializing forces of the place.

one song ended, another singer would immediately start a song of his or her choice. Everyone would listen through the first "verse" and then join in if he or she knew it. If nobody did, the leader might sing alone until others picked up the refrain.

There are two general classes of song, *amambu* and *aiyawit* (which is the name of the first mountain listed in the mountain songs). The *aiyawit* songs are long, repetitious, and sung more rapidly. They are often the songs sung during the *alambakka* periods. The *aiyawit* songs consist of a refrain that is repeated with each of about eighteen mountains. The list of these mountains is known by the women who sing these songs, but the location of the mountains is only vaguely guessed at. My inquiries on this subject elicited long silences, whispers among informants, and then confessions of uncertainty but the feeling that a certain mountain was somewhere near Nambung (a plantation) or Randinggi (a place near the coast). I did not get the feeling that people saw the listing of these mountains as symbolic of a journey from one place to another, but simply as a structuring device into which a totally independent refrain could be placed and a song thus created. An example of such a song follows:

> I see all the others, I see them talking at Aiyawit
> I see all the others, I see them talking at Aningbumgi
> I see all the others, I see them talking at Gukanaka
> I see all the others, I see them talking at Akanas
> I see all the others, I see them talking at Akandasim
> I see all the others, I see them talking at Akamirurki
> I see all the others, I see them talking at Andurini
> I see all the others, I see them talking at Awaingilum
> I see all the others, I see them talking at Awananga
> I see all the others, I see them talking at Akaungulingu
> I see all the others, I see them talking at Ayakaringul
> I see all the others, I see them talking at Aikivaka
> I see all the others, I see them talking at Aruaka
> I see all the others, I see them talking at Akindiang
> I see all the others, I see them talking at Akiamegi
> I see all the others, I see them talking at Aningarurutka
> I see all the others, I see them talking at Akandam
> I see all the others, I see them talking at Akarung, with
>   Karias and Kaknuraka and all.
> I see all the others, I see them talking, and I think it is
>   true, and later he spoke out.
> I see all the others, I see them talking, he followed a
>   woman, he ran after her.
> I see all the others, I see them talking, he pulls a vine to
>   the ground, he went and fell down
> Because of the woman.

This is a song about either pre-marital intercourse or adultery, and suggests that the man felt shame when the others found out. I do not believe that the reference to the vine referred to suicide by hanging although the words could be so interpreted. Informants would not venture an interpretation, saying the composer was dead and they did not know what he had meant. Often people would just stop transcribing and translating songs because they said they did not understand them even though they could sing them with no problem.

A second mountain song ran as follows:

> I see my friends from Aiyawit
>
> . . . .
>
> I see my friends from Akarung
> I go up [the mountain] and I stay for the day at Aiyawit
>
> . . . .
>
> I go up and I stay for the day at Akarung.
> I go outside and he goes to the village, you see him, he is
>   looking up.
> He wants to go to Raunga, and he looks over there, but
>   he sees smoke [clouds] at Ininbum and Wasaka
> You see he looks over there, at the smoke at Lungisbanas
>   and Alinwir.
> You see he looks over there at the smoke at Auvung and
>   Lengisin,
> He goes in the house and the ashes cover him.
> There are fruit flies around him, and the fire is out, it is
>   out.
> There is rain on the mountain,
> There is rain over there and it holds him back.
> He wants to go.
> So he sleeps down below, he sleeps with the taro [in the
>   garden].

This is a song about how the rain prevents a man from going out and visiting or moving about.

> I see all my friends all from Yalom [village]
> I see all my friends all from Mungais [old village site]
> I see all my friends all from Siguravut
> I see all my friends all from Kalgal [a stone]
> I see all my friends, do you see he is speaking?
> All the good men will gather in one place, they will leave
>   all the bad men.
> I see all my friends,
> In the morning he got up and followed her

I see all my friends at Lungisbanas and he went around
  to find his wife.
I see all my friends, he came with talk for her,
He will speak out about his thoughts.
Will you call his name for me [so I can hear]?
Gulungiram and Solmit are he [one man who has two
  names].

This song refers to a communal meeting where a case of adultery
was negotiated. Many of these songs end with the request to call the
name of the song's central character, so although the acts to which the
song refers are often obscure, the actors are usually known.

Alambakka songs are not only *aiyawit*, or mountain songs. There are
others, which call rivers, trees, or mountains not in the *Aiyawit* series.
The previous song and the one that follows exemplify this.

I see *akalugi* [a bird], and he flies around here,
And goes around to Rangulit
And goes around to Lamis.
And the wind blows him, and he flies to Kaungum,
And he flies around Misseit
And he flies around Vulumbit
And he flies around Wasaka.
It is not his, it is the wild pig's.
Has Ngurel [a woman] gone?
She goes and she comes across them both,
Later she returns.
She came to the place and she told Malunga.
Later she told him, and sits quietly.
Later he will see it is true.
He held them both, the woman and the pig.
I want you to call his name for me, Ngingaiyi is he.

In this song, the bird stands for the man, Ngingaiyi, who is being
accused of chasing after women. It is unclear both to me and to informants what the pig and wild pig stand for in this song. The many
place-names represent the wide circle of the man's activities. Not all
songs contain lists of places as is evident in the following song. Even
this song, however, calls at least one place-name. It is supposed to be
a song about taro.

Angemengi [dove] went and came to Kaliagi
Angemengi went and she came, and she wrapped him [it]
  in her net bag
And she came with him [it].
Angemengi went and she came, and she wrapped him [it]
  in her net bag.

Angemengi went and she came, and she cooked him [it]
    and she singed him [it],
And he [it] cried for himself.
Angemengi went, and she ran away and left the taro
    which was soft.
Angemengi went, and now you call her for me. It is Lasuk-
    mutki.

In this song the dove stands for the woman Lasukmutki, who was
not identified until the end. The taro is referred to as "him," as if it
were a person, which is why it could cry and feel sorry for itself, but
it was not interpreted as being representative of anything else in this
instance.

Baining songs are not about a single type of thing, but they do tend
to be about things that depart from the norm in some way. This can
be something as mundane as rain, which restricts a person's normal
gardening activities, or as extraordinary as an elicit sexual liaison. People frequently write songs about themselves and their experiences, but
there is nothing preventing someone from composing a song about
someone else. Songs are a special genre for the Baining in which they
talk about the personal traits of themselves or others.

Despite the appearance of publicly airing events and situations, people often pay little attention to the content of a song. They may know
all the words but not know who they refer to, or what happened to
inspire the song. Of course, this is not exclusively the case; sometimes
people do know that a song refers to the time Sambung threw ashes
over her father when he tried to get her to marry Nguinga, or the time
when Kurik spoke out when people were gossiping about her, and
that a song was written for the departure of Uvian, the anthropologist.
Whether or not people pay attention to the particular content of the
songs, the general content is symbolically important for understanding
the dynamics of the dance events.

Back Piercing

While the women are getting started on the dance plaza, the men
gather back at the *akusak* in the bush. This is when they pierce the backs
of the men who are going to wear *akip* spears. There are several men
who are acknowledged to be skilled in this job, but it is only experience
and not magic that singles them out. One by one the men lie down on
the ground on some banana leaves while several men crouch over
them. One man draws a line with lime powder along the spinal column
where the puncture should be (they try not to place a new hole in
exactly the same spot as an old one). Then two men pinch the flesh on

either side of this mark so that they are holding a fold of skin between their fingers. The specialist then takes a tool made of a sharpened piece of a cassowary leg bone, and using this as an awl, pushes it through the fold of skin. As he does this, everyone mumbles *"alarus, alarus,"* which means cucumber, the association being that the flesh should be as easily pierced as that of a cucumber. When the bone has appeared on the opposite side of the fold, the men slide a rope through this hole. The rope is then temporarily knotted so it cannot slip out and the whole area is bespat with sugar cane juice, which is said to relieve the pain. The whole operation is referred to as *ta trasir* (they pierce) or *ta kut* (they shoot [as with an arrow or spear]).

In Yalom people complain of the pain of this operation at every stage from start to finish, whereas in Raunsepna people say that it does not hurt when they pierce the skin initially, nor when they put on the spear and dance. Only when they take off all the paraphernalia does it hurt "a little." Although it is not explicitly said that people should not cry out in pain, I did not hear anyone cry out.

The day as a whole alternates between the continuous singing and dancing in the village plaza, and the periodic disappearance of groups of men and women to the fringes of the village to prepare for the next event. This account will assume the basic continuity of the plaza activity, and will follow the different groups through their preparations and displays.

Aramariki

The first group of men, those who carry the *aramariki* or *aisingaigi*, do not have to make extensive preparations. As said before, the *aramariki,* although not heavy, is carried in by as many men as can fit around it. In Yalom it was twelve men. These men decorated themselves with a leaf fringe around their necks, waists, and even in some cases their heads (those who did not wear leaves had cloth wrapped around their heads). They wore lime (or talc) on their faces.

Before they left the bush, one of the ritual leaders spat bespelled ginger over the dancers. He then led the group into the plaza, where he stood in front of the chorus spitting ginger. The men carrying the shield were also chewing and spitting ginger and they advanced in a cloud of spittle. Their step was a slow kicking walk. As they entered, the chorus began the *aramariki* song.

> My friends they say to me, the *avudamgi [aramariki]* will
>   come up to me.

Plate 9.4   *Aramariki*

It is from the *akusak* [bush place]
The wind travels with it, and it goes inside Aisingim [a
    place].
I did not want to learn this work before
But I could make one like this
Now I want to reciprocate this work, with flowers [decora-
    tions] to them all.

When that song ended and the women started another song, the men
danced into the plaza with the shield. They made two circuits of the
area before one of the men carried the *aramariki* off to the sidelines; the
dancers continued to dance around the circle. This whole event is said
to *suwup ama aluwupki*, that is, to "sweep the place."

Aisingaigi

As I mentioned earlier, the *aisingaigi* is more or less interchangeable
with the *aramariki,* and it too can "sweep the place." The *aisingaigi* like
the *aramariki* is carried by as many men as can fit around it, often as
many as twenty to twenty-five. It is carried over the dancers' heads.
These men do not dance with a kick step, but they do chew ginger

root. They are also adorned with leaves around their heads, necks, and waists, and are surrounded by ginger spray spat both by dancers and helpers. They carry in the mask, stand in front of the chorus for a song, and circle the plaza once or twice. The *aisingaigi* also has a song of its own, which refers to the breath or wind of the snake. It is this breath or wind that the ginger spray is supposed to neutralize. In addition, the song makes reference to the fact that *aisingaigi* is attracted to the dance ground by the singing and pounding of the women's chorus.

The *aisingaigi* unlike the *aramariki* does not enter the dance ground alone. It is accompanied by one or more pole "masks" (*aravukulka* [her sticks]) (Hesse and Aerts 1978: 28). The most prominent of these is the *angwarumgi*, which only appears at this time. The pole mask dancers wear fringed banana leaves or *anis* around their necks and waist, they have powder on their heads and faces, and they carry shreds of grass in their fists while they hold the pole ropes.

After the opening events, the *Assarikatki, Akip,* and *Anaru* are spaced throughout the day. If there is more than one line of these dancers, they may alternate with one another. The *Akurikuruk* come at the end of the day.

Both the *aramariki* and *aisingaigi* are said to "sweep the place," but no informant could volunteer what was cleaned or cleared out. I suggest that what is swept away are the transformative ambiguities of the previous ritual phase, most notably the intermeshing of bush and place, day and night. This dance activity then sets up new clean boundaries between these domains. However, these domains are bridged and mediated by some of the acts and regalia that follow. The dance pieces are anomalous creatures who mediate these domains.

The *aisingaigi*, whether a python or an eel, is a mediating creature. The Baining do not classify the python as a snake because it is arboreal rather than terrestrial; it sits in trees and pounces on its victims. Similarly, the eel is like a snake but in the wrong habitat; it lives in water not on land. These creatures are anomalous, but the combined habitats that they refer to encompass the trees, ground, and waters. The accompanying *angwarumgi* is a creature who simultaneously represents all these anomalous habitats; it is the name for a tiny insect that sits in trees and produces a type of foamy spittle that rains down from the tree it is in, as well as the term for the whirling foam found on fast-flowing rivers. This insect thus simultaneously evokes references to both forest and rivers. The connection between these companion pieces is underscored by the fact that eels are believed to eat this foam.[7]

---

7. The *angwarumgi* has yet a third feature which makes it a good symbol for the day dance, a plumelike tail called *aniski*, also the word for women's skirts. See the above discussion of this term. Pool (1971) saw this as symbolically important.

Assarikatki

After the *aramariki* or *aisingaigi* depart from the dance ground, the *assarikatki* dancers and their accompanying kin melt away from the dance. This group gathers on the edge of the village, to which the dance regalia was carried; here, the dancers proceed to adorn themselves. They paint their faces red and put a touch of white powder just over the ears. The women and other men chew sugar and spit its juices over them to make their bodies glisten, and then attend to one another in the same way.

The *assarikat* as well as most of the subsequent dancers complete their preparations by chewing sugar cane and spitting the juice over one another. Informants said this was to make their bodies glisten and shine as if they were sweating. Throughout the dance ginger and sugar juice are used as symbols of work and sweat. Ginger is "hot" and thus can symbolize the transformative agent, heat. Ginger, however, is not a transformative agent; it does not cook things. When the Baining say that the heat of the ginger neutralizes the "wind" or "breath" of the bark cloth, a powerful transformation is suggested, but all that is involved is a metaphoric reference to such transformative activity. In the same way, sugar cane is only a cosmetic to suggest sweat (heat), and not the agent itself (see chapter 5 for further beliefs about the transformative powers of sweat). The dancers thus represent aspects of transformation and mediation in the world, but in a "play" and not a "work" context (here I use "play" in the sense of a dramatic performance).

The *assarikat* dancers are adorned with *anis* and necklaces of cordyline leaves around their necks, arms, and waists. They are helped to put on their headdresses and to balance them securely with the ropes in their hands. This done, they slowly walk forward, all four dancers abreast with the rest of the crew hovering around. As they appear on the edge of the village the chorus switches from a general song to one about the *assarikat*.

> She broke the cordyline leaves at Aiyawit
>
> . . . .
>
> She broke the tanket at Akarung
> She broke the tanket, she shredded it and fastened it to a
>   rope
> Do you see? She puts it in back and it lights up [flashes].

This song makes an analogy between the tanket (cordyline) leaves tucked into the *assarikatki* and those used by the women to make *anis*.

Plate 9.5   *Asariratki*

Thus, the song tells about how a woman makes an *aniski* and puts it on, at which point the tanket leaves light up (literally, become sunlike). This quality of tanket leaves to be bright and shiny is obviously very significant, for it is repeated in a number of songs.

While these songs are being sung, the dancers come and stand in front of the chorus for one song, during which time they dance from one foot to the other with a swaying step. When the song ends, a faster song begins and the dancers start around the circle with a running step. After completing two circles, they are relieved of their cumbersome headdresses by men from the sidelines, but they continue to dance around the circle until the end of the song. At this point, these dancers leave the plaza, and the general singing and dancing continue.

Akip

After the *Assarikat* ends, the dancers designated for the first line of the spear dance, *Akip*, slip away to adorn themselves. The men first paint each other with a black paste made from ashes. They do this carefully, rubbing the paint on their arms, faces, back of the neck, back, stomach, thighs, calves, etc., helping each other by applying it to the places they cannot reach themselves, and by carefully examining one another to make sure no spot has been missed. After they are completely smeared with black, they begin to chew sugar cane and spit on one another to make the paint shine as if with sweat.

After painting themselves, the men don various accessories; they wear a hat or piece of cloth wrapped around their heads and they often put on rattles made of nuts, which are worn just below the knee or around the ankle. The women of a dancer's household fasten *anis* or strings of cordyline leaves around his neck and arms. Each man also provides himself with a staff of some kind: a traditional war club *(angalipka)*, a cordyline sapling, or a stalk of sugar cane. Some men have bunches of betel nut or even corn hanging from their necks or the tops of their spears. After these preparations are completed, the dancers get ready to put on the spears.

They first place the cradle between their legs and hold it there by pressure from their thighs. On the front and back prongs of this cradle they place the rosettes. Then the *akusakaigi* (cone base), is placed into the sprocket in the cradle. Finally, the long *araseulka* is placed in the top of the cone base. The string that pierces the dancer's flesh is now tied around the assemblage, where it holds the cone and spear upright and takes a good deal of the weight of these pieces, especially since the spear is designed to wave and sway with every dance step. The weight of all the components generally pulls the pierced flesh outward, so it forms a loop, which occasionally breaks.

While the ordinary *akip* dancers are decorating and preening, the *akavuganan* dancers are also readying themselves. These men are painted like the *akip* dancers, but they have red faces. One of the men carrying an *akavuganan* on top of the long spear gets ready a little faster

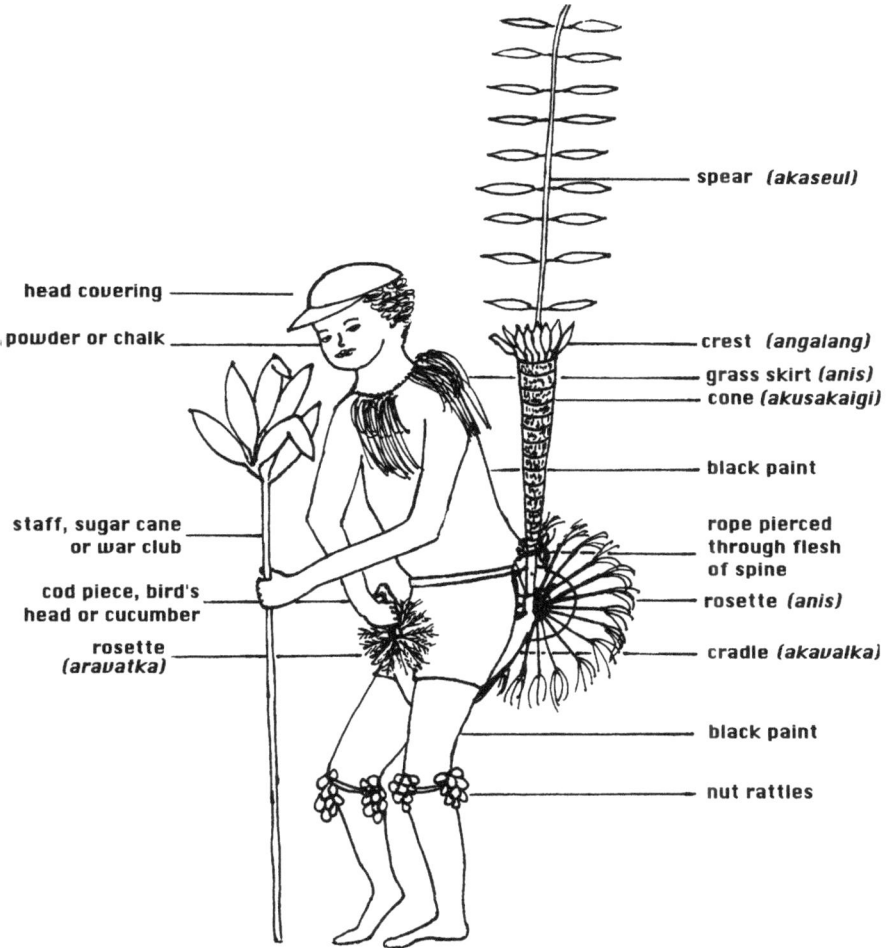

spear *(akaseul)*

head covering

,powder or chalk

crest *(angalang)*
grass skirt *(anis)*
cone *(akusakaigi)*

black paint

staff, sugar cane
or war club

rope pierced
through flesh
of spine

cod piece, bird's
head or cucumber

rosette *(anis)*

rosette
(aravatka)

cradle *(akavalka)*

black paint

nut rattles

Figure 9.8   *Akip* dancer

than the others. He is the one who will go ahead to tell the women
that the dancers are coming. This role is called *aspaska* (which means
"the one who goes first"). His *akavuganan* is said to be the "mother"
of the regular *akip* spears. When the others are just ready to unwrap
their *akip* bases and open the rosettes, this dancer proceeds to the plaza.
He runs into the plaza, dances before the women in the chorus, and
runs back to the bush where the rest of the line is waiting. Upon the
return of the *aspaska,* all the dancers line up to proceed single file to
the plaza.

While the men are decorating, with help from the women, the women also adorn themselves. They decorate their faces with dots of lime (some of the ones I witnessed also used red pigment) and spit their bodies with sugar juice. Now that it is time to depart for the plaza, these women go slightly ahead of the dancers' line.

The men's dance step is a sort of hopping step in which each leg is kicked out behind. When the dancers are dancing in place, they lean heavily on their staffs and kick forcefully. They usually hold the prong of their cradle in one hand, which may help to counterbalance the weight of the spear. When they are moving, the step becomes more of running kick. Commonly, the *akip* dancers come into the dance ground at a point opposite the chorus. Here the single file fans out into a line, which then dances backwards towards the seated orchestra. The women who have accompanied them go immediately to stand by the chorus; the pole *avuganan* do not go to stand by the chorus, but start immediately to dance around the circle. It is very difficult to balance these long poles, especially as the dancers quicken their pace, so it is not long (maybe only half a circuit) before the poles start to topple. As they do so, they are taken off by helpers or spectators who claim them, and the dancers continue their dancing without the poles.

The line of *akip* dancers, as we have seen, proceeds backwards towards the chorus. When the dancers arrive, they turn around and face it, and dance in place. At the arrival of the spear dancers, women in the chorus may stand up and sing and dance in place, by shuffling from foot to foot. It is said that they do this because they are *awilas* (hot), which certainly in this instance has connotations of excitement. In the first few minutes of the dancers' presence on the dance ground, women and children from the audience go up to them and remove various parts of their regalia; first and foremost, some of the women remove the *anis* from the men's necks and arms; children often strip them of their leg rattles; and anyone can come and take the betel nut, corn, or sugar cane. Even the cucumber from the codpiece may be taken and eaten. The explanation I was given for this behavior was simply that anyone could take the things, and people took them because they wanted the item. These "exchanges" have nothing to do with the particular individuals involved or the relations between them, nor do they initiate any relationship (i.e., it is not a sexual advance).

After the two songs during which they remain in front of the chorus, the dancers begin to dance around in a circle, outside the women's circle, which has continued uninterrupted. The women who have been standing with the men either go and join the women's circle or sit down with the chorus.

At this point, the event—as I witnessed it in the different villages—diverges considerably from region to region. In Yalom, all the men started their dancing, galloping around in a circle, but after only a couple of circuits the dancers began to flag, and bit by bit they dropped out of the circle to go to the edge of the plaza and have their spears removed. Thus lightened, they came back and danced for a longer time. Not one of the dancers that performed in Yalom lasted more than fifteen minutes, and even this was seen as tremendous martyrdom and endurance.

By contrast, the *akip* dancers at Raunsepna continued their dancing for about two hours. During this time they both danced around in a circle, and came and stood and danced individually in front of the chorus. Occasionally a dancer would leave the field either because the flesh holding the rope had torn or a piece of the paraphernalia had broken. Usually after adjustments had been made the dancer returned, spear and all. If this was impossible, he would return to dance without the regalia. Dancers occasionally took short rests on the sidelines to chew betel nut without removing their spears. I noticed once that when a dancer returned to the plaza a woman dancer asked him for his partly chewed wad of betel nut, which he handed over.[8] Sometimes a dancer decides to wear the spear regalia for a whole day. This dancer will then enter with the first line of the day, but will continue dancing through all the sets of the day. This seems to be a personal decision, and so far as I could tell it does not bestow any particular status on the performer. Barring this exception, the dancers tend to continue for about two hours, frequently yielding their ground as a new dance line arrives.

As with all the paraphernalia for these dances, the decorations are removed to the sidelines where anyone who wants them can claim them. People rarely carry off whole pieces intact, but guests frequently cut the bark cloth off pieces and take it home. Spectators might also claim parts of the *akip* decorations in order to salvage the feathers used. If no one from outside claims these feathered objects, the hosts will usually dismantle them to save the feathers, and maybe even the cone bases, for their next festival. Those objects not claimed and not salvaged by the bush workers are simply thrown away in the bush.

There are numerous songs that refer to the *akip* and *akavuganan,* and these are sung from the time of their arrival on the plaza until they leave, although in the case of a long performance other songs may be interspersed. The songs refer variously to the colors, height, and dance step of the dancers.

> I see the line of *akip*
> All the birds drop, shed [feathers] for it.

8. Other observers (Klemensen 1965: 188–89) have described this sort of behavior as having sexual innuendos, but I could find no basis for this either in observation or in informants' accounts.

They pluck the cassowary, it sheds [feathers] and they
    put them down below [on the rosette].
The lorikeet sheds for it
The cockatoo sheds for it
And the hornbill sheds for it.

I see the *kavuganan*, the child of the birds
When it is nearly time, they shed their feathers for it.
The hornbill, the parrot, the cockatoo and the lorikeet.

I see the line of *akip*
Like this they turn around and around between the
    houses here
And they jump [dance] just like the tumbuan [masks]
Following the road alone.

They drop the ginger with the *avuganan*
They paint the skin black,
They put on nut rattles
They put on lime
They put on powder.
The clouds are covering the sky here.

This last song introduces a theme that is frequently heard in the *akip*
songs: the association of clouds, rain, and thunder with the dance line. I
specifically asked if there was a causal association, whether the dancers
were supposed to attract the rain or represent it. The answers were
invariably "No"; the rain just came, and was considered a problem.

I see the line of *akip*, and they sing for them the *maruvarit-
    kina* [clouds]
There is a rainbow for them, the same as this, a rainbow
    on all the men.
And you see they are moving beneath it all with the *maru-
    varitkina* [clouds].

Thunder comes with the line of *akip*
The *avuganan* comes with the clouds
Thunder comes with the line of *akip*
The *avuganan* comes with the clouds.
It turns around and around with the red and the feathers
    and the *arasulki* is taller than the houses.

Some of the songs emphasize the pain of the dancers who have had
their backs pierced.

They surprise all of us, with their line of *akip* there is sick-
    ness here
They tie them, and they pull the rope through them.
And they dance with them.

A lot of the songs refer to how the feathers are taken from the birds. There is a definite association between the *akip* dancers and various birds, both in the feathers they wear and in the dance steps.

> You see the cassowaries,
> They all dance and scratch the ground underneath the
>   *aunga* [fruit tree]
> They jump and they dance
> They dance around the singers.

> It is cold and the lorikeets are sitting on top of the coco-
>   nut at Klinwata
> Everyone calls out to them
> Because they want to draw them here for the *akip*.

One informant said in reference to the first song that the *akip* is like a cassowary and the *avuganan* is like the *aunga* tree because it is held above the cassowaries. The cassowaries stand down below these trees and eat the fruit that has fallen off.

Spears and Birds

The *akip* dancers have the most complicated regalia of all, whose symbolism is complex and multivocalic. As we have seen, this costume consists of numerous components. It is only on the final day that all the pieces are assembled. The overall constructions are called spears and they resemble the weapon in some ways. Spears penetrate the boundaries of the prey, and in this sense they are mediators. They also mediate the boundary between life and death. The Baining call the act of threading the rope through the flesh "to shoot" or "to pierce." By penetrating themselves, the dancers identify both with the spear and the victim—they carry the spear, but are also pierced. I suggest this is one set of meanings associated with the regalia.

The *akip* dancers and the songs that accompany them are both visually and linguistically associated with birds, and this contributes another set of meanings. Not only are the dancers' costumes covered with bird feathers, but the songs refer to how the birds of the forest shed their feathers for the dancers. In addition to using bird materials metonymically, the regalia seem metaphorically to represent bird qualities (e.g., the long spear projects into the air and mediates between earth and sky).

Birds do not just mediate earth and sky, their lateral flight is significant as well. In Baining stories, birds presage events in the social world. The appearance of certain birds (cockatoos and parrots primarily) is seen as a harbinger of human action. The cry of a cockatoo can fore-

warn people of a raid; the flight of a lorikeet is interpreted to indicate
the pathway of people en route to the village. The cry of a bird represents loneliness, hunger, or death. Birds live on the periphery of the
Baining social world and are omens of change or disruption in that
world. They mediate the boundaries of that world. The association between *akip* and birds evokes comparison with the relations between
bird and song among the Kaluli (Feld 1982), but the Baining do not
associate themselves with birds as directly as do the Kaluli, either in
myth or ritual. Baining references to bird association are implicit and
vague.

The *akip* dancers represent not just flighted birds such as parrots,
cockatoos, and lorikeets, but the flightless cassowary as well. As in
other Melanesian cultures (see Bulmer 1967), the cassowary is not
classed as a bird but as a distinct kind of feathered creature.[9] Its feathers
are an important component of the *akip's* costume. The basket that the
dancers clasp between their legs is compared to the body of a cassowary; the spine of the basket is said to resemble the spine of that bird;
and the rosette that comes out of the rear is thus analogous to the cassowary's tail. Songs and stories describe how the cassowary must wait
beneath fruit trees such as the *aunga* for other birds to knock the fruit
down. This is also evoked in the regalia. The cassowary feathers used
in the dancers' rosettes, are worn low down on the dancers' bodies
beneath the spear, the *akavuganan* or the pole-held *avuganan,* any of
which could represent the tree. The backward kicking step of the *akip*
dancers may imitate the movement of a scratching cassowary.[10]

The cassowary is not a bird, but it shares an important feature with
the birds. Birds and cassowaries both have feathered tails called *aniski.*[11]
The rear portion of the woman's grass skirt is also called *aniski,* as is
the rear rosette of the *akip* dancer. The repetition of this term suggests
a common element in all these usages, and one which Pool (1971) sees
as central to the meaning of the dance.[12] He believes that the multitude
of objects called *anis* highlights women's roles within the relatively
male-dominated realm of the dance. The men make *anis* out of cassowary feathers, while the women make their own *anis* out of leaves and
plants. Those that the women make are not worn exclusively by them,

9. The Baining have a "just-so" story about the cassowary and the lorikeet, explaining
how the lorikeet tricked the cassowary into staying on the ground.

10. I did not think to ask whether this step had such significance, nor did anyone
mention such a meaning in describing the dance to me. This is, therefore, my own interpretation.

11. Dog or pig tails are called avilanga.

12. Pool (1971) suggests that the dance is a celebration of the relationship and interdependence of male and female, specifically of husband and wife.

however; they are worn by the male dancers as well. Yet when worn by men these *anis* are not worn on the buttocks, but around their arms, necks, and waists. In these positions they are accessible to anyone who chooses to remove them. The *anis* are thus mediators and media of exchange. The manufacture and transfer of the different sorts of *anis* in the dance are a way of bridging multiple domains at once: nature-society, male-female, and up-down.

There has been a lot of speculation about the "sexual" imagery of the long spear implements (Klemensen 1965; Poole 1941–42). People have interpreted these as long phallic images that emerge out of the women's symbol, the *anis*, and the cradle basket called *akavalka*. The dance has been seen accordingly as a fertility cult (Klemensen 1965; Corbin 1976). Pool (1971: 81) suggests that the multiple uses of *anis* refer to a covert expression of an interdependence between men and women, which is at the heart of the ritual. I think that the *anis* articulates a wider range of domains: up and down, bush and place, male and female. My own interpretation discounts the importance of sexual or fertility symbols per se, but contextualizes them in the larger process of social reproduction, which includes the production of male- and female-gendered identities, the social units of family and community, and the productive domains of bush and place.

The *anis* constitute a theme running through all the dance acts. The first reference is the pole "mask," *angwarumgi*. The little insect, *angwarumgi*, is said to have a plumelike tail called *aniski*. The *akip* dancers wear *anis* in several places; cassowary rosettes called *anis* are worn below their spears, and women's skirts are worn around their arms. The pieces brought in jointly by the men and the *anepkusakta* women are called *anisingring*, which can be translated as "the flat *anis* of the women" (Pool 1971). These pieces are not worn as skirts, but are carried on high poles where they mediate earth and sky. In this position, they evoke associations with bird tails, trees, and nests. Lest these associations be severed from other *anis*-related meanings, however, the pieces are connected by means of vine ropes to women helpers who wear two types of *anis*. The rope ties together the several referents of the word *anis* from bird to cassowary tail, from insect plume to women's skirts.

Anisingring

The *anisingring* (women's masks), do not appear alone on the dance ground. They always accompany another line of dancers, most frequently the *akip* dancers or the *akurikuruk*. Each piece is attended by two people: a man who carries the pole and a woman or young boy who holds a single rope that hangs from the top. These women are all *anepkusakta* or "women of the bush." As mentioned above, each woman has on a new *aniski* and on top of this she wears a small oval of painted bark cloth also called *aniski*.

The *anisingring* dancers come up to the dance ground at the same time as the *akip* dancers, but they cannot really be said to dance. The most that can be said for them is that they sway slightly. While the *akip* are dancing backwards or in place in front of the chorus, the *anisingring* stand together towards the edge of the plaza. When the *akip* move away from the chorus and begin to run around the circle, the *anisingring* also move to the center of the plaza, where the *anepkusakta* and young boys join the inner or women's circle. They proceed about twice around the circle, after which they carry the poles to the sidelines. The *anepkusakta* may then return to the circle to continue dancing with the women.

Anaru

The poles and figures of the *anaruka* (scaffolding) decorate the dance ground all day. From time to time, between other events, a line of pole dancers enters the plaza and takes up position in front of the scaffolding. At this point several helpers clamber up onto the stand in order to help untie and position the poles on the dancers' heads.

Once the pole is in place, the dancer launches forward and proceeds to circle the dance ground, outside the women's circle. Some dancers proceed quite sedately on their rounds, while others try a running step. Whatever their technique, few dancers succeed in making more than two or three circuits before the pole starts to topple, and many do not survive the first few steps away from the stand. When the dancer feels the pole begin to fall, he may try to put on a burst of speed and run outside the circle. Wherever the piece falls it is abandoned, and the dancer returns to continue around the circle. Helpers remove the pole to the periphery. As each dancer is launched into the circle, the men on the scaffolding proceed to fit another one, but because of the speed with which these poles fall, there are rarely more than two in action at any moment. The shorter poles, especially the ones with the eggs on them, are danced by young boys.

There are several songs that refer to particular types of *anaru* pieces (i.e., the bat or the cassowary). The women sing these songs when one of these pieces is launched. They may repeat the same song several times in an afternoon. The song of the bat that I recorded at Raunsepna was a simple one.

Plate 9.6   Scaffold of pole masks

They carry the bat and it stops here,
It has lost everything
And now it stays here with nothing.

The cassowary song is similar to one of the *akip* songs sung in Yalom.

You see the cassowary, it comes up and scratches at the
ground at the foot of the *aunga* tree.
You see the cassowary, it comes up and scratches at the
ground at the foot of the *aunga* tree.

Akurikuruk

The last dancers to appear during the *Asarai* day dance are the *akuri-kuruk*. These dancers disappear into the bush a couple of hours before their appearance because their decoration is incredibly elaborate. The dancer's entire body is painted, not like the *akip* dancers who are painted in a solid black, but in complex designs of white, reddish brown, and maybe mustard yellow clays. These designs are curvilinear, often outlining the stomach and ribs in white, then filling in the areas with brown or yellow. The only covering they wear is a small genital covering, and pandanus leaf coverings over their calves, similar to the "chaps" worn by the *Atut* dancers (see chapter 10). Just above these calf coverings they wear rattles of nuts. These dancers are the only ones during the day who are not bespat with sugar juice. I think this is because they are supposed to be arriving after a long and arduous journey, and they are hungry, hot, and dirty, but not brilliant or glistening.

When everything is ready, the dancers are led towards the dance ground. These dancers are said to need stewards to direct them since at the beginning they cannot see well through their headdresses, and later, after they have removed their masks, they are obliged to hold their arms and leaf bunches in front of their eyes. When the chorus sees them coming, it begins a series of special songs about the *akuri-kuruk*.

The dancers begin their characteristic dance before actually entering the clearing. The dance has several steps, which alternate. They move forward with a slow side-to-side motion, which is then interrupted by a low crouching step that can be combined with several steps backwards. As they crouch down, the dancers suck in their stomachs to exhibit the hollow created by their weeks of fasting. Once they have danced all the way to the front of the chorus, they dance there for a while alternating between dancing upright with a side-to-side step, and crouching and moving backwards. The crouching and moving gives the dancer an undulating form, which informants said was like the foam on a flooded river. The songs frequently refer to the boiling, rising, and ebbing of different rivers, and this movement is related to the hunger of the dancers. The dancers cannot remain stationary because of their hunger. The songs also do not remain stationary, but call out a progression of river names from distant places moving closer and closer to Yalom. There are several metaphors that accompany these masks: flooded rivers, depleted gardens, and long hot journeys. These images appear in the songs but not in the way the people talk about the masks or dancers.

The first song sung for the *akurikuruk* was composed when the Yalom people were first learning to do this dance.

> My friends are bringing something new to me,
> They call it *akurikuruk*,
> From Panus [the name of a particular mango tree]
> From Aswainbumba [a place-name, incorporating a vegetable name]
> From nyimgalumbit [a mango tree] from Yalom
> From Vangarram [place]
> From Guraka [place]
> From Yaiyo
> From Haiyit
> From Kusak [bush place]
> And he is hot,
> His mouth is long
> They dance and sit down [crouch].
> Later my stomach goes inside [gets hollow].
> They paint *avutik* on it
> And it turns around and around.
> The hat turns on top, at Kanangpit [place] in the bush.

> The wind comes with us from the *akurikuruk*
> It is underneath [below] Asuwanyit [river]
> It is underneath Auvungum [river]
> It is underneath Rangeis [river]
> It is underneath Biyatnamas [river]
> It is underneath Avdaska [river]
> It is underneath Kalkki [river]
> It is underneath Gulum [river]
> It is underneath Kalas [river]
> From the bush
> And it is hot
> Its mouth turns up
> And they paint designs on it [it is pretty]
> And they remove it at Changbit [place] in the bush.

The foam appeared and it boils
It comes up at Mandres [river]
It comes up at Takwas [river]
It comes up at Rumgi [river]
And it is at Arambungdiyingi [river]
And it is at Arumbum [river]
And it comes up in the bucket and it is in all their water
    and in all the waters.
It does not sit down properly, it rises and ebbs.
It does not sit down well, it sits down and stands up.
And they speak to it about its garden
But it just stays where it is and sits on the bed
And it sits in the village and it sits in the house.

The last song refers to the hunger of the *akurikuruk*. The words attribute the movement of the dancer to his hunger, which in turn is caused by the *akurikuruk's* not making a garden; he has not heeded the suggestion of those who talked to him and instead of going out to work in the gardens, has just continued to sit around in the village.

After several songs, assistants help the dancers remove their headdresses. As soon as the headdresses are lifted off, the dancers raise their arms up to their heads and cover their eyes with the leaves still held in their hands. In this position, they continue their swaying and crouching step as they are led from the dance ground by other men.

The *akurikuruk* dancers are endowed with the most defined attributes of all the pieces. Although they are fanciful creatures, they both share and negate aspects of the human domain. In fact they often seem to represent the antithesis of the socialized Baining person. This negative aspect begins with the fast that the dancer undertakes before the dance. As we have already seen (in chapters 5–7) food is the principal medium of Baining sociality, and fasting or food taboos (as may be done after a death) are statements about the dissolution of social bonds. Hunger directly correlates with one's distance from society. Through these means, the *akurikuruk* proclaims that he is outside the social order. This marginality is further exemplified by such attributes as being hot, dirty, and blind.

The songs primarily recount the long journey of the *akurikuruk* from a distant point over mountains and across rivers to arrive at the village, hot, hungry, and exhausted. These sensations are all common Baining predicaments, but the *akurikuruk* does not share them for the same reasons. His heat is the product of a long walk through the bush and forest, and not the by-product of productive labor. He is hot and dirty,

Plate 9.7   *Akurikuruk*

but not sweaty; he is the one type of dancer who is not bespat with
sugar cane juice, and informants specifically said this was because he
was supposed to be dirty. This information harks back to the Baining
beliefs about hot, cold, clean, and dirty, which were discussed in chapter 5: in short, the dirt (represented by the mud paintings) blocks the
dancers' ability to sweat and be productive. All of the rivers he has
crossed are flooded and thus muddy, and therefore not places to drink
and wash off the dirt to regain sociality.

   In addition to this, the dancer is blind. This attribute alludes to the
distinction the Baining make between the bush as a place that is tangled

and blocked, and the "place," which is clear; night as a time when one cannot walk without stumbling, and day as the time when everything is clear. Vision and blindness are opposed in the same way, as are clear and closed, blocked and stumbling. The *akurikuruk* stumbles because of a combination of the bush and blindness. He heads towards the "place" but his progress is erratic; he goes backwards almost as often as he goes forward; he bobs up and down across mountains and valleys; his pace is hindered by all those things antithetical to communal social life. Nonetheless, by the end of the dance he arrives in the village and his entry symbolizes the successful resocialization of the errant traveler. Here he will end his fast. His negative qualities are gradually erased and he becomes a full social being. In this sense, I suggest, the *akurikuruk* dancer represents all those men who have been devoting time and energy to ritual preparations rather than to garden labor. By his reincorporation, the *akurikuruk* symbolizes the return to secular values and practices. This interpretation is supported by one of the songs in which the *akurikuruk's* hunger is attributed to his laziness about making a garden. He is thus seen as refusing to participate in those activities which the Baining highly value. His hunger reflects his problematic behavior.

As Corbin says (1976: 57), the *akurikuruk* regalia represent a creature that is half-animal (possessing eyes, mouth, face, etc.) and half-plant. He interprets the cone on the back of the dancer's headdress as a growing tree, which he suggests is a sign of fertility. I am intrigued by his idea of the cone as a tree, which apparently his informants suggested, although mine did not. I do not, however, concur with the rest of his interpretation. If in fact the cone represents a tree, I think it illustrates the bushlike aspects of this creature: his natural, unsocialized qualities. In addition, I would suggest that the tree being represented is a coconut. I suggest this for two reasons: the first is that the cone on the mask is set back at about a 45-degree angle from the upright, an angle that suggests the leaning posture of coconut trees; the second is that the Baining have a story (referred to in chapter 4 and recounted in the appendix) in which a coconut grows out of the head of a deceased ancestor, and this mask could be an illustration of such an idea. In both these instances the coconut represents an interface between the natural (in one case, the bush; in the other, death) and the social; it is planted on the edge of villages; it is planted on graves; and it is often eaten raw (not transformed by cooking). In all of these aspects, it mediates between the domains of the Baining world, and as such it articulates all of the themes and events of the day dance. When the dancer takes off his mask, he sheds this ambiguous quality and enters the social world completely.

Asavangaka

After the *akurikuruk* the women continue singing, and the circle of women and men, which has continued all day gradually enlarges for the last event of the day. This is the *asavangaka*, which closes the dance. This event consists of two special songs, at least one of which is about the bird, *asavangaka*, which Pool (1971: 99) translates as swiftlet. This bird leaves its nest in the cliffs at dawn and circles in the sky all day long. I have heard Baining refer to this bird's activity as "play." Just as the birds circle the sky from dawn to dusk, so do the women circle the dance ground all day. This endless circling, also called "play," is brought to a close by the swiftlet's song. During these songs the circle of women reverses its direction five or six times. The song is one of farewell and seems to suggest the scattering of the people after the dance.

> They say farewell to the *savangaka* [bird]
> They say farewell to the Chunemba [flower]
> To the mountains
> They say farewell to the *savangaka*
> They say farewell to the Chunemba
> To the place
> They say farewell to the *savangaka*
> And send it off from the school and the buildings
> And send it off from the people's houses.
> They say farewell to the *savangaka*
> They make magic for it with *sagang* [leaves]
> And place them in the running water so one can drink
>   from it
> And look clearly at the blue mountains.
>   (Hesse and Aerts 1978: 45)

Hesse and Aerts say "while flying in groups they [the birds] suddenly change direction, and it is this sudden turnabout . . . that has probably inspired the song" (1978: 46). It certainly seems to correspond to the choreography of the last dances. At the completion of the last song, the circle breaks up and the mass of women and men move forward to the front of the chorus where they throw bits of flowers, leaves, and even twigs at the chorus. The dance is now over. At this point the women and children move back from the clearing and lean-to and make way for the men's chorus and later the *Atut* dancers.

In the closing act, the pieces thrown at the chorus are leaves, twigs and grass; these are all bush items similar to the raw materials used in the day-dance regalia and deposited on the heap outside the bush clearing. By throwing these things away, the dancers are relinquishing the regalia and their bush associations. The "play" and mediation be-tween bush and place is over. Leaves and grass become rubbish to sweep away; day turns to night; and the women quit dancing and sing-ing ("playing") and return to their homes to work (in the most immedi-ate sense, to cook).

At the conclusion of the dance, all the regalia that have been so pain-stakingly produced are unceremoniously discarded or given away. The utility of the objects is used up and their potency depleted. Up to this point these objects have stood in for the social person; now they be-come symbols of the deceased. The masks and regalia are left to decom-pose and become part of entropic nature, while the social dancers re-turn to their homes and food relations. This is the third and final phase of the dance.

As I concluded in chapter 8, the dance cycle parallels not only the life cycle, but also the production and reproduction of society itself. By moving from the domain of daily life to that of ritual the processes of production have become more transcendent. What emerges from the dance ritual is a conceptualization of society as collective domain of meaning. The process of socialization embodies the creation of the so-cial person. The ritual, which is analogous to the socialization process, thus analogously generates society. The creation of society is socializa-tion in its most encompassing sense. In the dance we see the application of the form of this process to itself.

As a society that has no enduring institutions (e.g., lineages or corpo-rate groups) that ensure continuity or collective organization and soli-darity beyond the span of the lives of its individual members and fam-ily-based domestic units, the Baining lack the means of defining their society and its constitutive processes on a collective scale. The con-finement of effective social organization to the lowest possible level, that of the individual person, the family household, or the hamlet, means that social life must be continually reconstituted through the everyday activities (i.e., work) of the members of these units. There are no higher-level, enduring structures to carry part of the burden of sociality.

What the monotonously concrete and repetitive activities of hamlet life and work are unable to do is define and revalidate their character as social forms. The repetitive pattern of daily life is only reflexively recognized as repetitive when the process is framed. It is precisely this that is achieved, on a collective social scale, by the dances (see T. Turner 1977). It is the women and children, not the male mask-bearers, who are the perfect symbolic embodiments of the everyday work of which Baining social life consists. Ironically, the real heroes of the dance are the most boring and repetitive actors; the ceaseless circling of the women in the face of all disruption represents the strength of society. It is framed and validated by the visitations of the fantastic masked ritual celebrants, which appear and then disappear again, leaving its continuity reinforced but unchanged. As the embodiment of self-definition and as the performed creation of the patterns of everyday life, the dance achieves meaning for the Baining—a meaning not verbalized, but directly embodied, like social life itself, in a praxis of self-making.

I thus came to realize that in trying to understand the Baining rituals, so apparently mysterious and remote from ordinary social life, I was actually studying socialization in its most encompassing sense. The dances, I finally understood, are the symbolic cultural forms through which the Baining mediate the social relations of production of themselves. I did not achieve this perspective until I had finished my analysis, because both the symbolic forms and the socialization process involved were very different from my expectations. I had thought that I would be using ritual to help me interpret aspects of the socialization process, not that I would need to undertake a thorough analysis of the socialization process in order to understand the ritual. I certainly had not expected that the central concern of Baining social ideology would take the form of a theory of socialization, extrapolated as a theory of work into a theory of ritual as play and from there into a theory of society as a whole. Nor had I expected that this formulation would explain why the Baining push "play" right out of the society into the marginal domains of the natural and dangerous, where it becomes the ritual means of framing and thus renewing the form of society itself.

10   Atut

The drama and excitement of a Baining Fire Dance are extraordinary. Phantasmagoric masks flit in and out of the shadows created by an enormous fire in the middle of a clearing. The dancers are accompanied by a chorus of male singers who sing in an extremely rapid falsetto style with a kind of yodeling refrain; they accompany themselves with hollow bamboo tube instruments. The scene is periodically shattered and at the same time highlighted as one or more dancers jump(s) into the fire and run(s) through it sending sparks and coals cascading among the dancers, and even the spectators.

This description holds for virtually all the Fire Dances I saw. It appears to be true for those of the Central Baining as well as those of the North Baining.[1] As I mentioned earlier, the Fire Dance of the North Baining, called *Atut,* is not believed to be indigenous to the area, but is thought to have been borrowed from the Central Baining in relatively recent times (Pool 1969–70: 58).[2] A Fire Dance is the kind of event that cannot help but attract attention, even though no attention is given to any other aspect of Baining culture. For this reason, Baining Fire Dances are known throughout Papua New Guinea. They have been

1. I only saw one Central Baining Fire Dance, but I have read and heard descriptions of many others. These dances are often referred to as Snake Dances (Read 1931–32; Bateson 1931–32; Poole 1941–42). They are now performed primarily as a tourist attraction, with tour buses bringing spectators out to watch for a couple of hours. The dances have consequently been modified to suit spectators' demands: they are shortened but sustain a greater dramatic intensity while they last. The one dance I did see was not a tourist attraction, but took place in the village proper several miles from the usual locale. Our group contained the only non-Baining spectators present, although every Fire Dance is attended by numerous Baining who do not participate, and thus fill the role of spectator.

I attended between eight and ten Fire Dances among the North Baining. Some were well-planned events, for which preparations were made weeks in advance. Others were spontaneous events, and the inspiration to perform occurred at the most one or two days before, or even on the same day. These were far less formal and often came as a surprise to the majority of villagers.

2. The North Baining do not use snakes in their Fire Dances, although informants said they used to. This is one significant difference between the dances of the two regions.

filmed for television and movies, pictured on a national postage stamp, and are a major tourist attraction for visitors to Rabaul. All the articles published in English about the Baining (Read 1931–32; Bateson 1931–32; Poole 1941–42; Corbin 1982; Hesse and Aerts 1978; Clarke 1977) are about these dances. Despite the interest and attention it has commanded, however, the Fire Dance remains little understood. In this chapter I explore the Fire Dance in its cultural and social dimensions, in an attempt to understand its role and importance in Baining life.

Atut

Atut is always performed on the evening following an *Asarai* day dance. It can be, and frequently is, performed independently of the day dance, however. When done in conjunction with a day dance, preparations for *Atut* begin weeks ahead of time, approximately when those for *Asarai* begin (see chapter 9). The preparations include the construction of the masks, paints, and body decorations—which are performed in seclusion in the bush, away from the women; and song rehearsals—which are performed publicly in the village at night and are a focus of village attention. When the Fire Dance is performed apart from the day dance, many of the preparations are foreshortened: masks may be reused from previous dances; and rehearsals, if undertaken at all, may take the form of a couple of hours of singing in the evening instead of all-night sessions. In this description I will focus on the preparations that were made for a Fire Dance held in conjunction with a big day dance at Yalom.[3]

I was unable to witness or participate in the *Atut* preparations in part because I am a woman, and also because I was actively participating in the *Asarai* preparations, which were occurring simultaneously. I thought, wrongly as it turned out, that there would be ample opportunities to attend *Atut* preparations later in my fieldwork; and I was even given promises to this effect. On later occasions, however, preparations were made secretly so I would not find out and petition to attend. They were even kept secret from my closest friends so they would not betray the information. The following description is therefore based on informants' accounts, most particularly those of my friend and assistant, Paul Tovi. Tovi kept a field notebook during the month of preparations in which he noted attendance and the sequences and materials of mask construction. He did not describe the procedures of construction, but from other accounts these appear to be very like those employed in *Asarai* preparations, which I did witness.

---

3. The two events were scheduled to celebrate the completion of my house.

Preparations

The bush site for *Atut* is a permanent place located about a half-mile from the village. It consists of an open sided shedlike structure called *akusak*, the same term used in *Asarai* (Hesse and Aerts [1978] call it *avemgka*). Unlike the *akusak* built for the day dance, the night dance *akusak* is maintained continuously, and masks, feathers, paints, and other paraphernalia are stored there between events. The work of preparation does not, therefore, need to commence with building a house, although the roof frequently needs repairs. Because of its permanent nature, this section of the bush is continually out of bounds to Baining women, who know where it is and keep away.

The preparations for *Atut* are the domain of the young men of Yalom. It is basically the youths between twelve and thirty who stage this event. Men of all ages rehearse and sing in the chorus. The young men, however, organize the preparations and make the regalia. These youths are not, on account of this, excluded from the day-dance preparations; in fact, they occasionally help out in the *Asarai* bush site too, sometimes moving back and forth through the sites to exchange materials, borrow shotguns, or sit and chew betel nut. The older men, on the other hand, rarely go to the *Atut* site.

Within the bush site there are no real bosses or leaders; those with more experience teach those with less. As Tovi said,

> If a man is already big and has gone many times to the bush, then he has more knowledge about these things. There is no boss. Whoever has more knowledge teaches the newcomers. The newcomers watch and learn.

Novices are called *asunasta* (pl.) (*asunaska* [sing.]). They are seen as needing to learn new skills, but the acquisition of this knowledge is not formalized in any way. There is thus no "initiatory" aspect to this process, nor is there any sense that a person acquires new status through it. Engaging in *Atut* (preparations or dancing) is not obligatory in Baining society, and is done simply out of individual desire and is termed play.

The *Atut* dance consists of three types of masked figures: *alaspraka*, *anguangi* (or *atutki*), and *avriski*. Each of these wears a different headdress, and it is the construction of these elaborate headdresses that occupies the majority of the time in the bush.

Avriski

The *avriski* is the simplest headdress. *Avriski* is said to be the shape of the wild taro leaf, but the mask neither resembles this leaf nor uses it in its construction. Corbin (1976) says the name refers to the "spirit"

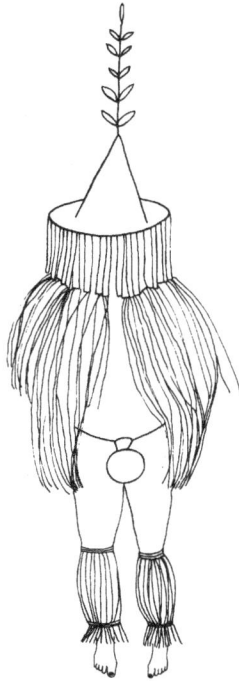

Figure 10.1   *Avriski*

of the taro, but nothing I got suggests the Baining have any concept of spirits of this sort at all. Since Corbin did not learn the language and was working through translators, I am hesitant to accept this claim.

The headdress consists of a cone-shaped hat with a brim (see fig. 10.1). At the point of the hat, a stick protrudes. This stick, *avulvulka*, is decorated with feathers and occasionally with a three-dimensional superstructure of any design, from abstract (circles, triangles) to realistic (e.g., fish, bird, helicopter, numbers). The brim of the hat is fringed with pandanus leaves. Traditionally, this hat was painted with blood spat from the tongues of the workers. Today the leaves are painted with store-bought red enamel paint, which looks glossy and wet.

An *avriski* dancer is covered from his shoulders often as far as his knees with a cape of pandanus leaves. Protruding through this cape is a pubic decoration made out of bark cloth and looking like a mushroom or a drum skin on a tube. This phallic covering is called *alamingel* (also a word for mushroom); nowadays the *alamingel* is tied on with a string around the buttocks. A bark-cloth flap called *aniski* (tail) hangs down over the buttocks. In the past, this piece of paraphernalia was not tied on, but sewn to the pubic hairs in front and pinned to the flesh at the base of the spine in back. From the ankles to the knees the dancer's calves are covered by leaves called *akamarat;* these leaves are like chaps and are intended to protect the dancer's legs from the fire. The body is painted with black ashes and a white earth paint called *arangulka.* The body paint is covered with a spittle of sugar cane juice that gives it a glossy sheen.

Corbin (1976) and Hesse and Aerts (1978) remark that there is usually only one of these masks per dance line and that it is supposed to lead the line and act as a steward to the other dancers. This is not in accord with my experience, since I saw several *avriski* (Corbin calls them *alingen*) masks appearing together, and they did not necessarily enter first. Informants told me that either *avriski* or *alaspraka* could enter first or last, the real restriction being that the *atutki* masks could not lead or end the dance line. Their explanation for this restriction was that the *atutki* is the "father of the other masks" because it is stronger than these others. Under questioning, they revealed that this strength was based on its being made entirely of bark cloth and therefore being more enduring than masks made of pandanus leaves. There was no other explanation for this ordering.

Anguangi

The *anguangi* or *atutki* headdresses are more like helmet masks (see Corbin 1976). These masks are more naturalistic in configuration than either of the other two. They frequently appear to represent the heads of animals or other creatures, although these creatures might well be fantastic and imaginary. The most striking features of these masks are the eyes and mouths. The eyes (usually two, but there may be only one) are unusually large, and are outlined with wood framing and painted with concentric circles. The mouths are usually protruding, giving the appearance of broad bills (like a platypus) (see fig. 10.2). The top and bottom bills create an opening through which the dancer can see. These masks are composed of a wooden frame covered with bark cloth and painted with varying degrees of design. They are made of relatively permanent materials and may be saved from one occasion to the next, although they can be discarded after only one dance. The *anguangi* or *atutki* dancers wear the same body covering as the *avriski* dancers: leaf cape, *alamingel* (phallic decoration), *aniski* (tail), and leaf chaps.

Alaspraka

The third type of mask is undoubtedly the most bizarre. It is a composite of a helmet mask similar to the *anguangi* described above with a

Figure 10.2   *Atut*

pair of huge rectangular frames like billboards, which instead of being hung on the chest and back are hung on the sides of the mask, completely obscuring the helmet mask within except when seen directly from front or back. This contraption is called alaspraka. The helmet mask inside is composed of a soft wood frame covered with bark cloth. It has an open mouth, out of which protrudes a long bamboo tube, which is blown as a trumpet. All of this is encased in a framework made of two panels (the "billboards"), each about four feet high by eight to ten feet long. These panels are made of the same flexible wood as the other mask parts. The placement of the horizontal and vertical pieces is scattered and varies with the designs. The panels are not solid wood, but openwork frames on which strips of pandanus leaves are sewn in an endless variety of patterns. These pandanus strips are then painted with lines or dots of red.

The designs on the panels of the *alaspraka* are complex and varied, and when young (or old) men are given pencil and paper, or even when spontaneously doodling with a stick in the mud, they tend to work out patterns for these panels. The two panels are held together on top by means of cross-braces, each about shoulders' width. From these cross-braces rise thin flexible sticks covered with white feathers. These sticks, called *avulvul*, bend and sway with the dancer's movements. Underneath this bizarre contraption, the dancer is dressed identically to those wearing the other masks. The fact that all the dancers are similarly decorated means that it is quite easy for dancers to exchange masks during the course of an evening, so that one who starts out wearing an *alaspraka* might later give his mask to another dancer and himself don something more compact like an *avriski*.

Hesse and Aerts (1978: 53) report that the *alaspraka* masks, which they call *vurbracha*, are conceived as cobwebs made by spiders *(asinipki)*, and that the variations in their design represent the "variety which one can find in the cobwebs of the forest." While this is a striking image, which to a degree makes sense of an otherwise fantastic design, I did not elicit any such referent, despite a lot of trying. At one point I heard the youths referring to the *alasprangut* (pl.) as *avut* (houses), and I asked if they were meant to be symbolically representative of houses, whereupon people laughed and said "No," adding that it was just a nickname among themselves, since the sides of the masks were like the walls (*asur* [wall, fence]) of a house. In fact Tovi said, "It is not like anything; it is just imagination" (he used the English word "imagination"). From this I am inclined to conclude that while people constantly see images and symbols in these fantastic creations, which they may use to describe and illustrate them, there is no culturally standardized referent for them. In this sense the masks are like a series of Rorschach ink blots into which people can read their own meanings.

Work in the Bush

The majority of the preparation time is devoted to the construction and refurbishing of these masks. In general the early weeks are taken up with the gathering of materials and the construction of the wood frames for the masks. The middle weeks are focused on finding, beating, and sewing on the bark-cloth coverings, and accumulating feathers. The final weeks are spent on the most perishable items: the pandanus leaf coverings, the leaf capes, the black and red paints, etc. This is not to imply that a whole *anguangi* mask can not be completed and set aside at the beginning, or that someone might not have the desire to start a whole mask from scratch in the last week or so. Mask construction is a combination of individual and collective effort. Usually one person begins a frame with some design in mind. Once he has achieved the basic concept, others might join him to finish it up. People do not necessarily build the masks they are going to wear in the dance. One person, perhaps an older youth, might initiate the construction of several masks, while younger boys will work as "crew" on a lot of different ones. Later the youths will divide the masks among themselves. Painting the designs on the masks is the one task that people see as requiring special skill (learned through experience), and according to Tovi's notes only he and one other man engaged in it. Many youths said they did not know how to paint, but I was told they could or would learn through watching others do it.

From the time preparations started in Yalom, about a month before the date of the dance,[4] work was carried out virtually every day. Not every person showed up every day, but some number of the group did. Those who did not might spend the day helping in their gardens, hunting or trapping (often with an eye for birds to provide feathers for the masks), or catching up on sleep after the all-night song rehearsals. There were over fifteen youths actively involved in the work. Although there was no typical pattern of activity, there were certain constants. The young men began to arrive in the early morning, often before 7:00 A.M. Those who were in the middle of a project might resume work on it where they had left off the day before. Others might organize expeditions into the bush for wood for frames, lianas with which to bind the frames, or vines for the same purpose, bark from two kinds of trees, from which to make bark cloth *(atuptam),* and bamboo for trumpets. These materials are all to be found in the bush, several of them in the deep forest, and one—the bark-cloth tree—on the lower slopes of the mountains nearer the coast. It therefore takes some time to amass all the necessary items.

While gathering these materials, it was important that none of the scavengers should encounter any women. It is considered taboo for a woman to see any of the materials used in preparation of the masks: if one were to do so, the materials would have to be discarded. It is also considered harmful and dangerous to the woman, but to what

4. The date of the dance was loosely scheduled for the end of November. As the time drew closer and preparations progressed, it was set definitively as November 23, 1977. The scheduling of this particular event became important because there was another big dance scheduled for November 25 at the neighboring village of Raunsepna. I very much wanted to attend both and found it ironic that the two events were so closely scheduled; I was worried that things might not be ready at Yalom and that they might decide to postpone the dance a day or two. The dance at Raunsepna was scheduled by the Catholic mission to dedicate a new health center, so I knew it would occur on schedule. As it happened, the two dances occurred as planned, two days apart, and I left Yalom the morning after the *Atut* and went to Raunsepna in time to see that performance. I was unable to view any of the preparations at Raunsepna, however, because of the time squeeze.

degree is unclear. She will get sick and might die, but the nature of the ailment is ambiguous. Some said she would have respiratory trouble like a bad cold; others said they did not know. Other evidence seemed to point to gynecological problems of either conception or delivery, but only Tovi would explicitly state this. He said she would get "sik mun" (pidgin for "moon sickness" or menstruation) and that she would loose blood and die.[5]

Another taboo relating to women is that the workers in the bush are forbidden to mention the name of any woman while they work, particularly while they are using vines to bind the frames. It is believed that calling a woman's name will in some way put her in the power of the *atut* spirits (the idea of them as spirits is not explicit but is vaguely present all the same) and she will get sick. The antidote to this and the previously mentioned mishap is for the offending man to tie a knot *(arsong)*, on his costume or mask, or to carry a cut cordyline plant with its leaves tied in knots, on the night of the dance; the polluted woman is then called to untie the knot, thus extricating herself from the dangerous power.[6]

The men are also exposed to some sort of dangerous pollution while working on the dance masks. They are considered impervious to the dangers themselves, but as carriers they can indirectly harm women and children with whom they come into contact. For this reason all the workers ritually wash themselves before they leave the bush site at the end of the day. This washing ceremony has been described in chapter 9; informants, however, assured me it is similar in both bush sites except that the water in the *Atut* site has no magical spell spoken over it. This purification enabled them to move in mixed company without harming anyone. Food or drink (including betel nut or tobacco), which had been in the bush site remained taboo to women and children. After the women realized I was accompanying the men to the bush, most of them ceased asking me for tobacco or betel for fear of pollution. On one occasion, however, a good friend asked me for betel nut, and when I started to explain why she couldn't have it, she told me it was all right, it wouldn't hurt her. Her husband, who was sitting beside us,

5. I was told of a pregnant woman who carelessly gathered firewood near the *Atut* hut when no preparations were in progress. When she got back to her hamlet she fell ill, went into labor, and died in childbirth along with the baby. This illness was blamed directly on the *Atut* on which she had trespassed.

6. Informants frequently drew parallels between the taboos imposed on women with regard to the bush preparations for dances and those imposed on men with regard to the women's preparations of cane belts for their grass skirts. I heard this analogy made primarily in the context of the day-dance preparations, as I described in chapter 9, but Pool (1969–70) refers to it in reference to night dances as well.

confirmed that it was all right. I am led to believe that this stricture is not so rigidly followed in practice as in theory.

None of the bush materials used in the preparation of the masks can be taken out of the *akusak* area until the night of the dance. In contrast to the procedure for *Asarai* masks, all of the discarded and unused materials are disposed of by burning. The one exception to this pattern is in the collection of firewood for the dance itself. This wood is gathered and brought directly into the hamlet nearest the dance ground, where it is stockpiled until the night of the dance. The firewood used in Yalom (but not in Raunsepna) for the Fire Dance was a special kind called *alas*. It consisted of bundles of small twigs that burned rapidly, hotly and with lots of sparks. Hugh stacks of these bundles were amassed before the dance and were the only evidence of the men's activities observable in the village. It was usually the youngest boys who collected this firewood, but young girls seemed to help them. The youngest of those who were helping in the bush site were in charge of collecting the wood, but they were assisted in this task by the children who were not yet old enough (approximately eight to eleven years old) to go to the bush.

Preparations in the Place

While all these preparations are made in the bush, parallel preparations are made, in the form of song and dance rehearsals, in the village. Here, as in the bush preparations, efforts are divided between the day and night dances. On certain nights the women gather to rehearse songs for the day dance. They sing from shortly after sundown until dawn, then they break up and go about their daily work. Boys, girls, and even men might dance in a circle around the house in which the women are singing. On nights when the women are not singing, the men might sing. As the day of the dance approaches, more and more people dance outside, and these rehearsals grow closer and closer together so that there are usually rehearsals two days out of three; Pool (1971: 85) reported rehearsals every evening, which alternated between the men and the women. People consequently get very short of sleep.

The men's rehearsals usually began somewhat later in the evening than the women's, about 9:00 or 10:00 P.M. (after some of the men had napped), and continued until dawn. Almost all the men were present, even those who were planning to dance rather than sing during the actual event. This was the occasion when new songs were learned and old ones remembered, so that the dancers remained abreast of the repertoire for future use. Young boys and girls, and some adolescent women danced around the house in which the men were singing.

The effect of all these rehearsals was to create an atmosphere of heightened activity, communality, and energy in the village. The nighttime activity contrasts with normal daily life, when people generally stay in their houses after dark and go to sleep early (about 8:30 or 9:00 P.M.). Because this atmosphere is itself so different from the regular routine of life, I concur with Pool (1971: 84) that it is itself part of the ritual.

> It is true that they serve many of the same functions as rehearsals. . . . But in addition to this rehearsal aspect, these sessions are part of the ritual. Though the ritual is primarily a one-day affair, there is a gradual ritual build-up which commences with the beginning of mask-building in the bush. . . . The tempo and atmosphere of the ritual increases day by day until it comes to a head on the day of the dance.

Because of these singing sessions, the *Atut* preparations are not as isolated and separate from village life as they appeared at first. One half of the preparations occurs in the village, while the other takes place in the bush. These two aspects remain separate, however, until the night of the performance.

The Dance

Atut is principally considered a fun occasion. Although, as I have described, there are taboos and restrictions on the procedures surrounding the event, the event itself seems to have very little in the way of symbolic referents. *Atut* is performed more frequently than the day dance. A day dance might be performed once every two or three years, while a night dance might be performed as often as once a month (Pool 1971: 60). In Yalom these dances did not occur this often on the average, but there was a week when two night dances were performed. People attributed this abundance to the desire of the youths, and on this occasion to the desires of the boys who were home from school on Christmas vacation. Whatever the pretext, the motive for the performance seems to be simple enjoyment.

On the night of the dance, the chorus usually begins singing at about sundown. Some of the men and boys build a big fire in the middle of the dance plaza, and the singers gather at the edge of the area, often under a lean-to shelter (built to protect the daytime chorus from sun or rain). They play their long bamboo instruments by pounding them against a log or stone. They select at whim from the repertoire of night-dance songs and continue singing even if the dancers have not yet arrived.[7]

Often those on the dance plaza will hear the loud echoing sound of the *alaspraka* trumpet emanating from the forest, and everyone remarks *"atutki."* These sounds may herald the arrival of the dance line, or may just be made periodically to build atmosphere. The trumpet sound is indeed eerie and resounding, and it works well to create a mood of anticipation. Before the masked dancers arrive, women and children may dance around the plaza to the music. Women dance their slow shuffling step, while the children (especially boys) imitate the wilder gyrating step of the *atut* dancers. When the masked dancers arrive, the women are supposed to disappear or keep their distance, but once the dancing is really under way they can return.[8] They move off to the periphery of the dance plaza, where they form a little circle of their own. They never seem to share the dance plaza with the masked dancers, not even to stand by the fire to warm themselves, as do many uncostumed men.

The masked dancers usually appear in a long line somewhere on the periphery of the plaza. In Yalom it was by the top of a small rise just beyond the houses. One or two dancers might be visible while the rest of the line remains out of sight in the bush on the other side of the knoll. Occasionally, however, before the dancers appear, a group of actors might come up and enact a little skit, which informants described as being in the nature of a joke. Typically, one of the young men dresses up as an old man with white hair and dirty skin, and comes up and tries to beg tobacco or betel from the chorus. If they give it to him he goes away and tells the dancers to begin. If they do not give him any, he threatens or cajoles them, and tells them that he is sorry to have to report that things in the bush have gone awry, and that there will be no dancers. He keeps up this harassment until they give him what he wants, and only then does he depart. This little scene is called *asuaka*, which means old man.

A variant on this drama was reported to me by Tovi, who said that at a dance which had occurred about seven or eight years earlier, he, Tovi, had been dressed up as a young girl, with a woman's *aniski* (grass skirt), bark-cloth breasts painted with red paint, and a woman's basket with betel nut, lime, and pepper leaf. He was brought in by an older man who had marched up to the chorus and demanded that they stop

7. The dancers should not arrive before it is totally dark, although at one Raunsepna dance they came in while it was still dusk. I gathered then that this was not proper by listening to the amount of comment it generated.

8. Pregnant women are not supposed to attend the dances, but informants said that if the women stand at a distance it is really all right.

Plate 10.1   Dance line

singing. He said, "Stop singing! First I want to ask if any of you men want to marry my daughter," and he paraded Tovi back and forth. Tovi said that all the young men started to sweat and wanted to drop their bamboo instruments and run away. Tovi started to cry. Finally, one old man agreed to marry her, and the duo went off and called forth the dancers. I never saw any such enactment, nor do I think it is very common;[9] it is, however, evidently an available variant, which can be performed when desired.

After the dance line arrives on the periphery of the plaza, the chorus begins a special song, which serves as an introductory number. It has a rapid, staccato, pounding rhythm with yodeling interludes. At each staccato part one masked figure should dance into the plaza, and dance in place in front of the chorus. When the music changes to the undulating wail, that figure dances away from the chorus to the edge of the circle, where he dances in place while the other dancers make their entrances. The length of each interval varies at the whim of the chorus, and the dancer must stay as long as the verse lasts before being released to join the flanking line. Gradually the dancers outside the plaza dwindle, and the line of masks dancing in place grows. Only when all the dancers have entered does the music change and the line of dancers flanking the circle break up.

At this point, the masks begin to dance wildly around the fire. They dance mainly in a counterclockwise direction except when crashing through the fire (Pool, however, saw clockwise dancing). Individual dancers vary their movements by coming and standing in front of the chorus and dancing in place to the music, then drifting away and beginning around the circle again. The dance consists of the alternation between circling and dancing in front of the chorus. The costumes, music, and firelight nevertheless combine to make it an unearthly and dramatic scene. This atmosphere is heightened and excitement grows when dancers enter the fire. The mood created is somewhat contagious. Long periods might go by with no fire dancing, but once it starts others may get drawn in and participate too. In general nobody really walks or dances in the fire. The action is usually that of running through it and maybe kicking branches or embers to create a shower of sparks. Occasionally, a dancer might pick up a burning log or coal and whirl or throw it into the surrounding crowd. This creates an even bigger stir, and people may scatter, but there are usually men and boys standing near the fire who push and shovel the fire back together and keep feeding new logs and brush to keep it going.

9. Neither Pool (1971), Corbin (1976, 1982) nor Hesse and Aerts (1978) ever mention(s) this sort of performance.

Plate 10.2   *Atutki*

Although once the dancing and circling begin, they continue virtually unaltered until morning, there are a few variations that can serve
to break up the night. Dancers may tire and leave the circle for a rest
(they go behind the knoll where they remove their masks and smoke,
chew betel, or even eat). Occasionally the whole chorus will stop singing for a fifteen- or twenty-minute break, at which time the dancers
leave the place and wait out of sight until the music starts again. If any
portion of a mask breaks off in the dancing or jumping, it is immediately collected by one of the men or boys around the fire and thrown
into the fire; these pieces must be destroyed. A dancer can continue to

Plate 10.3   *Alaspraka*

dance with a mask that has been slightly damaged. If a mask gets too damaged to dance in, however, or if the dancer gets tired, he can return his mask to the bush house, wash, and return as a spectator to the plaza.

The masked dancers are occasionally called upon for other tasks. Women or children prone to sickness, crying, temper, etc. may be pushed under the legs of an *atutki* dancer. Young children are often handed to dancers, who carry them around the circle, striking terror into the hearts of both the victim and other children watching. It is an extremely common threat for adults to tell a child that the *"atutki ki tal nyi"* (the *atutki* will get you [literally, "will carry you"]). These threats are very similar to Western threats about the bogeyman except that in this case the *atut* actually appear in person and do sometimes "carry" children. On one occasion I saw an *anguangi* dancer holding a thin stick, which he used as a whip to hit a young girl whose parents said she should be punished. This act is related to other encounters with *atut*, which will be discussed later.

Fire Dances are often the occasion for house razing. Baining houses are made of wood, bamboo, and thatch, and they need to be replaced every four or five years as best I could judge. Often old houses are left

Plate 10.4   *Atutki* and child

standing as new ones are gradually built. When a dance occurs, these old houses may be scavenged for flammable materials (thatch, bamboo walls, rafters, etc.) to keep the dance fire burning. On one occasion I witnessed, however, a house was just set afire in its place and burned to the ground.

The *atut* dance lasts until the sun comes up. Some time before it gets light, between 5:15 and 5:45 A.M. the masked dancers leave the plaza. Usually they do this in an individualistic way, one at a time as the desire strikes them, but informants also said that it is possible for the opening song to be repeated and for the masks to leave one by one to the music. The dancers must be gone by the time the sun rises. Corbin (1976) reports that the dancers must extinguish the fire by stomping on it before they leave, but I never heard of this nor saw it happen. The chorus continues to sing after the masks leave, until about 6:00 A.M. Then it closes with one particular song, *Elasaka*. This and the introductory song are the only songs that are obligatory for the dance and the only ones that have fixed positions in the sequence of events. *Elasaka* means life.

Analysis

The most important thing to understand about the Fire Dance is the concept of *atut*. *Atut* refers to the dance as a whole; it is the name for the event. Within that encompassing domain, *atut* also refers to a particular kind of mask, the headdress type, which is also called *anguangi.* Outside the context of the dance, the term *atutki* is used very like a synonym for *aioska* (in Yalom informants said that *atut* are *aios* although they have both words in their dialect). This is particularly true when *aioska* refers to a bush spirit that frightens people in the bush or at night.

Children who misbehave or cry incessantly are frightened and cajoled by threats of *atut* coming to take them away. In fact the threat of these *atut* can be realized at times other than dances. Twice during my stay in Yalom, the quiet of the evening was broken by loud thumps on the outside walls of the houses. People inside got very excited and shouted *"atutki, atutki"* and pushed the younger children outside. There, standing and shuffling in a semi–dance step in the moonlight, was an *atutki (anguangi)* figure, mask, leaf covering, body paint and all, holding a bundle of twigs (actually a vine called *anguruk*) in his hand. Parents pushed their children towards him and he lashed their upper arms with his sticks. Occasionally, adolescents or adults would also present themselves for whippings, and in these cases the *atutki* would whip them and then hand them the lashes so they could whip him in return. Nobody could explain why this was done. The *atutki* is here being used in a dual role. Children who are not properly socialized are being punished by those beyond society. In a sense they are being shown where their sort of behavior leads. In contrast, the fully social members of society, adolescents and adults, are showing that they can confront these natural forces by taking the whipping. They then reverse the relation and whip the *atutki* and send it back to the bush. They are setting an example for the children, who are petrified of the *atutki*, by showing them that adults can match the power of the *atutki* and that they should emulate these role models.

The relationships between Baining and *atut* are analogous to those between Baining and *aios* described earlier. One gets the feeling that there is no real distinction between *aios* and *atut* within a range of shared meanings. (Informants vaguely acknowledged that the dead are *atut*, but I never heard a corpse or specific deceased person referred to as *atutki*). I would venture to say that people think of *atut* as a species of *aios*, most particularly those creatures who live in the bush and chase or terrorize people. People fear *atut* just as they fear *aios.*

These attitudes are in keeping with the fact that *Atut* is essentially focussed on what Van Gennep (1960) calls the liminal phase. The little skit called *asuaka*, where actors dress up and come in to tease the chorus, might be seen as a rite of separation. In these scenes young male actors take the roles of old men or young females. The roles that they play are the inverse of their own on some important social dimen-

sion (age or sex). The chorus and the spectators must accept these inversions as real, that is, they must commit themselves to an inverted
world before the dance can proceed. Once the audience has accepted
these basic inversions, they have entered the liminal phase and the
dance begins. Although this little drama is only occasionally performed, its existence fills the structural role of a separation rite within
the ritual process. The rarity of its performance illustrates how much
of the structure and meaning of these performances is present only by
allusion.

As a ritual of the margins, *Atut* is composed of a series of segregated
domains. It only occurs at night; it begins after sundown and ends at
sunrise. In *Atut* the sexes are already separated; the men alone sing
and dance. If the women also want to dance, they can only do so in a
corner away from the central plaza. The ages are also segregated, and
it is specifically the young men who perform *Atut*. What is important
is how this segmentation is opposed to the normative patterns of cooperation and integration. Not only are the normal social contexts of age,
sex, and sociality pared away, but the cosmological distinctions that
normally accompany these social distinctions are also eliminated. The
separations of bush and "place," night and day, human and animal,
alive and dead, male and female are elided, and bush creatures in the
form of *atut* (alias *aios*) invade the plaza. The *atut* represent the supernatural creatures, *atut/aios*, which inhabit the bush and are created out
of bush materials. These materials are transformed by human hands
and are then inhabited by humans. Informants also said that once preparations in the bush house have commenced, the real *atut* that normally
live scattered in the forests will gather by the bush house to watch the
proceedings. Thus, these objects represent a convergence of supernatural creatures and man-made creation.

The various dimensions of the Baining world are called into question
by the *atut*. They are bush creatures who invade social space; they are
humans who dress up as natural and/or supernatural beings; they are
men who take on the identities of creatures whose names have feminine endings. Their dance is disorderly and chaotic, by contrast with
normal life and other dances. But the dissolution of the normal boundaries between domains provides certain rewards to offset the chaos that
it engenders. The processes occurring during *Atut* open new avenues of
interaction between normally separate domains, and the mediation of
these relations is considered very potent. The *atut* are thus believed to
have powers that they can bring to bear on Baining society. In this sense
again, the *atut* are similar to the *aios* because they are the mediators of
the same sort of natural power. There are fleeting references to the
forms this power takes as when the *atut* carries and handles the vine

whips or when people crawl under the dancers' legs. I believe, however, that the real mystique and power of the *atut* lies not in these actions or this paraphernalia, but in the fire.

It is the fire and the dancers' ability to penetrate it that captures the imagination in *Atut*. For the Baining, heat (e.g., fire) is the transformative agent par excellence. The Baining use fire to transform things from natural to cultural, from raw to cooked, cold to hot, bush to place (as in the making of gardens). Mature social actors are people with stores of internal heat (manifest in their ability to sweat). Old people sit close to a fire to warm themselves, thereby making themselves more social (see chapter 5), and fire is used at night to provide light and ward off the cold. The *atut* do not use fire as a tool in any of these ways; their fire is not a mediator, but a direct extension of themselves—a shared essence. *Atut* do what no Baining can do: they walk on, pick up, and play with, fire. They do not warm themselves next to it; they enter it directly. They do not use fire to transform food into social essence, the fire itself is their fuel. It is their external heat source, and in this way it is especially potent, because it can be alienated from its possessor. For this reason it is especially efficacious for curing people. Not only do the *atut* use and relate to their fire differently than do the Baining, but the fire itself is different. This fire is not an agent of transformation that can be used in a controlled fashion to alter substances, but the reverse—a force of destruction and consumption, as can be seen when the fire consumes whole houses or bits of masks. Yet even this is not the true essence of the *Atut* fire. I believe that the *Atut* fire is powerful because it burns without appearing to consume. It is an ever-present blaze, which goes through no cycles. Normal fires are started slowly, blaze hot, and then die down, in a fashion analogous to the life cycle; the *Atut* fire burns brightly from start to finish. It is constantly replenished, of course, but the effect of this feeding is to sustain an unceasing fire. It represents the invariant essence of transformation. Into this conflagration move creatures who are immune to the destructive force of the fire, and indeed are identified with it. It is as if the fire burns without consuming them. Even more, the fire threatens to overwhelm everything when the dancers begin to wield the fire as a weapon, to fling sparks, and scatter embers. This is a far cry from a fire contained on a hearth. In this respect the fire seems to represent the domain of nature that is ever present in Baining cosmology; it is raw fire.

It is because the fire represents nature so completely during this dance that it is so incompatible with sunlight. It is not the same fire that cooks food, warms people, and makes gardens during the day; in fact it is antithetical to these uses (note that the women never go near the fire to warm themselves at night, and the men are there ostensibly to feed the fire). Instead of being a useful tool in their control, the fire is a raging force out of human control and dominated by supernatural beings who share its power.

The *atut* dancers share the powers of the fire. They are the antithesis of social personae; they are the dead, the natural spirits, and the embodiments of disorder and chaos. They threaten the whole socialization process in their attacks on children and people in the bush. They are the antithesis of fully social male adults, those who must enact their roles.

The natural and chaotic qualities of *Atut* are reflected in other aspects of the event as well. The dance movements themselves are disorderly and chaotic by comparison with those of other Baining dances and with normal Baining life. They are indicative of raw energy, uncontrolled by social form. In other Baining dances, the dancers form lines or circles, which orient one dancer to another, and all of them to the available space, in patterns that are suggestive of social relationships. In *Atut*, after the initial introduction, the dancers are independent of one another, and each dances where or how he pleases. Other than a general counterclockwise directionality, the dancers move at their own speed, on their own paths; they can dance in front of the chorus as much or as little as they like; they can dance into or through the fire; they can stop or rest of their own free will.

The chorus is situated in opposition to these dancers. The chorus is not individualistic, nor is it chaotic. It maintains a socially patterned presence for the duration of the night. That the chorus and dancers are opposed is evident in a number of ways. The chorus has consistently maintained its presence in the village, where it rehearsed and where it now sings. The chorus can begin singing before sundown and continue after sunrise. It sings in concert, according to prescribed patterns, and sits in one place, often under a rude shelter. The *atut* dancers show their opposition to the chorus both by their chaotic dancing and also by their dancing in front of the chorus. There, they seem in a sense to be baiting the chorus, confronting its members with their natural essence. These confrontations are indicative of the whole event: one individual acting on his own whim against a group acting in unity according to preordained patterns and structural concord; the chaos of one night in opposition to the daily social pattern of the rest of the year.

Although the chorus has very little control over the dancers at the height of the frenzied night dance, it does exert control at the beginning and end of the event, when it calls the dancers in one by one, and equally when it dispatches them one by one at dawn. It also controls the event in another and far more important way: the chorus must continue to sing until dawn, whether or not there are any dancers remaining on the plaza. Here we can see that the chorus is not just an accompaniment for the dancers, but is an important structural element in the whole ritual design. The chorus must not only greet the day, thereby mediating the realm of the night and *atut* with that of the sun and of Baining society, but it must do so with a special song called *Elasaka*. The shadows of night, death, and destruction are thus swept away and encompassed by this incantation to daylight, life, and creation.

> I sing *elasaka* and I will finish it [the dance]
> I sing *elasaka* and I will finish it
> I sing *elasaka* and I will finish it
> There is no more [no more songs]
> I sing *elasaka* and I finish it, the sickness
> I stay after it, the cold is gone, the sweat is gone.

These last lines refer to the cold of the night, which is now over, and the sweat of the dance, which is finished. Daylight, health, and life have emerged. Another text that can be sung at the end is as follows:

> I close [stop] myself with *elasaka, elasaka* here
> I close [stop] myself with *elasaka, elasaka* here
> I close [stop] myself with *elasaka,*
> I get rid of them with the songs [*sumup*]
> I get rid of them with the songs [*amambu*].

This song refers directly to the departure of the *atut* ("I get rid of them"), and suggests that these songs of life *(elasaka)* are anathema to the *atut* and can send them rushing back to the bush (if they have not already left) by their very performance.

The closure of *Atut* is, as we have seen, not greatly elaborated. In most cases, the dancers betake themselves from the plaza at whim, thus strengthening the illusion that the *atut* make their home in the forest by day. Nevertheless, their departure does begin the transition to normal time, in which bush and place, night and day, and death and life are segregated. With the domains separated once again, the chorus concludes its performance by greeting the day with the song of "life." After this the men and women resume their normal tasks, and a new day of work begins. The Baining have once again asserted some form of dominance over the forces of nature.

Songs and Singing

Although within the context of the dance the singers and dancers are structurally opposed, the levels of opposition are still more complex.

On one level, the singers represent society in contrast to the dancers from the bush, but within this activity lies another opposition manifest in both the form and content of the songs themselves. *Atut* music is wilder and less constrained than other Baining music. It consists of an extremely rapid, high-pitched, full-throated chant, accompanied by energetic pounding of bamboo on wood. Song sessions are intense activities, which sometimes seem to produce heightened emotions in participants (see chapter 6). Not only the form but the content of the songs contrasts with normal Baining values. The subjects of the songs are not those found in normal daily discussions. The song texts are more in the nature of gossip than anything else. They narrate and reflect on situations and behavior that in the Baining world are classified as private, natural, shameful, and problematic. They are composed by individuals, and, although learned by the group, their referents are not part of a communal store of knowledge. People do not need to know particular songs, or even any songs, to be active members of the society.

It has been disconcerting to anthropologists (Bateson 1931–32; Pool 1971) that the songs *(asunup)*, which are so exotic a part of Baining culture, and which are the focus of so much enjoyment, have such mundane texts. "The songs contain no reference to ancestors or other religious concepts. They are simple little lyrics referring to incidents of daily life, to love affairs and to dreams" (Bateson 1931–32: 338). The songs certainly do not talk about the great cosmological issues of Baining life. There is no reference to ancestors, birth, death, marriage, initiation, spirits, harvests, etc. Although they do not name great cultural issues, the songs are nonetheless reflections of the patterns and values of Baining life. In normal Baining routine, gossip is not very common. People do not comment or speculate on other people's behavior, disputes are infrequent, and the scandalous or shameful aspects of people's pasts are kept quiet, remaining perhaps in the memory of those involved or their witnesses, but not often referred to in subsequent discourse. This lack of gossip allows normal discourse and daily life to flow without too many personal disruptions. As we have already seen, this devaluation of the merely personal in favor of normative sociality is one of the dominant principles of Baining life.

Despite these intentions (and despite my original perceptions of Baining life, based on outward appearances), scandalous and shameful activities are not quite so absent as they first appear. Accusations, suspicions, and confessions of adultery, pre-marital sex, theft, even sorcery, do occasionally arise. It is characteristic of the Baining however, that they try to settle these issues quickly and forget them. Then, instead of spending hours analyzing or slandering people's characters, they might compose a song about the incident. As Tovi said, "Songs are where people put talk about what other people do." Often these songs are composed by the perpetrator of the infraction him- or herself, and enumerate his or her shame or badness.

> The others are talking of me here
> The others are talking of me here
> And they talk of him,
> And they talk of him.
> He is a thief and a trickster
> And they talk to each other about him
> They will send him to the prison
> They will put knowledge in his head [will teach him].

This song was composed by a young man about himself and his friends who were caught pretending to be *aios* and extorting food, money, and tobacco from others. Another man, involved in the same scheme, composed this song.

> Friend, you see the women
> And they are talking about the male flying fox
> Friend, you see the women
> And they are talking about the male flying fox
> And they talk of the taro
> And they talk of the money,
> Of the one who talks a lot ["mauswata" in pidgin]
> And the trickster.
> Later they will imprison them at Lassul.

In fact no one was imprisoned for this scheme, but they were made to feel ashamed and thus wrote these songs.

Another youth caught in adultery composed this song.

> And the flying fox cries here
> And the flying fox cries here
> He spreads talk of himself, how he is bad.

In these songs, the flying fox represents a man, and is a way of referring to someone rather obliquely, although everyone knows the convention.

> They talk of him, they talk of him here
> I am the flying fox
> They talk of him, they talk of him here
> I am the flying fox.
> They talk to him about the woman
> And they speak to him twice.
> But he does not like it,
> He does not want it,
> He is a stubborn man.

This song recounts how the elders tried to make this youth marry a certain woman, but he stubbornly refused.

> They stared at me,
> They stared at me
> You would have said they were frogs
> You would have said they were fish.
>   (Bateson 1931–32: 339)

This song was collected by Bateson. It was composed by a young man who had been taken to court for an offense against a small child. The words refer to the staring of the assembled men.

Baining songs need not refer to the specifics of the event to which they allude, and thus often those who sing the song have no knowledge of the meaning of the text. Nonetheless, such songs do always refer to a particular event.

As we have seen elsewhere (chapter 6), songs do not only refer to "scandalous" types of events, they can refer to sentiments such as loneliness, hunger, sadness, etc., or to other sorts of events outside of the daily routine. Visits by anthropologists, district officers ("kiap" in pidgin), people from other tribes, helicopters, ships might all be inspiration to a composer.

> One kind of work for us, and it divides us
> One kind of work for us, and it divides us
> Independence changes the Council, Provincial Govern-
>   ment, village court, village court.

This song refers to some of the confusions the Baining suffered after independence from Australia caused changes in local authority structures.

> We are sorry for her, later she will go from here
> We are sorry for her, later she will go from here
> We are sorry for her, later she will go, and
> The men and the women from Yalom they cry for her, it
>   is true
> They cry for her, it is true.

This song was written on the eve of my departure from Yalom.

These events and sentiments share the characteristics of being outside Baining society or of threatening the boundaries of Baining social patterns. Such events are carefully contained by the Baining. Whenever possible, they, and their disruptive influences are displaced from daily life and relegated to the domain of ritual, song, and dance. They thus become transformed into ritual "play"; as in other instances of play, the songs constitute a collective form for dealing with disruptive forces and behaviors that threaten social norms. These song texts and references differ strikingly from those Schieffelin (1976) and Feld (1982) discuss for the Kaluli because they are not designed to evoke affect.

At the point when the domains of nature and society are least distinct and the flow between them is greatest, the songs that are being sung refer to events and behavior that also transgress the boundaries of natural and social. The dance and masks themselves symbolically illustrate spatial and cosmological distinctions and transgressions; the songs refer to parallel distinctions and transgressions in the domains of social action and social relationships. Together, the dance and music encompass both domains of the Baining world in a moment in time without actually explicitly uniting or equating the two. The dance events are powerful but implicit expressions of the supreme values and concerns of Baining culture and society.

11   Anarchy as Structured Antistructure

When I set out to begin my fieldwork the Baining were notorious for being "unstudiable," or, as Bateson put it, for "lacking any formulable culture." From my acquaintance with the Baining, I certainly agree that the concepts of social and cultural structure that Bateson and Poole attempted to apply to them do not in fact work. This, however, is not the result of some deficiency on the part of the Baining; the problem has lain all along in the shortcomings of the theories so unsuccessfully imposed upon them. Baining social life does not lack structure, nor does Baining culture lack form. The theoretical value of the Baining case is precisely that it challenges the anthropologist to rethink basic concepts of social and cultural anthropological theory and come up with new concepts capable of dealing with the structures of Baining society and cultural consciousness.

Taking up this challenge, the analysis of the immanent principles of Baining social practices and cultural forms of consciousness presented in this book departs from much conventional anthropological thinking in five specific respects. First, it treats the production of the social person as subject, agent, and social identity as embedded in social organization, rather than as a unit of analysis separate from it. Second, it takes social activities and transformative processes (e.g., work, the life cycle, etc.) as the primary units of social and cultural structure alike. By identifying underlying schemas and invariant constraints within these processes, the locus of structure is located within the processes and not outside them. This approach contrasts with social anthropological conceptions of structure as unchanging institutional form *external* to the processes and activities that "flow through" it. It also differs from synchronic structuralism's goal of abstracting the paradigmatic relations of the semiotic elements of activities from the syntagmatic forms of the activities. Third, in stressing the social nature of activity, my analysis distinguishes the social components of subjective activity from the psychological components of the same activity (e.g., my distinctions of sentiment from emotion, value from motivation, and the symbolic forms of mediation of social interaction from individual "cognition").

This point, of course, is a familiar tenet of the Durkheimian tradition, but it has been ignored by much recent writing on the cultural formation of "emotions." Fourth, in critical opposition to Durkheim, I have sought to emphasize ways that cultural forms of consciousness of social relations and personal actions alike may distort or misrepresent them by projecting the subjective contributions of acting subjects onto objective forces or entities. The result is that socially stereotyped representations of social and personal relations often fail to correspond to their objective forms. This results from the socially determined perspective of the actor, which renders invisible aspects of the pattern or situation of interaction in which he or she participates. Fifth, I have tried to reconceptualize the nature and role of social values in order to reintegrate value theory into both the cultural and social aspects of the analysis. My approach starts from a focus on social forms of productive activity and examines the interdependence of the different productive activities those forms define and promote. The cumulative result of these analytical and theoretical moves is that the distinction between social and cultural analysis disappears, as objective cultural and social structures alike become grounded in the subjective forms of social activity, and vice versa.

In recent years the theoretical concepts of structure, society, and culture have been widely repudiated by "postmodern" approaches, which have claimed to supplant or dissolve them in various ways. While my critique shares certain points of departure with these postmodern formulations, it moves in a fundamentally different direction. Merely jettisoning the notions of structure, or of objective cultural or social reality, or indeed of subjective agency, as many of these approaches do, succeeds only in turning them into unwitting caricatures of the theories they reject. In contrast, my project has been to reformulate the notions of structure, society, and culture, as well as those of the social person, cultural subject, and value, as immanent features of socially organized practical activity. I attempt to demonstrate how these interdependent features can be discovered and analyzed through ethnographic observation of interpersonal interactions. My analysis is thus explicitly conceived in the anthropological tradition of approaching general theoretical issues by way of immersion in ethnographic particularities.

Formulating the Structures of Baining Life

The first step toward uncovering the social and cultural structures of Baining life is to recognize the kinds of patterns that exist in Baining social interactions: something Bateson and Pool largely failed to do

because they were looking in the wrong places. Living among the Baining, I fell easily enough into the repetitive and orderly routines of everyday social life. I only felt disoriented when I tried to think of these
manifest regularities in terms of the anthropological notions of society,
structure, and the individual I had brought with me to the field. Eventually I gave up trying, and devoted my efforts simply to recording
the routines of the daily life going on around me. I began to notice that
many of these routines were concerned in one way or another with the
making or affirmation of aspects of personal identity. A prime example
of this, which became the thread I followed to unravel many of the
basic patterns of Baining life, was the practice of adoption. Baining
adoption, I saw, was not a unique event or instantaneous jural redefi-
nition of personal relations and identity, but a cumulative process of
repetitive exchanges, involving the provision of food by the adopting
parents to the adopted child, considered by the Baining to be ultimately
repaid by the adopted child in adulthood in the form of support for
these aged adoptive parents. The valued identity of "adopted child"
was defined in terms of the activities through which it was produced:
not its abstract jural relationship to the adopting parents but their repetitive actions of producing and giving food.

As a paradigm of the patterning of Baining social life, the example
of adoption thus suggested that the social identity of the individual
(i.e., the "person") constituted, at least for the Baining, a fundamental
category of social organization. From this standpoint, it appeared that
the organization of social activities involved in "making" a person
could be seen simply as the complement of the aspects of personal
identity produced by those activities; and further, that these same activities created the household as a social unit. The basic constituents
of such complementary patterns, at both personal and social relational
levels, were not abstract norms or jural rules but material activities.
These activities have the same underlying transformative patterns:
they are *schemas* rather than norms.

The Baining person and Baining social activities thus appeared to
constitute complementary (and equally "social") aspects of a single
comprehensive pattern, rather than separate and incommensurable
levels, one "social" and one "individual." Trying to grasp this pattern
as immanent in material activity, I gradually came to see the social
person as itself merely the schematic organization of the material body,
considered as a set of bodily processes and qualities that are themselves
produced by the schemas of Baining social activity. The body, in other
words, serves as the material interface between the internal schematic
pattern of personal identity and the external social activities that produce it. The social production of the body, in its various culturally de-

fined aspects, thus emerged as a primary focus of Baining social organization.

It took me much longer to realize that the relations among the various sets of schemas involved in the production of the body/person themselves constituted a sort of metaschema, which acts as an invariant constraint on the transformations embodied in the individual schemas. This realization came as I increasingly attempted to integrate the constructive side of Baining social life and personhood with its complementary deconstructive or disintegrative aspect. The Baining recognize that what is put together through their concerted efforts to "make themselves" must eventually come apart. The life that progresses through successive stages of "making" until it becomes, in its turn, a "maker" of other lives, eventually loses its ability to keep making and finally to keep itself together. At this point, it enters a "second childhood" in which others must care for it, and it eventually dies, in an ultimate dissipation of the energies that have created and sustained it. The negentropic process of production (of social persons and relations) is ultimately balanced, within the span of each person's life, by the reverse—entropy. This inexorable balance regulates the transformations that constitute the complementary phases of the Baining life cycle, and thus coordinates the schemas constituting the pattern of Baining personhood and social relations. Taken together, the schemas comprised in the Baining social universe thus form a structure in the dynamic sense of Marx (1947) or Piaget (1970) (as a set of transformational processes regulated by invariant constraints) rather than the static sense of the functionalist-positivist and structuralist concepts of structure.

Like the schemas of which it consists, this structure is immanent in the daily material activities of Baining life and personhood. It is, in short, a "deep" structure rather than a transcendental formal pattern. It is a structure in constant motion, maintaining a constraining balance between constructive and disintegrative forces. This structure is infinitely replicable in social time (in practical terms, reproducible in the same form from generation to generation) and social space (i.e., applicable across social space from the "making" of an individual person to the relations among the families comprising a homestead, and ultimately to the collective relations of society as a whole to the natural world as expressed in communal ritual).

Discovering such replication is what allowed me to recognize and abstract the underlying patterns or schemas that form the basis of Baining life. This model and the schemas it comprises are embedded in everyday activities: work, family life, and rituals. These activities produce the relations and linkages that give form to Baining life. Among the Baining, the moments of production and generation are not separable from the mundane activities of daily existence. Nevertheless, the form and meaning are deeply embedded in these events and are not easily recognized.

Work as Cosmology: Nature into Culture and Back Again

The basic principle informing the pattern of Baining activity is the transformation of natural entities into social products. This process is the underlying schema of Baining life, and it delineates the most basic values in Baining culture. Activities that produce this transformation acquire value. In the Baining case, the most valued products of this transformation are social persons, and the most valued activities are those which transform unsocialized beings (i.e., children) into social persons. The ability to engage in this transformative activity is the most valued quality that can be attributed to an individual. What prestige there is accrues to the people who socialize others. Baining persons do not permanently embody this ability, however; instead they gradually lose it by passing it on to others. They "use it up" by engaging in the work of "making" others, and become relatively less social as they age.

Baining concepts of bodiliness reflect this concept. The body is both natural and social, and constitutes the primary interface of natural properties and socializing processes. All the main processes of socialization and desocialization are bodily processes: working and sweating; eating food and growing; sex and reproduction; aging and death. Even the apparent exception, adoption, defined as the replacement of natural bodily reproduction by a purely social relationship, is pragmatically effected through the substitution of one set of bodily processes (nurture, work, sweat, and the provision and eating of food) for another (sexual reproduction). Baining society, culture, and personal identity are thus all constructed as scenarios of the drama of the social appropriation and loss of the natural body. As a biological product of sexual reproduction, imbued with energy, strength, and reproductive powers, the body is the primary natural raw material of social production. Through its activities of work and growth, it is at once the primary instrument and the main site of this productive process and, as the material aspect of social personhood, its principal product. Finally, through its loss of flesh and blood, it ages and eventually dies; it thus becomes the mere natural waste or residue of the socializing process. Analogously, the ritual masks, the construction and animation of which constitute the focus of Baining ceremonial, are themselves virtual bodies. They are laboriously produced (socialized) and subsequently discarded to revert to the natural bush from which they came when their part in the social drama is finished.

There is thus a common underlying pattern to all the activities the Baining call work: the transformation of a natural into a social entity, defined as a person or product integrated into Baining society and participating in the activities that sustain the social milieu. To a greater or lesser extent all of Baining life is concerned with manipulating movement and transformation between natural and social domains. The boundaries between nature and society are not permanently fixed; they are constantly negotiated by actors as they move through their environment encountering, transforming, or succumbing to natural forces (e.g., through farming, hunting, or other interactions with animals or *aios*). These encounters lead to a variability of individual experience both over time and over space. The Baining are constantly altering the boundaries of the natural domain as they transform segments of it into gardens, hamlets, or ritual bush sites. As they walk across the landscape they are continually crossing the margins between natural space and socialized space. These margins are not fixed, but change and alter as social action and time work in different ways upon the landscape. The boundaries and characteristics of actors are likewise relative and not fixed.

In general, there are broad categorical definitions of what nature is and where it is found, and of what society is and where it is found. There are also general criteria for determining who are socially mature, active people. These broad principles, however, do not necessarily apply uniformly in all instances. Baining actors are constantly encountering and transforming the boundaries of these domains. Through their actions they actively create the boundaries of their world.

This cyclical pattern, or master schema, is at once highly adaptable and also extremely stable. Because it is a schema of incorporation, which acts on elements from one milieu and converts them into transformed products in another, the basic pattern can encompass a wide range of new elements. New crops such as corn, cucumbers, or beans can be subsumed into the garden domain without challenging the values the Baining give to garden work. New activities like growing coconuts, cocoa, cardamom, or coffee for cash can be introduced and subsumed into the garden schema.

In this case, the product of the work of planting, nurturing, and harvesting is not food; it is not directly used to nurture and instill social values in children. Instead, these crops are sold for cash. The cash, however, is used primarily for nurturing and socializing. It is spent on store-bought food, clothing, and school fees, each of which is an extension of traditional activities. The food and clothing are a form of nurture, while school has become an extension of the parental activity of teaching children to work and to value work. By providing school fees, the parents instill a new but compatible value of formal education into the roster of activities that children need to master in order to become social actors in their own right. The Baining myth about the origin of the coconut now includes a new phrase in the father's dying words: "This plant will provide you with food *and money*" (see appendix). Each of these items is the legacy of parents to children.

Baining social organization is composed of schemas based on the same principle of transformation embodied in work. Much of what we would call Baining social organization is manifest in elementary family relations; the nuclear family functions as the principal unit of residence, production, consumption, and social interaction. The "natural" relations within the nuclear family are transformed into "social" ones by key activities such as adoption, which creates the social and cultural aspects of family relations; socialization, which creates social actors out of "natural" beings; garden work, which both transforms natural space into a social milieu, and produces the principal medium of exchange in the society, food; food exchange, which generates the social bonds between both individuals and groups; and ritual, which abstracts all of these relations to produce a model of and for social reproduction. These activities simultaneously generate both individual persons as social actors and the social-cultural system within which they act.

Food giving is a mundane and repetitive daily activity, but it is valued among the Baining because it creates and renews the social bonds between parents and children. The medium, food, that produces such bonds is therefore imbued with social value. The social value that accrues from food giving and exchange is then generalized and pervades the entire domain of Baining social relations. Everyone engages in food exchange, but the role a person plays alternates over the life cycle. In general, children receive food, while adults give it, but adults also exchange with peers on a regular basis, switching between the roles of giver and receiver. Elders who are no longer productive gradually revert to receiving food more often than they give it, and become more childlike.

The basic pattern of food giving underlies two quite different productive processes. The first is the replacement of social actors by their successors, each generation replacing itself through the socialization of the succeeding generation. In the course of the exchange between an adult food giver and a young child, the child is simultaneously instilled with social values (e.g., work and parenting) and with social substance (food). This is a productive process. Through it, the child comes to incorporate the values, attributes, and actions of a social person. As each new social actor goes on to participate in the production and so-cialization processes, he or she replicates this pattern in his or her rela-tions with the next generation. The reenactment of the schema of per-sonal experience thus becomes social reproduction.

Food giving also constructs and maintains the bonds that form the fabric of Baining society. When adults proffer food and betel nut, the gesture is usually immediately reciprocated and in most cases in a strictly symmetrical pattern. This is very different from the asymmetri-cal exchange between generations. This pattern of immediate exchange extends the ties of sociality between individuals and households. It creates social bonds (see Fajans 1993a). In a society such as the Baining, in which there are no corporate groups and important extrafamilial roles and relations, the ties between people have to be constantly con-structed and renewed on an ad hoc basis. Because of the social values embedded in food, it is used to create and perpetuate the social nexus in which people live and act. By exchanging this highly valued sub-stance, people create the web of relationships that defines and binds them; this nexus is society. The daily exchange of food and betel nut has nothing to do with reproduction in the sense of replacement, but everything to do with the ongoing reproduction of the social relations that constitute communal society. When people stop engaging in these activities, the ties wither. In such circumstances actors become progres-sively less social. Aging and dying are processes that attenuate and then terminate the ties that bind. The Baining social system is thus a pattern of relations that must constantly be recreated through the activ-ities of its members.

This takes steady work. Work continually consumes raw energy in the forms of food and heat. The Baining acquire energy by trans-forming natural products into social ones. Nature is the raw material for social production. This aspect of production is symbolized by the heap the men make as they enter the ritual bush site each day. With these energy-providing natural materials, the Baining produce social products and relations. Raw materials and energy, however, are not enough. The social input, provided by human action, transforms this material and energy so that it can be utilized to achieve social goals. It is the striving for and attainment of these ends that in turn invest the transformative processes with sociocultural value. Garden work, socializing, cooking, and sharing are the processes through which raw potential energy is abstracted from nature and converted in order to be utilized and consumed by society. This energy is bound into the matrix of social relations and their concrete transformations. The sys-tem needs a constant replenishment of this energy because society con-tinually consumes it. This dissipation occurs in the consumption of food and the expenditure of energy in work, through the use of fire to heat and cook, through the production of sweat in gardening, and through the transference of human energy to others by way of childbirth and socialization. Society is the transformed state in which adopted, socialized people live in cleared villages heated by fires and eat cooked food that is exchanged among households, etc. Society is what people make, and by making it they make themselves, their ultimate product.

Although society persists, its individual components do not: cooked food is consumed to provide energy to work and socialize; social persons are also consumed through the act of producing other social persons. Bits and pieces of society are used up over time, and drop out. Socialization and production are part of a cycle, the latter half of which is a reversal of the former. In this latter phase, people die and revert to nature; food is consumed and expelled as feces; unused food decays; garbage is thrown away and reverts to nature; the forest reclaims the swidden plot; and the masks rot and return to the bush from whence they came. These latter transformations are not produced by human activity, but are not conceived as the products of active natural processes either; rather they are considered to result from a lack of effective action or transformative energy. This aspect of life is symbolized by the heap that the men make as they leave the ritual bush site each evening.

These aspects of death and degeneration constitute a mirror phase to socialization. As components of society dissipate their energy, they become transformed in reverse: gardens revert to natural bush; people age and die; domestic pigs run wild; and children play in the mud or steal cucumbers. These elements revert to "nature" in the residual, entropic, sense of the term: that is, not nature in its aspect as fecundity and raw potential, but in its aspect as chaos and sterility. "Nature" here, is entropy, the dissipation of energy. Elements of this natural, entropic milieu are characterized by the loss of energy and heat, and their inability to reciprocate in social interaction; in this domain, food is transformed by rotting instead of cooking, gardens are overgrown with bush instead of socially nurtured crops, semidomesticated animals run wild, and people may become *akambain*. In many instances the reversion may be only temporary, of greater or lesser duration: *akambain* people usually recover and rejoin social groups; garden plots lie fallow and then are remade into swiddens. The transformations in these instances are reversible when there is an investment of additional energy into the system. Sometimes, however, as in the case of death, such transformations are permanent and irreversible.

Although the Baining appear to divide their world dualistically into bush and place, nature and society, animal and person, life and death, this dyad is actually a triad. The Baining world is a linear sequence of phases that are related as antecedent and subsequent stages of the same process. Passage between phases is effected by human activity (or lack of it). Nature in the form of potential, the first stage, is utilized by social actors who transform it into social products, constituting the second stage: human society. These products eventually get used up or worn out and become aspects of entropic nature, the third and final stage. Because it is their labor that effects the changes between and relations among these aspects or phases, the Baining see their labor as the source of the values associated with them. The social milieu is the most highly valued because of the work required to produce it. This estimation is reflected in the value given to adopted children and garden produce. Relations that the Baining create through their own actions are more esteemed than those determined by kinship or locality. Work, the set of activities that sustain Baining life, is highly valued.

For the Baining there is no implied connection between the two (initial and terminal) domains of nature. There is no linkage at the base of the triangle between the contrasting aspects or phases of "nature" produced by yet another set of transformations. The dead do not eventually get reborn, nor are manure and compost (or even swidden ashes) consciously used to refertilize the natural world. The two domains are at opposite ends of the linear temporal spectrum. There are, of course, many societies where these domains are linked in just such a manner, and the system becomes a continuous cycle of transformation and metamorphosis (Weiner 1976; Kahn 1986). For Baining society, the system remains a broken triangle without continuity. As a consequence of this orientation, there is no indigenous explanation for the constant replenishment of society by nature. The Baining do not recognize a feedback mechanism in their system through which entropic nature is regenerated, that is, transformed back into potential nature. There is no counterpart to our notion of the cycle of organic decay and natural growth, in which time and the sun's energy collaborate to revitalize the domain of nature as the well of potential social energy. This phase of the cycle is structurally invisible to the Baining. I would suggest that this invisibility occurs because the Baining have evolved a sociocultural perspective framed exclusively in terms of motivated human action.

This primary emphasis on human productive activity underlies the secularity of the Baining world view. The Baining see themselves, the living actors, as the transforming agents in their society and have no place for supernatural, or even natural, causality. They recognize no other agents of transformation working in tandem with themselves to produce Baining society. Thus, they describe their ritual process as "making themselves."

Values

"Work" as a category of productive activity mediates between two forms of dependent consumption, that of children and that of the aged and infirm. Work is thus identified with social agency, and as such contrasted to dependency of infants and the aged as social patients. The latter, however, are implicitly differentiated into opposing types of dependent patienthood: infants as potential producers whose raw capacity is in the process of developing as a result of the transformative process of feeding; and the aged, who are burned-out producers in the process of losing their productive powers and thus their social character as agents. This pattern is replicated in the cosmological schema according to which society mediates between the two opposing forms of nature (raw potential and entropic disintegration, respectively). The two relationships, work-dependency and society-nature, are clearly only different manifestations of the same basic schema. This schema defines, in the one case, the internal structure of society, and in the other, the cosmic structure of relations between the social and the non-social world.

In each of these relations, one of the elements is given greater value than the other. What I have referred to above as positive and negative transformations result in products with positive and negative value. Values, as I define the term, are qualities produced by the relative amounts of activity invested in producing various outcomes. The amount of labor invested is not necessarily the amount necessary to do a job, but the amount of time deemed culturally necessary, which often exceeds the minimum necessary to get the job done. This investment must be measured against all the other activities people perform in the total production of the social whole. The value attributed to certain tasks is, thus, a relative measure of its socially defined importance. The Baining consciously invest all their labor in work and socialization, whereas they do not even recognize dependency and nature as products of their own labor. Instead, the latter are seen as the result of the lack of investment of labor. They are thus negatively valued, while work and society garner positive value.

The Baining as Materialist Anarchists

Although work is a highly valued activity, the Baining do not have just one category of value. A second category of value is a commitment to egalitarianism and the construction of individuality within the limits of such common social values. All the positively valued transformations that the Baining call work are equally within the capacity of all active adults. As a result, the moral commitment to the values of work is equally shared as a value of Baining identity. Any development of distinctions of value between social persons, then, would undermine the value of the common identity of all Baining. Egalitarianism thus becomes a kind of invariant constraint preemptively forestalling individual expressiveness.

The apparent "flatness" and monotony of Baining life follow directly from the radical character of Baining egalitarianism, which holds not only that all social persons are equal, but also that social interaction is grounded purely in their shared moral commitment to the same set of social values and forms of relationship. The uniformity of this moral commitment precludes anyone's deriving unequal advantage or distinction from their common interaction: any form of hierarchy, status distinction, or relation of domination and subordination is felt to be antisocial and thus immoral. The high degree of voluntary conformity of Baining actors to their consensual patterns of interaction tends to prevent any differentiation of persons in respect of their relative social value or degree of dominance. The apparent monotony and repetiveness of Baining social life becomes a measure of the success of the social and cultural mechanisms that inculcate this attitude. The result is that social meaning is tightly condensed into a few cogent activities and ideas, which remain stable because they are so basic to ongoing daily life and are so uniformly shared in by everyone.

Mask as Fetish

The Baining know that they and their society are wholly their own products. To a degree almost unparalleled in the ethnographic record, their culture promotes the consciousness that productive work is the source of all social value. Together with their relatively egalitarian sexual division of labor and lack of exploitative relations of production, this makes them as close to an unalienated society, in Marxist terms, as can be found outside the pages of utopian novels. That the communal life of this society is centered around the ritualistic production of an elaborate and varied array of fetishistic masks ("fetishistic" in a Marxist sense, for the Baining who make them have no consciousness of their social symbolism or meaning), including some of the most gigantic and flamboyantly grotesque figures known to primitive art, thus appears, on first exposure, as an ironic ethnographic joke.

I have sought to demonstrate, however, that a thorough analysis of these masks, the process of producing them, and the rituals in which they are employed reveals that they comprise a faithful replication of the forms of Baining social production and personhood. In ritual, these forms are applied to a radically asocial content: the "natural" forest in its capacity as a reservoir of unsocialized potential powers and raw materials. The rituals are in effect dramas of socialization on a metasocial scale: replications of the social form of adoption through which society as a whole "adopts" nature (the bush) and through work and sweat transforms it into socialized beings (the masks), in the process reflexively constituting itself as a social totality.

To the Baining, of course, all this is "just play," with no deeper interpretation or exegetical meaning. In one sense, this dismissive label appears as a limit of social consciousness: in effect, as false consciousness. In another sense, however, it seems profoundly true. The imitation of the forms of social activity abstracted from their effective social content is one kind of play; such imitative play is a normal activity of children in almost all cultures, although ironically not of Baining children. Imitative play is frequently unselfconscious: the players do not step outside the forms of their existing social relations or identities, but simply imbue these forms with an alien—often fantastic—content, as a way of gaining mastery over the forms and processes they imitate. The focus of play is not on bringing to consciousness the constituted nature of the forms, and thus their susceptibility to transformation through human agency, but rather on asserting the player's expertise in their performance and control over their use. Thus, the ironic result: in making play out of their work of "making themselves," the Baining end by fetishizing as "just play" their most fundamental productive power: the ability to make the social forms in which they produce themselves.

The resulting bifurcation of social consciousness becomes the framework of Baining culture and social life. On the one hand, the uniform repetition of forms of self-productive labor comprises the virtually exclusive contents of secular social life and personal identity. The Baining have an almost pellucid self-consciousness about their productive powers, but their production yields a monotonous daily existence. On the other hand, there are brief interludes of ritual "play" characterized by the creation of ceremonial social patterns and masked identities of surreal variety and panache. The Baining are unselfconscious about what is produced, but such activities yield great collective excitement.

Baining ritual "play" does have its empowering, and even indirectly productive, aspects. The projection of forms of ordinary social production beyond the boundaries of society (the "place") onto the extraordinary natural content of the "bush" becomes a sort of playful tour de force, a ritual sport through which the everyday work of socialization becomes transposed into a vicarious adventure of capture, conquest, and domestication of alien powers. This is, of course, a man's game. The projection of social form onto asocial content becomes, reflexively, a mock reproduction of social form. The metaproduction of the form of social production (and thus of society as such) is a power men arrogate for themselves. They need, however, to take along a token woman, whose ritual transformation into a man establishes the necessary symbolic connection between the actual process of socialization and the virtual analog the men are "playing" at.

It is important that, as play, the men's ritual activity be collective, in contrast to the individual level of everyday productive activities in the domestic household. Men, it seems, need to come together to play. Rituals constitute the primary (and in precontact times virtually the only) positive occasion for gathering and concerted action by all the members of the community. Thus, although the men's playful replication of the formal process of "making themselves" makes no pragmatic contribution to the growth or socialization of any child, it does have a pragmatic social effect of another sort: the concrete enactment, in the mode of orchestrated ritual performance, of the social totality.

"Habitus," Agency, Consciousness, Culture

Setting out to analyze a society as a system of activities, in the context of contemporary social theory, immediately suggests convergences with the recent development of "practice theory" (Ortner 1984) and above all the work of its most influential practitioner, Pierre Bourdieu (1977). Bourdieu's concept of the "habitus" as a set of "dispositions" to act, formulated from the egocentric perspective of the actor, and integrated through their acquisition as activities of the actor's own body, seems in these respects well suited as a theoretical framework for my account of Baining society as an emergent system of activities (1977: 72). Like the forms of activity constituting Bourdieu's "habitus," Baining activities as I describe them consist of conceptual forms of activity immediately bound up with the concrete activity they represent. As Bourdieu rightly insists, activities in this sense must not be confused with abstract conceptual "rules" for acting, but consist rather of contextually bound patterns of action formulated from the actor's subjective point of view: in a word, "schemas" as I use the term in this book. Given my convergence with Bourdieu on this fundamental point, it might seem that my project of an ethnographic description of the Baining in terms of their collective patterns of interaction might fairly be defined as an ethnography of "habitus."

Even at the level of description, however, there are fundamental dif-

ferences between my account of Baining patterns of activity and Bourdieu's concept of "habitus." A brief review of the contrasts between
my treatment of Baining activities and Bourdieu's "habitus" may serve
as a useful way of highlighting specific aspects of my approach.

Bourdieu developed the concept of "habitus" as the basis of his am-
bitious attempt to surpass the mind-body dualism of received philoso-
phy and social theory, together with its corollary oppositions of structure and action, and signification and intention (meaning). Mauss had
used the term "habitus" in his essay "Bodily Techniques" to refer to
a society's repertoire of culturally patterned ways of using the body
(Mauss 1960: 372). The point of that essay was to develop the idea of
the social patterning of bodily activities as the mediating link between
the objective forms of social and cultural structure and the subjective
production of social relations and cultural representations. The patterning of bodily movement and action, for Mauss, became the material
vehicle for the internalization of social morality and moral discipline
("sang froid"), a process he saw as entailing the repression of the id-
like spontaneous needs and urges of the body ("l'emoi envahissant").
Bourdieu took over Mauss's notion (minus its psychoanalytic trim-
mings) as the core of his concept of "the socially informed body,"
which he posited as the "unifying principle" of the array of practices
(i.e., collectively standardized activities), which, following Mauss, he
too called the "habitus" (Bourdieu 1977: 124).

As I have related, embodiment (the production of the body in a variety of culturally specified respects, by means of culturally specified
activities, which in turn draw upon culturally defined bodily capacities) is a basic paradigm of sociality for the Baining. Viewing embodied
activity as the organizing principle within which formalized activities
comprise the life-world of a society is another respect in which Bourdieu's (and Mauss's) concept of "habitus" anticipates and converges
with the Baining data. My account of Baining sociality, however, differs
from Bourdieu's and Mauss's formulations in several crucial respects.
For both Mauss and Bourdieu, the internalized forms of bodily activity
are unconscious, and this unconsciousness is an essential corollary of
their assumption that the embodied subject takes no active role in the
internalization of socially standardized bodily techniques or forms of
activity. Bourdieu's "socially informed body" is a passive tabula rasa
that receives the stamp of objective regularities in social behavior and
then imposes them, as a sociological counterpart of the unconscious,
as motivated "dispositions" on the activities of the subject. For the
Baining, by contrast, the body consists of active processes (e.g., work,
sweat, etc.), which directly constitute the subject (as, for example, a
worker or a socializer). It is by means of these active capacities and

processes that the embodied subject engages with others, simultaneously shaping itself in conformity with their patterns and in turn shaping others. The conscious, active production of the body by the body (i.e., the active *forming*, as well as the passive *informing* of the social body as embodied subject) is thus the heart of the Baining cultural approach to socialization. The Baining, in sum, do not separate the body (as unconscious) from the socialized subject (as conscious), but rather directly identify the two, thus ironically realizing Bourdieu's theoretical goal of overcoming the mind-body split more completely than Bourdieu himself, whose demotion of the "socially informed body" to the level of the unconscious in effect preserves the Cartesian division in another form.

A major point of difference between Bourdieu's concept of "habitus" and the account of social activities presented in this book thus turns on the role of consciousness. The main socially shared patterns of interaction among the Baining are conscious. Collectively shared Baining forms of activity are consciously taught and learned, associated with conscious ideas of social propriety and valued personal qualities, and oriented toward conscious purposes by actors who are aware of what they are doing and why they are doing it. For Bourdieu, by contrast, the dispositions of "habitus" are absorbed unconsciously, through mimetic repetition of common, iterative modes of conduct, without the intervention of conscious reflection or intention. This means in practice that culture, the whole apparatus of socially shared symbolic constructs, values, and meanings, plays no active mediating role in the process; like the symbolic architecture of the Berber house in Bourdieu's account, it serves at best as an arbitrarily imposed set of contours, or map, to which the pathways of activity comprising the "habitus" conform, simply because they are there (Bourdieu 1977).

To point to the significance of the ethnographic fact that the Baining consciously draw upon public cultural values and forms of interaction as schemas for the conscious direction of social activity is not, of course, to imply that the Baining are totally conscious of themselves, their society, or the symbolic constitution of their cultural representations. It is merely to emphasize that their conscious activities, and the conscious meanings and values for the sake of which they undertake them, are a fundamental and constitutive, rather than an epiphenomenal or derivative part of their social and subjective reality.

The problematic separation of cultural "structure" from social "habitus" is directly related to a more general problem with Bourdieu's formulation that has been pointed out by several critics. The essential problem is that Bourdieu begs the fundamental question of how the patterns of "habitus" are learned, and once learned, motivated so that the acting subject is led to repeat them in the same form. Bourdieu nowhere explicitly explains how the leap from statistically regular objective social pattern to preconscious subjective dispositions is accomplished. He seems to rely implicitly on a behaviorist, or perhaps Durkheimian positivist model of internalization and replication of the internalized forms by the actor, with the actual mechanisms of learning and motivation left as a "black box" (Jenkins 1992: 95–96; cf. Bourdieu 1977: 77). To the extent that "habitus" is a genuinely social product, rather than a mere accumulation of private patterns of unconscious reflex imitation, its replication in "practices" must be accomplished through activities consciously directed toward the production and realization of social values rather than merely driven by unconscious psychological motivations. This means that the subjective consciousness of actors (what they think they are doing and why they think they are doing it) becomes crucial to a description of the activities involved.

We thus come to the fundamental question of the relation of "habitus" to the subject as social agent. The unconsciousness of "habitus" for Bourdieu is directly connected with his assumption that social activity is universally driven by the striving of actors to maximize their self-interest through strategies designed to advance their status in hierarchies of domination and subordination. The symbolic content of representations of action and value is theoretically redefined as "symbolic capital" to be deployed in the strategic competition for status distinction. Problems arise when actors as subjects are not themselves conscious of such a motivation. Bourdieu's treatment of the "habitus" as unconscious is a convenient way of avoiding these problems. The unconsciousness of the "habitus" and the reductionist discounting of the cultural content (and, one might add, forms) of symbolic mediation and representation as epiphenomena of the universally predetermined struggle for status distinction and domination thus appear as consequences of Bourdieu's assumptions about the intrinsic, precultural nature of the subject.

Without questioning the brilliance and cogency of Bourdieu's analysis of the activities of French academics and intellectuals in terms of these concepts, I suggest that a case like the Baining reveals the ethnocentric limitations both of Bourdieu's concept of "habitus" and the fundamental assumptions about the nature of human subjects and social action that appear to underlie them. First, and most important, Baining social action is not directed toward competition for status or dominance. There is no established form of hierarchy in Baining society beyond the central role of worker and food giver. Rather, the Baining belong to that subset of human societies that attempts to suppress all distinctions of relative value among social persons in order to make common sociality the exclusive basis of social interaction. In this respect, the Baining bear resemblance to certain hunter-gatherer societies (see Woodburn 1988; Lee 1976; Howell 1984; Myers 1986, personal communication). Pierre Clastres has described certain Amerindian societies in general theoretical terms as avoiding internal hierarchy and subverting all forms of domination and power in their internal relations (1977: 167–86). The very constriction of the range of social interaction and communication that strikes outsiders as an extreme form of monotony can be understood, in Baining terms, as the positive product of their struggle to sustain egalitarianism. To the extent that they succeed as egalitarian anarchists, the Baining belie Bourdieu's assumptions about the intrinsic nature of actors as competitive social atoms, struggling for distinction and domination over their fellows.

At the end of the day, there is no room for subjectivity, agency, consciousness, cultural symbolism, or meaning in Bourdieu, save as reflexive determinations of a self-reproducing social structure and the eternal competition for relative distinction within it. "Activity" for him is merely the enactment of an objectively predetermined script. Bourdieu's concept of "doxa" (1977: 164) seems to be an attempt to bridge the chasm between his functionalist conception of the self-reproducing social system operating through "habitus" and the subjective collaboration of actors as agents in this process. "Doxa" is the quasi-perfect fit between the objective structures (i.e., statistically regular patterns of behavior) and the internalized structures of agents, which make the "structures" in question appear to the subject as "natural" phenomena to which no social alternatives are conceivable (1977: 166). The "doxa" is thus beyond discussion because it is the unquestioned form of consciousness rather than comprising contingent contents of consciousness. "Doxa" and "habitus" are thus presented as two sides of the same coin; "doxa" is habitus's "appearance of naturalness," its quality of being beyond question, because of its uniformity and taken-for-grantedness among all normal members of the society, and "habitus" is the unquestioning reproduction of the "doxic" order. No more than he does for "habitus," however, does Bourdieu provide an account of the process by which "doxa," as the subjective naturalization of the social order, is produced. "Doxa," like "habitus," thus turns out to be a mere name for an effect rather than a conception of the process or causes through which the effect is produced.

The fundamental reason that Bourdieu is unable to speak meaningfully about the social production of subjects, either as agents of activity or as consciously self-directed actors, it seems to me, is paradoxically that he places too much of a load on the individual subject as the source of motivation and activity, and thus ironically fails to grasp the nature of the contribution of the social and cultural system to the production of subjectivity itself. Baining forms of activity are publicly mediated by cultural formulae: not individual symbols, but schematic constructs of symbols, categories, meanings, and values that define the forms of interaction through which subjects can objectively realize themselves as social persons. Social values comprise a critical part of these public cultural representations. The Baining values of sociality and work, for instance, constitute qualities that inspire a large proportion of Baining social interaction, in various ways that I have described in detail in the foregoing chapters. The point I wish to make here is that these values are not reducible to "motives" or psychological phenomena. They are, rather, cultural representations of productive activity. Values are representations of how activity is channeled and distributed in the forms and proportions necessary to reproduce Baining social relations and persons.

The desire for social value motivates the Baining to engage in the material activities that produce it. The Baining channel and focus their psychological processes, including both conscious and unconscious intentions and cognitions, into the production of one another's personal identities and the mutual relations that connect them. The relations between motivation and intention and their social forms as values are dialectically produced through these activities. By ignoring the fundamental constitutive role of cultural representations in the production of subjective agents, Bourdieu forces himself to fall back on unconscious psychological processes and intrinsic, acultural strategic behaviors that cannot account for the phenomena he sets out to explain: socially reproduced patterns of subjectively oriented social activity.

They Make Themselves

As self-conscious producers of themselves, the Baining constitute a collective counterexample to Bourdieu's concept of the individual subject as constituted, in its essential nature as a competitive, dominance-seeking social atom, independently of and prior to society. The activities that make up Baining social life are preeminently processes of producing social actors. Whatever their other cultural limitations, they are aware that they are the agents of their own creation: as they say, "they make themselves." For the Baining, then, human agency, as the capacity for willed, consciously directed activity, is the central quality of human social life that links the complementary aspects of social persons as the products and producers of one another, and their shared social world. As this implies, the Baining do not conceive of this capacity or its products, their conventional forms of activity and personal identity, as "natural" in the sense of Bourdieu's "doxa." On the contrary, they conceive of themselves and their society as social because they know them as products of their own activities, which for them is precisely what distinguishes human society, and the persons who compose it, from nature in its various forms and meanings. On these fundamental points, I take my theoretical cues from the Baining rather than Bourdieu. By contrast, Bourdieu's conception of the nature of the subject as given independently of any specific cultural content or social relations commits him to a "natural" theory of human nature. In these terms, Bourdieu's theory thus ironically becomes another "doxa," grounding an "objectivist" conception of culture and social action in an imputed universal pattern of social behavior, whose unquestioned naturalness seems to follow from its universality.

The "ensemble of social relations," to use that expression for the forms of interaction constituting the Baining counterpart of "habitus," constitutes both Baining society, as an inclusive system of relations, and individual Baining, as social persons and agents. It is immanent in both, but is also, as a set of forms of activity, analytically distinct from either. It may be said, then, that the ensemble of Baining forms of social activity mediates between society as a whole and the individual as person and actor. It is important to be clear about the difference between this proposition and Bourdieu's formulation that the "habitus" mediates between "structures" and "practices." For Bourdieu, "structure" is located outside "habitus," which merely formulates the perspective of a subject acting from a point located within a social order determined, as it were from above, by the "structure." The various forms of activity making up the "habitus" do not so much themselves comprise a structure as represent a refraction of a structure from the egocentric perspective of a situated body; the structure itself is conceived as located on a higher level, an ideal plane abstracted from all subjectivity, perspectives, and activities. In my analysis, on the contrary, "structure" arises directly from the coordination of activities among different subjects with their contrasting perspectives and roles; to the extent that it exists, it is a product of the actors' organization of activities rather than the other way around.

Social Change

Over the century that the Baining have had fairly continuous contact with colonial and national cultures, they have somehow resisted interpellation by the state. There have been many intrusions into the structure and fabric of their world. Despite these influences, the tenor of Baining life does not appear to have changed very much. This persistence has not been overtly ideological or assertively resistant. Instead, the Baining have continued to interpret the world through their own familiar schemas. These schemas are so basic and general that even fairly alien beliefs and practices have been assimilated. When the values of alternate systems have caused a clash in values and motivations, most Baining have rejected the new and returned to the old and familiar. This has been true of most of those who have lived, worked, or studied outside the community.

As the above suggests, the Baining are able to incorporate a range of new experiences and objects into their traditional pattern of life. At the same time, the ready incorporation of the new into the old tends to subsume the new into the same basic patterns. Despite an influx of new ideas, new products, and new opportunities, Baining life has remained remarkably close to its traditional form. In fact, the Baining seem to value these new activities according to the same criteria they used for the old. They have not abandoned their traditional patterns, but have abandoned a number of new activities (new crops, new housing patterns, new occupations) for a return to the old. The basic conservatism of Baining life is an expression of the constriction of the range of Baining personal activity to forestall the possibility of social differentiation and hierarchy. It is this commitment to radical egalitarianism and common sociality that gives the Baining system its great strength to resist disruptive change. It is this strength that has made them seem "undeveloped" in the eyes of the rest of Papua New Guinea, but the converse of this effect has been the strong continuity of Baining life and community, as seen in my discussion in chapter 3.

The Baining as Melanesians

As an ancient group with a unique culture, speaking a non-Austronesian language, the Baining are of interest to Melanesianists with respect to their differences from and similarities to the general features of Melanesian societies and cultures. In many respects, the Baining appear to be almost as isolated culturally and socially as they are linguistically from other Papua New Guinean societies. They lack such widely shared Melanesian traits as big men or chiefs, elaborated exchange systems based on specialized valuables, ancestor cults, initiation rites, men's houses, elaborate forms of gender asymmetry and pollution beliefs, and routinized warfare.

It is nonetheless interesting that the Baining possess a series of traits that might be interpreted as rudimentary forms of some of these characteristic Melanesian features. They are clearly an extreme case of what has been called in the Melanesian literature a "loosely structured" society (although I have tried to show, in my interpretation of the structures of their social and cultural system, that the term "loosely structured" reflects more about Western anthropological preconceptions about the nature of "social structure" than any intrinsic lack of "structure" per se). Rather than forming groupings and relationships on the basis of prescriptive rules of descent, marriage, or residence, they create (and terminate) social relations through optative relations of exchange (adoption, taro, and betel nut exchange in casual interaction, and mortuary feasts may serve as examples) (Fajans 1993a; Foster 1993, 1995; Schieffelin 1976; Battaglia 1990). Most of these exchanges employ food products (mostly garden produce, with some pork and betel nut) as media for the creation of kinship relations, personal identity, and social values, a common Melanesian practice (Goodale 1995; LiPuma 1988; M. Strathern 1988). The Baining form of these practices is in the order of a basic schema that has reached greater elaboration in other societies.

The values that accord prestige in this society—nurturance, socialization, and work—are ones that are very often associated with female gender roles. Among the Baining, these roles have been gender neutralized, in large part through adoption, so that males and females participate equally in them. To some extent, this cooptation of women's productive and reproductive activities has stripped women of their exclusive role as prestigious social actors, but it has also resulted in a near-egalitarian social order. This equality on a daily basis is set against the asymmetry of ritual activities in which men assume the role of reproducers on behalf of society as a whole. This alienation of women's activities and powers is a theme repeated in a number of other Melanesian societies where flute cult myths tell of the theft of flutes from women or where men imitate menstruation as a means to engage in reproductive activities (Herdt 1981; Tuzin 1980; Hogbin 1970; Lutkehaus 1995).

Finally, the ritual use of masks among the Baining resonates with the widespread use of masks among many of the societies of contiguous areas of New Britain and the Duke of York Islands, and many other Papua New Guinean peoples (Errington 1974; Gell 1975; Tuzin 1980). I suggest that this may reflect a common use of masks as "virtual bodies" in the sense I have used the term in my interpretation of Baining ritual, reflecting the centrality of the body in the social and cultural systems of these societies as ordered sets of transformations of nature into society and back again.

The Baining are thus not really culturally and socially isolated from other Melanesian societies. Rather, they manifest aspects of widespread if not universal social processes found throughout the area. Understanding the simple and repetitive forms and processes of Baining life therefore provides insight into the underlying schemas and patterns of numerous other Melanesian societies.

That the Baining share many of the same basic social schemas and cultural forms as other Melanesian societies but have not elaborated them into forms of asymmetrical status differentiation—whereas most of the other societies of the area have produced far more dynamic and elaborate versions of the same forms together with intensified patterns of individualistic assertiveness, social inequality, competition, and hostility—suggests a conclusion of general relevance. The Baining have created one of the closest approximations to an anarchist utopia on record: they are radically egalitarian, even in most aspects of gender relations, and they have achieved social cohesion and solidarity while forestalling the development of politics, hierarchy, or institutionalized violence. They have paid a price for their utopia, for it is bought at the cost of a remarkably thorough and effective suppression of individuality and (with the apparent exception of the masked rituals) cultural elaboration. Perhaps utopia is practicable only as monotony? This, however, is an outsider's reaction. To the Baining, their lives are fraught with interest and moral purpose. Living with the Baining, one feels that they would answer that their gentle and sociable way of life is worth the price.

Appendix

The Origin of Coconuts (Baining story as told by Langerkan)

I will tell the story about the men and the coconut palm. A long time ago, there were two parents, a man and his wife, who lived with their two children. There was nobody else around. They lived alone with their two children, two boys. One day, the father told the boys, "When I die, you bury me; bury me and then keep cleaning [weeding] the hole [the grave]. Later, if you watch, a sprout will come up, come up from my head. Take care of it, and it will grow and grow into a tree. This tree will bear many fruit which you can use for cooking your food. Later it will also provide money for you." Thus the father spoke of the tree.

Some time later, the father died. The mother and the two children buried him. They buried him outside the front of their house. Each morning they took turns cleaning the grave. They waited and waited. Finally one of them saw a small sprout coming up from the father's head. He came and told his mother about the sprout coming up, growing like a tree from the father's head. She said, "You two leave it. Later, much later, it will be as he said—a tree, a good thing, will grow from his head. It will bear many good fruit." Then she said, "Let us wait." Each day the two children continued taking turns cleaning the area. The tree grew, and got bigger, and it grew some more and got bigger still, until it reached way up.

Meanwhile, each day the mother would take her two children to the gardens with her. They went to the gardens and worked. After that, the mother would leave first. She would leave the boys working in the garden. She would harvest some taro and some greens for the three of them and would leave before them. She went home and cooked the taro and the stones for the greens. First she would wrap the leaves up and would go and get some water at a small water hole. She poured this water, which had salt in it, over the greens and cooked them. When the two boys came home later, she would give them food, and they all ate. But the boys tasted these greens and thought, "This does not

287

taste good. What has our mother done to it?" They thought badly of their mother for this. They didn't know about salt; they thought their mother had urinated on the greens. The boys started to hide their greens and later to throw them away in the bush. They did not like to eat them. This went on for a while. Every day the mother left the garden with their food, fetched the water and cooked the food. Later she fed this food to her sons, but they threw away the greens.

While all this was happening the coconut tree was growing bigger and bigger. Finally, it started to bear fruit. First it only had flowers, then it only had green coconuts with no flesh inside them. The mother kept telling her sons to leave it alone. "Wait," she said "it is not ready yet." All this time she kept going to the gardens and coming home and cooking the greens with saltwater. The boys still did not like this sour food and whispered to each other about their mother. They continued to throw away their greens and go to sleep hungry.

Finally, one day the smaller boy came back from the coconut tree and announced that some of the coconuts were already dry [mature]. The boys cut down a bunch of coconuts, and they husked one and cut it open and drank the liquid out of it. Then they cut it in half and scraped the flesh. Their mother scraped it and gave the boys some scrapings. They ate it and said it was good; they ate it all. They scraped and scraped the flesh from the shell, until only the shell was left. The mother held the shell [like a bowl], and tried it, and said, "Maybe later we will use it like this." Her two thumbprints were imprinted on the shell from where she held it. They said, "This is a good tree." Later they tried cooking their food in coconut milk. The boys scraped and scraped the coconuts and their mother cooked their taro in the coconut milk. This food was good. They said, "Our tree is good! Hereafter, we will eat its fruit."

They continued cleaning and weeding the tree and it kept bearing fruit. It did not fool around, but bore more and more fruit, until the coconuts were lying all over the ground where they fell. The mother told the boys to put the nuts in piles. They put the nuts into piles and left them to sprout. Then they planted them. Each morning they piled the coconuts into heaps—many, many heaps. Then they went to the garden.

One day the boys decided to follow their mother and watch her when she left the garden to cook. They followed her home, but hid in the bush alongside the house. When they saw her leave to get the salt-water, they followed her again. She did not see them. She went to the water hole. It was a very small water hole, and it was covered with a small cloth. She lifted the cloth and the water boiled up to the surface. She filled her small bamboo tube with saltwater and headed home. The two boys were curious, and after she left, they went down to explore. They lifted up the small cloth on top of the hole and the water boiled up. They did not quickly cover the hole again, as their mother had done, and so the water boiled out of the hole. It boiled up and up; it spilled over the edges and started running all over the land. The boys got scared and started running away from the hole, and the water started following them, like a big flood. The boys went on and on and on and on, further and further and further. They made a circle, a big circle with the land on one side and the sea on the other surrounding this land. The boys' mother ran down to meet them, shouting and shouting at them to put some mountains on the land, to hold back the water, and to put some islands in the water, and some reefs in it as well. And the boys went off and made lots of islands and reefs. They were gone a long time, months and months. Finally they came back to their mother, and they went back to the small water hole out of which all the salt water had come, and they covered it up. The water stopped flowing then.

Some time after this, the mother died. The boys buried her next to their father. They were by themselves then. They continued going to the garden each day, and coming home with their taro and their greens; but now they had to cook for themselves. One day they decided to go fishing. They said to each other, "We'll go and we'll try and we'll see. Will we catch some fish?" So they went down to the mangroves, to the sea, and they tried to catch hold of some fish [they tried to catch the fish with their bare hands]. As they stood in the water a small piece of a stick came up and poked one of the boys in the back of the knee. He said, "This piece of stick pokes me here. Why?" He picked it up and threw it away, but it floated back and poked him in the back of the knee again. Again he threw it away, but again it came back and poked him once more. This time he picked it up, and they carried it home with them.

When they got home, they planted the stick just outside the doorway of their house. It sprouted and two little shoots came up from the base. It grew quickly into two pitpit plants. The one furthest from the house flowered first, then the nearest one followed. The boys wanted to try it, as before they tried the coconut, and the fish, but it was not ready yet. They continued to go to the garden. Each morning they cleaned their parents' graves before going to the garden. Then they went and worked, and when they came home they brought two taro with them. They brought these two taro and put them in the corner of their house. Then they took the two they had brought the day before and cooked those for their meal. They did this every day.

One day, while they were gone, a woman jumped down from the

pitpit stalk outside their door and went inside. She went in the house and took the two taro. She cut them from their stalks and lit a fire on the older brother's hearth. Then she cooked the two taro. When they were done, she laid one on the elder brother's bed and the other on the younger brother's bed. Then she went back outside and climbed back onto the pitpit stalk. When the boys came home, they saw this. "Who cooked these two taro of ours?" they asked. "Not our mother. She is dead. So who, who cooked them?" The next day the same thing happened. After the boys left, the woman again climbed down and cooked the taro. She chopped firewood, and lit the fire and cooked the taro, and then she laid one on each brother's bed. When she was done, she left and climbed back up her pitpit stalk. When the boys came home as usual, they looked into one another's eyes and said, "Who did this for us? Who cooked our taro?"

The next day, the elder brother said to his younger brother, "We will go together to the garden. You will stay there, but I will come back here in order to see who is cooking for us." So they lied and talked about going to the gardens, and they went. Then the elder brother turned around and came back, and hid inside the house. He hid in the corner. The woman thought that they had both gone to the garden, but that was not so; one brother had come back and had hidden in the house. Not knowing this, the woman came down from the top of the pitpit plant and went inside. She did not see the brother. She came in and sat down. She cut the taro—first the elder brother's and then the younger brother's. She lit the fire as usual and put the taro on top of it; she cooked the taro. Then the brother jumped towards her. He came next to her and sat down on the bed next to her. She thought, "But where did he come from?" She thought they had both gone to the garden, but then he appeared. She saw him and wondered what should she do. She couldn't find the way out in time. Then he came and sat down next to her and said, "You can't hide, now. Don't be afraid, no! You will stay here now. We will live together." Then the other brother appeared. He had come back from the garden after his brother. He wanted to see what was happening. He saw them together over there, his brother and his *aruera* [taboo relative, in-law]. They called out to him, "You come in," and he came inside. He wanted to see, and he saw his brother and his sister-in-law. His brother was going to stay with her. His brother said, "No, I do not know where she came from." They all talked to each other and gave each other betel nut. When that was done, they made the beds up to go to sleep. The elder brother made his bed with his wife. The woman told the younger brother to make his bed ready too. She said, "You make your bed too. There is a woman up there, and later I'll go up and get her." So the younger brother made up a bed for himself and his wife, and when he had finished, she went out and up to the top of the pitpit and got her younger sister to come down. She said, "You come down and we'll go into them. Don't be afraid." Then they came down and the two sisters came inside to their two husbands and to their own beds. They came in and they talked to each other. They exchanged betel nut, and chewed, and after that they ate the taro that the woman had cooked earlier. They ate, chewed betel, and later they slept.

Glossary

ahakugi	Grandmother.
Aharaigi	Day dance from the coast.
aheirein	Anger or dispute.
ahindumgi	Taro and coconut cream dish served at feasts.
ahis	Food taboos.
aiga	Great-grandfather.
aios	Ghosts; spirits; bush creatures; vines; corpses; fireflies.
aisingaigi	Python or eel; large dance piece.
akakat	Baining name for themselves.
akalup	Shame.
akambain	Crazy; wild.
akarrutki	Food exchange with pitpit.
akaseul	Spear shaft for *akip* regalia.
akavalka	Testicle.
Akip	Spear dance performed during the day (*akipa*, the spear).
akurikuruk	The last act in a mountain day dance.
akusak	Site for dance preparations; cone for dance spears; ginger plant.
akusakaiginaka	Ritual leader.
alamingel	Mushroom-shaped pubic covering.
alaspraka	Mask worn in *Atut.*
aluska	Bark container for steaming vegetables.
Amambua	Coastal dance performed at night.
ambarka	Older boy, man.
ambarta	Big, older children.
ambias	Blood.
amerika	Betel nut; pig in a mortuary distribution.
aminok	Substance; body fluids.
amruawa	Taro bundles.
amungom	Seance; divination.
amuris	Good, industrious.
anaingi	Hunger.
anaruga	Pole mask.
anat	Taro in the garden.

andaka	Taro.
andum	Cooked taro.
angalipka	War club.
angirrup	Shame.
anguangi	Mask worn in *Atut;* bat.
angungi	Hot.
angurigit	Hand.
angwarumgi	Insect; foam.
aningaka	Head.
aninganingulta	A line or group.
anirka	Bamboo slit drum; great-great-great-grandchild; spouse.
anis	Tail of a bird; grass skirt.
anisingring	Women's pole masks.
anyimga	A watcher, helper in food taboo.
aramariki	Large shieldlike dance construction.
araninda	Old people who stay at home.
aratki	Basket.
aravakpum	Cane belt.
aravetdumga	A whole pig served at a feast.
arimbab	Home of the dead.
ariski	Hunger.
arsong	Ritual knots.
arum	Sadness.
Asarai	Day dance in the mountains.
asarik	Butchered meat.
asavangaka	Swiftlet.
aseirein	Anger or dispute.
asiengi	String bag.
asil	Ferns.
Asingal	Coastal dance performed at night.
asinipki	Spider.
asis	Paint design.
asleng	Garden.
asmas	Feast.
assarikatki	Dance headdress.
asuaka	Old man.
asuamga	Thief.
asunasta	Novices in *Atut* preparations.
asunup	Songs.
atalak	The play.
Atit	Food exchange with pigs.
atlo	Good, industrious.
atmiraka	Adopted child (masc.) (*atmiraigi* [fem.]).
Atut	The night dance in the mountains.
atutki	Masked figure.
avilanga	Tail of a pig or dog.
avriski	Mask worn in *Atut.*

avutik	Paint design.
awalsaing	Black body paint.
awatki	Female man; a woman who works on ritual regalia.
awilas	Hot, excited.
awis	Cold.
awubung	Belongings.
awumbuk	Tiredness; a social hangover.
awuringdang	Paint design.
awusinga	Great-great-grandchild.
engilka	Small, younger child (*engilta* [pl.]).
guaruimga	My son.
guaruimgi	My daughter.
gumam	My father.
gunan	My mother.
kalak	To ride on the shoulders.
kana	With; the household of "so and so" (masc.) (*kina* [fem.]).
kut	To shoot.
mama	Papa.
nana	Mommy.
nari	To hear, understand.
sis	To eat raw food.
talak	To play.
trasir	To pierce.

Bibliography

Primary Sources

Bateson, Gregory. 1927–28. Field Notes from the Central Baining. Unpublished notes, stored at the American Museum of Natural History. New York.

Brereton, M. J. 1965. Patrol to Coastal Bainings. Rabaul Patrol Report No. 6, 1965/66. Rabaul Subdistrict. Port Moresby, Papua New Guinea. National Archives.

Chamberlain, Robert. 1966. Patrol to the Inland and Coastal Bainings Census Divisions. Rabaul Patrol Report No. 2, 1965/66. Rabaul Subdistrict. Port Moresby, Papua New Guinea. National Archives.

———. 1967. Patrol to the Inland and Coastal Bainings Census Divisions. Patrol Report No. 3, 1966/67. Rabaul Subdistrict. Port Moresby, Papua New Guinea. National Archives.

D'Arcey, A. 1948. Patrol of the North Bainings. Patrol Report No. 6, 1947/48. Kokopo Subdistrict. Port Moresby, Papua New Guinea. National Archives.

East New Britain Office. 1991. Census Statistics from the 1990 Census. Unpublished interim report. East New Britain Provincial Report.

Hart, L. G. 1964. Patrol to the Inland Bainings Census Division. Patrol Report No. 1, 1964/65. Rabaul Subdistrict. Port Moresby, Papua New Guinea. National Archives.

Haywood, M. R. 1957a. Patrol to the Inland and Coastal Bainings. Patrol Report No. 4, 1956/57. Raunsimna Subdistrict. Port Moresby, Papua New Guinea. National Archives.

———. 1957b. Patrol to the North Baining. Patrol Report No. 1, 1956/57. Raunsimna Subdistrict. Port Moresby, Papua New Guinea. National Archives.

———. 1957c. Patrol to Wiliambempki-Poiniara Area. Patrol Report No. 2, 1956/57. Raunsimna Subdistrict. Port Moresby, Papua New Guinea. National Archives.

———. 1957d. Patrol to Wiliambempki-Poiniara Area. Patrol Report No. 3, 1956/57. Raunsimna Subdistrict. Port Moresby, Papua New Guinea. National Archives.

———. 1958. Special Patrol Report. North Bainings Area. Rabaul Subdistrict. Port Moresby, Papua New Guinea. National Archives.

League of Nations. 1938–39. *Report to the League of Nations on the Administration of the Trust Territory of New Guinea.* Melbourne, Australia.

Martin, J. D. 1955. Patrol to Maintain Native Administration in the North Bainings Area. Patrol Report No. 2, 1955/56. Kokopo Subdistrict. Port Moresby, Papua New Guinea. National Archives.

Martyn, J. F. 1955. Patrol to the North Baining Subdivision; Administration following outbreak of Cargo Cult. Special Patrol Report No. 1, 1955/56. Rabaul Subdistrict. Port Moresby, Papua New Guinea. National Archives.

———. 1956. Patrol to the North Bainings Subdivision. Patrol Report No. 1, 1956/57. Rabaul Subdistrict. Port Moresby, Papua New Guinea. National Archives.

Norton, J. E. 1966. Letter Accompanying Patrol Report. Patrol Report No. 2, 1965/66. Rabaul Subdistrict. Port Moresby, Papua New Guinea. National Archives.

Orken, M. B. 1954. Patrol to the North Bainings, Inland and Coastal Subdivisions. Patrol Report No. 1, 1954/55. Kokopo Subdivision. Port Moresby, Papua New Guinea. National Archives.

Parrish, D. J. 1946. Patrol to the Inland Villages of the North Bainings. Patrol Report No. 3, 1946. Kokopo Subdistrict. Port Moresby, Papua New Guinea. National Archives.

———. 1947a. Patrol to the Bainings Division of the Gazelle Peninsula: Coastal Division. Patrol Report No. K2, 1946. Kokopo Subdistrict. Port Moresby, Papua New Guinea. National Archives.

———. 1947b. Patrol to the Coastal Villages of the North Bainings. Patrol Report No. K3, 1947. Kokopo Subdistrict. Port Moresby, Papua New Guinea. National Archives.

Pentony, Patrick. 1940. Report on the Demographics and Health of the Baining, New Britain. Unpublished paper presented to the Department of Psychology, University of Western Australia.

Pool, Jeremy. 1969–70. Field Notes from the North Baining, Puktas and Wiliambempki Villages. By permission of the author.

———. 1971. Final Report to the Wenner-Gren Foundation: Field Work Among the Northern Baining, New Britain (1969–70). New York. Unpublished manuscript.

Port Moresby, Papua New Guinea. National Archives. 1904–5. *Annual Report on the Development of German Protectorates in Africa and the South Seas.* English translation.

———. 1907–8. *Annual Report on the Development of German Protectorates in Africa and the South Seas.* English translation.

Rohatynskyj, Marta. 1992. A Study of Minor Ethnic Groups in East New Britain. Unpublished report to the Provincial Government of East New Britain.

Sangkol, Moses. 1969. Patrol to the Inland Bainings. Patrol Report No. l-A, 1970. Lassul Bay. Rabaul Subdistrict. Port Moresby, Papua New Guinea. National Archives.

Williams, J. C. 1949. Patrol to Coastal and Inland Villages of North Baining. *Patrol Report No. KPO 5, 1948/49.* Kokopo Subdistrict. Port Moresby, Papua New Guinea. National Archives.

Secondary Sources

Bateson, Gregory. 1931–32. Further Notes on a Snake Dance of the Baining. *Oceania* 2: 334–41.

———. 1972a. Cybernetic Explanation. In *Steps to an Ecology of Mind*. New York: Ballantine Books.

———. 1972b. A Theory of Play and Fantasy. In *Steps to an Ecology of Mind*. New York: Ballantine Books.

Battaglia, Debbora. 1990. *On the Bones of the Serpent: Person, Memory, and Mortality in Sabarl Island Society*. Chicago: University of Chicago Press.

Bourdieu, Pierre. 1977. *Outline of A Theory of Practice*. Cambridge, England: Cambridge University Press.

Brady, Ivan, ed. 1976. *Transactions in Kinship: Adoption and Fosterage in Oceania*. Honolulu: University of Hawaii Press.

Bulmer, Ralph. 1967. Why is the Cassowary not a Bird? *Man*, n.s., 2(1): 5–25.

Cage, John. 1939. *Silence: Lectures and Writings by John Cage*. Middleton, Conn.: Wesleyan University Press.

Carroll, Vern. 1970. *Adoption in Eastern Oceania*. Honolulu: University of Hawaii Press.

Clarke, Peter. 1977. *Engini*. Rabaul: The United Church Press.

Clastres, Pierre. 1977. *Society Against the State*. Translated by Robert Hartley. New York: Urizen Books.

Corbin, George. 1976. The Art of the Baining of New Britain. Ph.D. diss. Columbia University.

———. 1982. Chachet Baining Art. *Expedition* 24(2): 5–16.

Democretos. 1948. *Ancilla to the Pre-Socratic Philosophers*. Compiled by Kathleen Freeman. Cambridge, Mass.: Harvard University Press.

Douglas, Mary. 1966. *Purity and Danger*. London: Routledge & Kegan Paul.

Durkheim, Emile. 1972. The Conception of Religion. Review of *L'Irreligion de l'avenir*, by Guyau. In *Emile Durkheim: Selected Writings*, edited by Anthony Giddens. Cambridge, England: Cambridge University Press.

Epstein, Scarlet. 1968. *Capitalism, Primitive and Modern: Some Aspects of Tolai Economic Growth*. East Lansing: Michigan State University Press.

Errington, Frederick. 1974. *Karavar: Masks and Power in a Melanesian Ritual*. Ithaca: Cornell University Press.

Errington, Frederick, and Deborah Gewertz. 1994. From Darkness to Light in the George Brown Jubilee: The Invention of a Nontradition and the Inscription of a National History in East New Britain. *American Ethnologist* 21: 104–22.

Fajans, Jane. 1985. They Make Themselves: Life Cycle, Domestic Cycle, and Ritual Cycle among the Baining of Papua New Guinea. Ph.D. diss. Stanford University.

———. 1993a. The Alimentary Structures of Kinship. In *Exchanging Objects: Producing Exchange*, edited by Jane Fajans. Oceania Monographs 43. Sydney, Australia: University of Sydney Press.

———. 1993b. Exchanging Objects: Producing Exchange. In *Exchanging Objects: Producing Exchange*, edited by Jane Fajans. Oceania Monographs 43. Sydney, Australia: University of Sydney Press.

Feil, Daryl. 1984. *Ways of Exchange: The Enga Tee of Papua New Guinea*. St. Lucia, Queensland: University of Queensland Press.

Feld, Steven. 1982. *Sound and Sentiment: Birds, Weeping, Poetics, and Song in Kaluli Expression*. Philadelphia: University of Pennsylvania Press.

Foster, Robert J. 1993. Dangerous Circulation and Revelatory Display: Exchange Practices in a New Ireland Society. In *Exchanging Objects: Producing Exchange*, edited by Jane Fajans. Oceania Monographs 43. Sydney, Australia: University of Sydney Press.

———. 1995. *Social Reproduction and History in Melanesia: Mortuary Ritual, Gift Exchange, and Custom in the Tanga Islands*. Cambridge, England: Cambridge University Press.

Gell, Alfred. 1975. *Metamorphosis of the Cassowaries: Umeda Society, Language and Ritual*. London: Athlone Press.

Goodale, Jane. 1995. *To Sing With Pigs Is Human: The Concept of Person in Papua New Guinea*. Seattle: University of Washington Press.

Greenberg, Joseph. 1966. *Language Universals with Special Reference to Feature Hierarchies*. The Hague: Mouton & Co.

Herdt, Gilbert H. 1981. *Guardians of the Flutes: Idioms of Masculinity*. New York: McGraw-Hill.

Hertz, Robert. 1960. *Death and the Right Hand*. Translated by Rodney Needham and Claudia Needham. Glencoe, Ill.: The Free Press.

Hesse, Karl, and Theo Aerts. 1978. *Baining Dances*. Port Moresby: Institute of Papua New Guinea Studies.

———. 1982. *Baining Life and Lore*. Port Moresby: Institute of Papua New Guinea Studies.

Hogbin, Herbert Ian. 1970. *Island of Menstruating Men*. Scranton, Pa: Chandler Publishing Co.

Howell, Signe. 1984. *Society and Cosmos: Chewong of Peninsular Malaysia*. New York: Oxford University Press.

Jenkins, Richard. 1992. *Pierre Bourdieu*. London: Routledge.

Jinks, B., P. Biskup, and H. Nelson. 1973. *Readings in New Guinea History*. Sydney, Australia: Angus and Robertson.

Kahn, Miriam. 1986. *Always Hungry, Never Greedy: Food and the Expression of Gender Relations in a Melanesian Society*. New York: Cambridge University Press.

Klemensen, Arvid. 1965. *Strange Island: The Noona Dan in the South Seas*. Translated by Joan Bulman. Sydney, Australia: Ure Smith.

Leach, Edmund. 1979. Anthropological Aspects of Language: Animal Categories and Verbal Abuse. In *Reader in Comparative Religion*, edited by William A. Lessa and Evon Z. Vogt. New York: Harper Collins, Inc.

Lee, Richard. 1976. *Kalahari Hunter-Gatherers: Studies of the Kung San and their Neighbors*. Cambridge, Mass.: Harvard University Press.

Leont'ev, A. N. 1978. *Activity, Consciousness, and Personality*. Englewood Cliffs, N.J.: Prentice Hall.

Lévi-Strauss, Claude. 1965. Le Triangle Culinaire. *L'Arc* 26: 19–29.

Levy, Robert I. 1973. *Tahitians, Mind and Experience in the Society Islands*. Chicago: University of Chicago Press.

Lipset, David. 1980. *Gregory Bateson: The Legacy of A Scientist.* Englewood Cliffs, N.J.: Prentice-Hall.

LiPuma, Edward. 1988. *The Gift of Kinship: Structure and Practice in Maring Social Organization.* Cambridge, England: Cambridge University Press.

Lutkehaus, Nancy C. 1995. *Zaria's Fire: Engendered Moments in Manam Ethnography.* Durham: Carolina Academic Press.

Marx, Karl. 1947. *Capital: a Critical Analysis of Capitalist Production.* New York: International Publishers.

Maschio, Thomas. 1994. *To Remember the Faces of the Dead: The Plentitude of Memory in Southwestern New Britain.* Madison: University of Wisconsin Press.

Mauss, Marcel. 1960. Les Techinques de Corps. In *Sociologie et Anthropologie.* Paris: Presse Universitaire de France.

Munn, Nancy D. 1986. *The Fame of Gawa: A Symbolic Study of Value Transformation in a Massim (Papua New Guinea) Society.* Cambridge, England: Cambridge University Press.

Myers, Fred. 1986. *Pintubi Country, Pintubi Self: Sentiment, Place, and Politics among Western Desert Aborigines.* Washington, D.C.: Smithsonian Press.

Ortner, Sherry B. 1984. Theory in Anthropology Since the Sixties. *Comparative Study of Society and History* 26(1): 126–66.

Parkinson, Richard. 1907. *Dreisig Jahre in de Sudsee.* Stuttgart.

Piaget, Jean. 1967. *The Psychology of Intelligence.* New York: Basic Books.

———. 1970. *Structuralism.* New York: Basic Books.

Piers, G., and Milton B. Singer. 1953. *Shame and Guilt: A Psychoanalytic and A Cultural Study.* New York: W. W. Norton and Co.

Pool, Jeremy. 1984. Objet insaissable ou anthropologie sans objet?: Field Research among the Northern Baining, New Britain. *Journal de la Societe des Oceanists* 40(79): 219–33.

Poole, J. 1941–42. Still Further Notes on a Snake Dance of the Baining. *Oceania* 13: 224–27.

Rascher, Matthaus. 1909. *Aus de Deutschen Sudsee: Miteillungen der Misssionare vom Heiligsten Herzen Jesus: Band I: Baining, Land und Leut.* Munster: Druck und Verlag de Aschendorffschen Buchhandlung.

Read, W. 1931–32. A Snake Dance of the Baining. *Oceania* 2: 232–36.

Rubel, Paula, and Abraham Rosman. 1978. *Your Own Pigs You May Not Eat: A Comparative Study of New Guinea Societies.* Chicago: University of Chicago Press.

Schieffelin, Edward L. 1976. *The Sorrow of the Lonely and the Burning of the Dancers.* New York: St. Martin's Press.

Strathern, Andrew. 1971. *The Rope of Moka: Big-Men and Ceremonial Exchange in Mount Hagen, New Guinea.* Cambridge, England: Cambridge University Press.

———. 1975. Why is Shame on the Skin? *Ethnology* 14: 347–56.

Strathern, Marilyn. 1988. *The Gender of the Gift: Problems with Women and Problems with Society in Melanesia.* Berkeley: University of California Press.

Turner, Terence. 1977. Transformation, Hierarchy and Transcendence: A Critique and Reformulation of Van Gennep's Model of the Structure of *Rites de*

Passage. In *Secular Ritual,* edited by Sally F. Moore and Barbara Meyerhoff. Amsterdam, Netherlands: Van Gorcum.

———. 1979. Kinship, Household and Community Structure Among the Kayapo. In *Dialectical Societies,* edited by David Maybury-Lewis. Cambridge, Mass.: Harvard University Press.

———. 1980. The Social Skin. In *Not Work Alone,* edited by Jeremy Cherfas and R. Lewis. London: Templesmith.

———. 1984. Value, Production and Exploitation in Non-Capitalist Societies. Paper presented at the American Anthropological Association 82nd Annual Meeting, Denver, Colorado.

Turner, Victor. 1967. *The Forest of Symbols.* Ithaca: Cornell University Press.

Tuzin, Donald. 1980. *The Voice of the Tambaran: Truth and Illusion in Ilahita Arapesh Religion.* Berkeley: University of California Press.

Van Gennep, Arnold. 1960. *The Rites of Passage.* Translated by M. K. Vizedom and G. L. Caffee. 1909. Chicago: University of Chicago Press.

Vygotsky, L. S. 1962. *Thought and Language.* Cambridge, Mass.: MIT Press.

———. 1978. *Mind in Society: The Development of Higher Psychological Processes.* Cambridge, Mass.: Harvard University Press.

Wagner, Roy. 1986. *Asiwinarong: Ethos, Image, and Social Power Among the Usen Barok of New Ireland.* Princeton: Princeton University Press.

Weiner, Annette B. 1976. *Women of Value, Men of Renown: New Perspectives in Trobriand Exchange.* Austin: University of Texas Press.

Wertsch, James. 1981. *The Concept of Activity in Soviet Psychology.* Armonk, N.Y.: M.E. Sharpe.

———. 1985a. *Culture, Communication and Cognition: Vygotskian Perspectives.* Cambridge: Cambridge University Press.

———. 1985b. *Vygotsky and the Social Formation of Mind.* Cambridge, Mass.: Harvard University Press.

White, Geoffrey, and John Kirkpatrick, eds. 1985. *Persons and Selves: Ethnopsychology in Pacific Cultures.* Berkeley: University of California Press.

Whitehouse, Harvey. 1990. A Cyclical Model of Structural Transformation among the Mali Baining. *Cambridge Anthropology* 13: 34–53.

———. 1995. *Inside the Cult: Religious Innovation and Transmission in Papua New Guinea.* Oxford: Oxford University Press.

Woodburn, James, Tim Ingold, and David Riches, eds. 1988. *Hunters and Gathers.* New York: Berg Publishers.

Index

activity, 9, 236, 264, 267
  as conscious, 278
  and identity, 11
  as material process, 11, 266–67
  mediate between society and actors, 283
  social nature of, 264
  as theory, 9, 10, 11
administration, influence of, 18, 48
  neglect by, 43, 44
adolescence, 59, 93–95, 108–9
  in *Atut*, 240, 255
  fear of marriage, 59, 94–95
  same sex groups, 59–60, 94
  work, 93
adoption, 20, 22, 27, 43–44, 63–68, 76, 77, 266, 268
  by childless couples, 67
  collapsing distance between generations, 75
  cultural sanctions toward, 64
  related to dispersion, 43
  after illness, 67
  exchange of infants, 66
  epitome of social relationships, 68
  feeding with milk substitutes, 66
  initiating a request, 64
  use of kin terms, 63
  as model for sociality, 71
  nursing an adopted child, 65
  providing nurturance, 64, 65
  of orphans, 67
  as productive activity, 266
  reversal, 65
  by single people, 67
  a social act, 63
  creating social households, 22, 270
  valued relations, 63, 117, 266, 273
  after weaning, 64, 65

Aharaigi, 31
aios, 8n, 88, 126–27, 129, 130, 132, 140, 142–43, 149–51, 160–61, 188, 189
  destructive powers, 206
  as entropy, 157
  minor role in mortuary ritual, 154
  in natural contexts, 126
  opposed to social production, 157, 207
  as players, 168
  and pollution, 206
  stealing from gardens, 69
  stories about, 126
Aisingaigi, 187–88, 216–17
  construction of, 188–89
akakat, name for Baining, 13
akambain, 89, 115, 127–28, 129, 132–34
  stereotypic behaviors, 133
  marked state, 133
  inversion of normal behavior, 128–29, 130, 133, 133–34
  displaced onto external agents, 134
  opposition of natural and social forces, 135, 272
Akip, 30, 129, 220–25
  construction of, 181–83
  use of feathers, 181
Akurikuruk, 30, 190–92, 230–34
  blind, 230
  construction of, 190–92
  marginal being, 234
  dirty, 230
  food taboos, 232
  hot, 230
  hungry, 230
  reintegration into society, 234
  antithesis of social person, 232
Alaspraka, 2, 240
  construction of, 242–44
  designs, 243–44

delayed, 74
immediate, 74
regalia, 167, 173, 206–9, 225
  embodying productive processes, 174,
    178, 206, 256
  left to rot, 235, 236
  metaphorical persons, 178, 206–7
  nonrepresentational, 174
  metaphor for transformations, 206
region, 31
regional ties, through dances, 170
relations, produced through activities, 74
relations with other Papua New Guin-
    eans, 39, 41, 80
  adoption, 79–81
replication, of schemas, 267
reproduction, 72, 82, 271
  through activities, 236
residence, 19, 72
  in cocoa blocks, 46
  post marital, 61
ritual, 162, 236, 270, 277
  fragmentation of social world, 159,
    205
  framing, 7, 236–37
  inversions, 249, 256–58
  liminal phase, 159, 255–56
  includes preparation, 198
  rite of separation, 249–51
  resegregration of domains, 159, 178,
    256, 259
  as socialization, 237
  and social production, 178, 276
ritual heaps, 175, 177
  destroyed, 204
ritual leaders, 171, 172, 173, 204
  lack of in *Atut*, 240
  female, 172
  male, 172
  song leader, 198
ritual pollution, 174. *See also* washing
ritual preparations, intensity increases,
    247–48. *See also* bush preparations
road network, 38
  cut taro on paths, 137, 140
  ambivalence toward, 48
  needed for cash economy, 48
Rohatynskyj, Marta, 15
rotting, 174–75
  analogous to death, 179

inverse transformation, 206
rubbish heaps, 175, 204

St. Paul's massacre, 37
St. Paul's mission, 35, 36
saltwater, need for, 33, 287–89
schema, 11, 79, 266, 286
  simultaneously adaptable and stable,
    269
  master, 11, 267, 269
  as structure, 11
  See also pattern
secrecy, 193
sentiments, 113, 116–22, 135
  demarcate the boundaries of the per-
    son, 116, 262
  in songs, 119, 262
  and value, 116
sex, 57, 59, 60
  premarital, 57–58
sexual imagery, 227
shame, 5, 53, 79, 116–18, 120, 123n, 124
  of biological ties, 54
  at boundaries of natural and social re-
    lations, 116, 117, 118
  in close kin relations, 117
  about pregnancy, 62
  premarital, 58
  in songs, 212
slavery, 33–35
Snake Dance. See *Atut*
social, valued over natural, 283
sociality
  creation and maintenance, 121
  destroyed at death, 154
  devalues the personal, 260
  individual vs. the collectivity, 154
  reestablished through mortuary rituals,
    138, 139, 156, 162
socialization, 53, 98, 110, 114, 270, 271,
    272, 283
  work to play, 237
social organization, 74–75, 267
  produced through transformations,
    270
social patterns, as conscious, 279
social person
  Akurikuruk as antithesis, 232
  Baining view, 85
  egalitarian view, 275

www.ingramcontent.com/pod-product-compliance
Lightning Source LLC
Chambersburg PA
CBHW022138020426
42334CB00015B/947